ANTI-RACISM
IN EDUCATION

Dedication

This book is dedicated to all those in higher education who have experienced and suffered from any and all forms of racism. We stand by them in solidarity and hope our voices contribute to a collective journey of healing through anti-racist empathy and action.

ANTI-RACISM IN EDUCATION

STORIES OF GROWING ACTIVISM

Edited by Geetha Marcus and Stefanie Van de Peer

LONDON AND NEW YORK

First published in 2023 by Critical Publishing Ltd

Published 2025 by Routledge
4 Park Square, Milton Park, Abingdon, Oxon OX14 4RN
605 Third Avenue, New York, NY 10017

Routledge is an imprint of the Taylor & Francis Group, an informa business

Copyright © 2023 Zaynab Akhtar, Anthony Ataekong, Caralyn Blaisdell, Olutayo Burrows, Jane Culpan, Arek Dakessian, Michelle L Elliot, Marion Ellison, Misbah Haqani, Simon Hoult, Kavi C Jagadamma, Judith Lane, Geetha Marcus, Bianca Mastrominico, Sandra Ndale, Anne O'Donnell, Joy Owojuyigbe, Georgina Pearson, MD Rezaur Rahman, Walid Salhab, Eurig Scandrett, Anthony Schrag, Stefanie Van de Peer and Emma Wood

All rights reserved. No part of this book may be reprinted or reproduced or utilised in any form or by any electronic, mechanical, or other means, now known or hereafter invented, including photocopying and recording, or in any information storage or retrieval system, without permission in writing from the publishers.

Trademark notice: Product or corporate names may be trademarks or registered trademarks, and are used only for identification and explanation without intent to infringe.

British Library Cataloguing in Publication Data
A CIP record for this book is available from the British Library

ISBN: 9781041054238 (hbk)
ISBN: 9781915713001 (pbk)
ISBN: 9781041054245 (ebk)

The rights of Zaynab Akhtar, Anthony Ataekong, Caralyn Blaisdell, Olutayo Burrows, Jane Culpan, Arek Dakessian, Michelle L Elliot, Marion Ellison, Misbah Haqani, Simon Hoult, Kavi C Jagadamma, Judith Lane, Geetha Marcus, Bianca Mastrominico, Sandra Ndale, Anne O'Donnell, Joy Owojuyigbe, Georgina Pearson, Walid Salhab, Eurig Scandrett, Anthony Schrag, MD Rezaur Rahman, Stefanie Van de Peer and Emma Wood to be identified as the Authors of this work have been asserted by them in accordance with the Copyright, Design and Patents Act 1988.

Text and cover design by Out of House Limited

DOI: 10.4324/9781041054245

Contents

Acknowledgements   page viii

Meet the editors and contributors   page ix

Foreword by Khadija Mohammed   page xv

Introduction
Silence is not an option
Geetha Marcus and Stefanie Van de Peer   page 1

Chapter 1
'And still I rise'
Geetha Marcus   page 17

Chapter 2
Whose knowledge counts in early childhood education and care?
Caralyn Blaisdell   page 33

Chapter 3
Changing worldviews through study visits
Simon Hoult   page 45

Chapter 4
Using critical dialogue to address racism, humanise the Other and create solidarity and praxis in the classroom
Emma Wood   page 61

Chapter 5
Decolonisation as public sociology practice
Eurig Scandrett   page 77

Chapter 6
The Scottish Centre for Social Justice
Marion Ellison   page 91

Chapter 7
Challenging dominant narratives about the Global South to address implicit bias and othering
Walid Salhab, Sandra Ndale and Emma Wood   page 103

Chapter 8
Film festivals and film studies: An anti-racist approach to curation and education
Stefanie Van de Peer   page 119

Chapter 9
Creative strategies for unknowing: Taking risks to encourage equitable relationships in the classroom
Anthony Schrag   page 133

Chapter 10
White is the colour of my name: Anti-racism in theatre and performance praxis
Bianca Mastrominico   page 149

Chapter 11
Mad studies and anti-racism
Anne O'Donnell   page 163

Chapter 12
Imagining defragmented university spaces
Arek Dakessian, Anthony Ataekong, Joy Owojuyigbe, Olutayo Burrows, Misbah Haqani, MD Rezaur Rahman and Georgina Pearson   page 177

Chapter 13
Critical conversations on decolonising the physiotherapy curriculum
Kavi C Jagadamma, Judith Lane and Jane Culpan   page 187

Chapter 14
Walking the talk: Changing and challenging the conversations in occupational therapy education
Michelle L Elliot and Zaynab Akhtar   page 203

Conclusion
Learning to love
Geetha Marcus and Stefanie Van de Peer   page 219

Index   page 225

Acknowledgements

The authors acknowledge the following sources for figures in this book:

Figure 1.1 – Teaching Resources

Figure 2.1 – Daramy et al (2022)

Figure 4.1 – United Nations

Figure 6.1 – Smith et al (2021)

Figure 15.1 – Statista (2022)

All figures in Chapter 9 are © Anthony Schrag.

Meet the editors

Geetha Marcus

Geetha Marcus is a senior lecturer in teacher education at the University of Edinburgh. She is a sociologist, feminist and teacher activist whose research and teaching interests focus on social inequalities within public education systems. She has extensive professional experience in the field of primary education, both in classroom practice and in senior management. As a practitioner-researcher, she believes there is an urgent need for teachers to employ education methods for justice-oriented social change.

Stefanie Van de Peer

Stefanie Van de Peer is an academic whose area of expertise is women in documentary and world cinema. She is a film historian interested in non-mainstream filmmaking, such as activist non-fiction and animation. Central questions in her research focus on power structures, identity formation and emancipation. She has professional experience with several international film festivals as coordinator, programmer, curator and board member.

Meet the contributors

Zaynab Akhtar is a graduate from Queen Margaret University, Edinburgh and is currently working as an occupational therapist within the National Health Service (NHS) Forth Valley's adult mental health team. As her studies progressed and her experiences evolved, so did her interests in where her occupational therapy role might lie. In the early stages of her career, she is excited to continue expanding her clinical knowledge and practice throughout the various sectors her profession has to offer.

Anthony Ataekong was a 2021–22 postgraduate student in the Institute of Global Health and Development at Queen Margaret University.

Caralyn Blaisdell (Cara) is a qualitative researcher, early years pedagogue and teacher/practitioner educator at Queen Margaret University. Cara's research explores how young children's rights, enshrined in the UN Convention on the Rights of the Child (1989), are lived and experienced by children within their many different social relations. She is particularly interested in how emotional relations shape children's rights as a living practice.

Olutayo Burrows was a 2021–22 postgraduate student in the Institute of Global Health and Development at Queen Margaret University.

Jane Culpan is a senior lecturer in health sciences at Queen Margaret University and a Health and Care Professions Council (HCPC) registered physiotherapist. She is interested in exploring the fit between the academic curriculum for pre-registration qualifying programmes and current challenges to effective healthcare practice.

Arek Dakessian is a research fellow in the Institute for Global Health and Development (IGHD) at Queen Margaret University. He is a sociologist who is interested in cultural production, material culture, racialisations and refugeedom. His research revolves around refugeedom and integration. Specifically, he is part of a team that investigates the role of social relationships and social connectedness in enabling integration, both from the perspective of the host and that of displaced communities. Arek is also a founding member of LIVED, an Edinburgh-based charity dedicated to researching refugeedom, as well as a member of the Social Network Analysis Group of Scotland.

Michelle L Elliot is an occupational therapist, occupational scientist and senior lecturer in the Division of Occupational Therapy and Arts Therapies at Queen Margaret University. She is interested in many facets of everyday experiences and occupations in different contexts, in particular the constructions and representations of narratives that influence identities, opportunities and processes of change. She is committed to the practice of inviting curiosity and her work often unearths more questions than answers.

Marion Ellison is Professor of European Social Policy at Queen Margaret University. Specialising and publishing widely in comparative social policy, work and employment, social work and public management and governance in Europe, Marion's most recent publication, 'The Cost-of-Living Crisis in the UK: An Economy on the Edge' examines the economic, social, and environmental conditions underlying the cost-of-living crisis and its impact on social and health inequalities in the United Kingdom. Marion also leads the Public Sociology Research Group, which houses the work of the Scottish Centre for Social Justice at Queen Margaret University.

Misbah Haqani was a 2021–22 postgraduate student in the Institute of Global Health and Development at Queen Margaret University.

Simon Hoult is the co-head of the Division of Psychology, Sociology and Education at Queen Margaret University. He has been involved in university-based teacher education for over 20 years, during which time he developed a keen interest in the potential of study abroad to influence students' worldviews, as well as his own. He has led study visits to South India for over a decade, collaborating with colleagues from a local university. This formed the basis of his PhD research, as well as a number of single and joint publications, including an edited text of Indian and UK students' scholarly work presented at a conference.

Kavi C Jagadamma began his career as a physiotherapist in India, then moved to Scotland to study for his doctorate. He is a senior lecturer at Queen Margaret University. His teaching practice focuses on entrepreneurship, innovation and research. He has a keen interest in the challenges of decolonising the curriculum and in exploring the complexities of creating space for all to feel a sense of belonging in education and practice.

Judith Lane is a senior lecturer in physiotherapy at Queen Margaret University, with over 20 years' UK and international experience in the development of pre-registration curricula across the allied health professions. Her teaching practice is focused on preparation for professional practice and research methods. She is committed to the development of contemporary physiotherapy practice and creating graduates who are future ready.

Bianca Mastrominico is a performance-maker and scholar. Since 2002, she has been co-artistic director of the performance laboratory Organic Theatre (www.organictheatre.co.uk). Bianca is programme leader for the MA in Digital Performance and BA (Hons) Performance at Queen Margaret University, where she is also co-leading the Practice Research Cluster. She is a member of the TaPRA Performance and New Technologies Working Group and is active within the Magdalena Project network of women in contemporary theatre.

Sandra Ndale grew up in Malawi, where she was a resident of the STEKA care home. She is now a filmmaker, photographer and entrepreneur who runs her own business. Although she undertakes a range of commercial opportunities, her focus is on getting poverty-experienced young people's voices heard in Malawi.

Anne O'Donnell is a lecturer in mad studies at Queen Margaret University. She graduated from the University of Edinburgh with an MSc in community education in 2007 and is currently undertaking doctoral studies on a project entitled 'Learning to Challenge Epistemic Injustice: Collective Advocacy in Scotland', also at the University of Edinburgh. Her teaching and research are both based on linking the personal and the public.

Joy Owojuyigbe was a 2021–22 postgraduate student in the Institute of Global Health and Development at Queen Margaret University.

Georgina Pearson is deputy director of the Institute of Global Health and Development at Queen Margaret University. She is a medical doctor and medical anthropologist by training, with experience in interdisciplinary approaches to research and teaching across biomedical and social sciences. She was awarded her PhD by the London School of Economics and Political Science. Before joining IGHD in 2019, Georgina was a lecturer in public health at St George's, University of London, and a research fellow in the Firoz Lalji Centre for Africa, London School of Economics, where she continues to collaborate on research projects as a visiting fellow.

MD Rezaur Rahman was a 2021–22 postgraduate student in the Institute of Global Health and Development at Queen Margaret University.

Walid Salhab is a multi-award-winning filmmaker and lecturer in media practice at Queen Margaret University. He was born and brought up in Lebanon, spent time in Iraq as a child refugee and, having experienced significant trauma, came to the United Kingdom as a student. He has lived in Scotland for more than 40 years, but his work is heavily influenced by his early experiences as a refugee and his desire to affect current discourse about refugees and migrants and their right to sanctuary. His short films foreground the voices of the marginalised and dispossessed, and have won accolades at film festivals worldwide.

Eurig Scandrett is a senior lecturer in public sociology with research interests in environmental justice movements, and a trade union representative with the University and College Union (UCU). He graduated and worked in environmental science research before spending 15 years in adult and community education, and was head of community action at Friends of the Earth Scotland. He recently edited *Public Sociology as Educational Practice* and (with Anne Harley) *Environmental Justice, Popular Struggle and Community Development*. He is a member of the project board of the Jimmy Reid Foundation and currently chair of the Scottish Palestine Solidarity Campaign.

Anthony Schrag is a practising artist and researcher and senior lecturer at Queen Margaret University. The central focus of his work examines the role of art in participatory and public contexts, with a specific focus on social conflict, agonism and ethics. He has worked nationally and internationally, including residencies in Iceland, the United States, Canada, Pakistan, Finland, the Netherlands and South Africa, among others. He has been the recipient of numerous awards and grants, including from the Royal Society of Edinburgh, the Hope Scot Trust, Creative Scotland, the British Council, the Royal Scottish Academy, the Dewar Arts Award and Standpoint Futures, as well as a Henry Moore Artist Fellowship.

Emma Wood is a senior lecturer at Queen Margaret University, and course leader of the university's MSc in Digital Campaigning and Content Creation. Her research and practice focus on ways in which critical dialogue can be utilised in the emancipation of marginalised groups through an understanding of their lived experience as expertise. Her model of critical dialogue creates an environment in which people can organise and communicate their views, and take action to challenge oppressive social norms. She is chair of the Scottish charity STEKAskills, which aims to connect Scottish communities with their contemporaries in Malawi to bring about social change. She works in close partnership with the grassroots Malawian NGO, STEKA, which creates sustainable futures for young survivors of human trafficking.

Foreword

The year 2020 will remain etched in our minds for years to come. Our world quite literally ground to an abrupt halt. We found ourselves in the midst of fighting two global pandemics: Covid-19 and racism. There were early indicators that the coronavirus was disproportionately affecting Black communities. It exposed the historical and contemporary inequities that Black families and communities experience every day of their lives. On 25 May, we learned of George Floyd's murder in Minneapolis by a police officer. The Black Lives Matter movement became a global phenomenon, with protestors taking to the streets in pursuit of racial justice with calls to dismantle systemic racism.

Closer to home, in Scotland, Shekhu Bayoh was killed in 2015 after being restrained by police officers. It was not until 2020 that the terms of reference were agreed for a public inquiry to examine the events surrounding his death and to consider whether race was a factor. These inhumane acts became the reckoning point for all activists. Indeed, I reiterate the words of Geetha and Stefanie as they introduce the powerful stories in this book: 'silence is not an option'.

I feel honoured to be invited to write the foreword to this incredibly insightful book, which includes stories of growing activism from academics working in higher education. As a BAME primary teacher, I spent many years of my teaching experience 'playing White'. My pupils and colleagues were White and I wanted to fit in. After all, I was the product of a curriculum where I could not see myself – I had learned that from my own educational experiences in Scotland. When I moved into higher education and began working with my students, who were early years practitioners and student teachers, I very quickly realised that I was again in the minority. I wanted to bust this myth of 'sameness': we need to see colour and we need to be responsive to it.

In 2020, I was invited to lead an expert steering group to respond to the publication of the European Human Rights Commission's (2019) report *Tackling Racial Harassment: Universities Challenged*, which revealed that racial harassment was a common experience for both students and staff. We created a safe space in which we declared our intention to stand in solidarity and interrogate the systemic racism in our institutions. We led discussions about difference and facilitated constructive conversations about race, racism and Whiteness. Leaders across our higher education and further education institutions endorsed a declaration against racism. '*Racism exists on our campuses and in society, so call it what it is and reject it in all its forms. We stand united against racism*'. This landmark moment in Scotland was a call for leaders and governing bodies to demonstrate leadership in and accountability for eliminating racism.

Geetha and Stefanie have masterfully collated the stories of resistance and activism. The stories in this book outline how academics strategise in their institution to educate, agitate and organise across disciplines. Use this book as a moral compass to transform the experiences of both your students and your colleagues of colour. The stories of activism in this book also provide colleagues with the strategies and skills needed for anti-racist interventions, and guide White colleagues to deal with the pushback they may face from colleagues who may see them as White liberal troublemakers.

In a phenomenal keynote, Dr Muna Abdi asked colleagues to consider how they use language in anti-racist spaces. Does it create conflict and tension or do we use it to create safe spaces to acknowledge, describe and dismantle racist discourses? Through their own storytelling, educators discuss how they deal with bias, privilege and discomfort. Their stories offer an anti-racist vision. Nesrine Malik's (2019, p 264) words capture the very essence of this book: '*We need new stories, but we also need to write them ourselves. It will not be easy and it will not happen overnight. But one thing is certain as far as the keepers of the status quo are concerned: it is too late. They will be hearing from us.*' Read these 'new' stories with care and compassion. Geetha and Stefanie share their concluding thoughts on 'learning to love' as one united in solidarity, creating loving moments in unloving spaces. What a beautiful way to reframe our thinking around anti-racist practice from one of discomfort to love in action.

Dr Khadija Mohammed
Associate Dean for EDI, UWS

References

European Human Rights Commission (2019) *Tackling Racial Harassment: Universities Challenged*. Geneva: EHRC.

Malik, N (2019) *We Need New Stories: Challenging the Toxic Myths Behind Our Age of Discontent*. London: Orion.

INTRODUCTION: SILENCE IS NOT AN OPTION

Geetha Marcus and Stefanie Van de Peer

Introduction

This book describes an ongoing campaign of anti-racist action staged by a small group of scholars and students from diverse fields. The chapters are written by a collection of academics at Queen Margaret University, Edinburgh who are at various stages of their careers and from a range of different fields, including media, communication and performing arts; health sciences; psychology and sociology; education; and global health and development. Each chapter describes a journey towards anti-racist teaching and activism. These stories are about the writers' own experiences of racism and how this translated into action – their own growing understanding of the impact of racism and their subsequent decision to take personal or professional action. Importantly, each chapter not only acts as a case study, grounded in relevant theory, but also shares with the reader a suggested platform of individual action that can be taken by anyone who is willing to make a start at being an anti-racist educator. Each chapter includes a few reflective questions and recommended readings.

Seeds of violence and growing frustration

George Floyd, Stephen Lawrence and Sheku Bayoh

In 2020, the murder of George Floyd and subsequent expressions of anger, frustration and grief at the continued existence of racism – particularly in the

United States – led to more sophisticated and honest conversations about its impact in the United Kingdom. The seeds for our book began then, but we did not realise it at the time. There was, of course, similar indignation when Stephen Lawrence was murdered in London in 1993, and again with the lesser-known plight of Sheku Bayoh, who was killed in Kirkcaldy in Scotland in 2015. Both deaths have prompted inquiries: the Macpherson Report issued as a result of the Stephen Lawrence Inquiry in 1999 (six years after his death), and the ongoing Sheku Bayoh Inquiry, which only began in May 2022 (five years after his death). Their families have fought tirelessly for justice. Lawrence's family has stressed that '*silence is not an option*' (Lawrence, 2021). Both the fact that only two of the perpetrators out of six were convicted for Stephen's murder, and the decision that the two police officers allegedly involved in Bayoh's death be allowed to retire on the grounds of ill-health are unimaginably frustrating for their families and communities. *Lament for Sheku Bayoh* is '*an artistic response to this tragedy, an expression of collective grief for the loss of the human behind the headlines; a non-apologetic reflection on and frustration with identity and racism in Scotland today*' (Lavery, 2021, p 2). We want to dedicate this book to George, Stephen and Sheku, and to others like them, who have not received the justice they deserve. We believe that anti-racist activism must start early, during education, and should be inherent to all higher education. Only then will younger generations learn about systemic racism and develop the tools and knowledge to become genuinely anti-racist. Being an anti-racist educator might be a form of irrational hope, but the authors argue the work must begin and continue despite institutional and personal setbacks.

Non-performance and glacial progress

Since the Macpherson Report in 1999, there have been multiple reports written about racism and racial justice in the United Kingdom over the past two decades: the Equality and Human Rights Commission's (EHRC) *Healing a Divided Britain* (EHRC, 2016); Theresa May's Race Disparity Audit (gov.uk, 2017); the Report of the Commission on Race and Ethnic Disparities (gov.uk, 2021), also known as the Sewell Report; the First Report of Archbishop's Commission for Racial Justice (Church of England, 2022); the annual *State of Hate Reports* (Hope Not Hate, 2022), to name just a few.

The EHRC has released 216 publications on race discrimination since 2007 (EHRC, 2022). Four of these were about racial harassment in British universities (EHRC, 2022). Apart from Boris Johnson's Sewell Report, which critics argue *'displays a basic (mis-)understanding of how racism works'* (Bhopal, 2021), nearly all of these reports profess urgency and the need to act; however, the structural and everyday racisms as well as the rise in hate crime show that meaningful progress remains glacial. Ahmed (2004) describes this kind of *'doing'* as the *'non-performativity of anti-racism'* – the busy acts of inquiring, gathering evidence and data, stating, reporting and policy-making are ends in themselves. It translates into an odd strategy of taking action not to take action.

This book reflects a zeitgeist of the impact of both the decolonisation and Black Lives Matter movements on our work and personal growth, and the realisation that, as academics, we must sharpen our focus on anti-racist practice. Since George Floyd's murder at the hands of a White police officer in Minneapolis, there has been a growing call within the university sector – one that goes beyond the inclusion of texts that represent diverse experiences and perspectives – to instil an anti-racist mindset and to decolonialise education curricula at all levels. This book seeks to build on the canon of literature on racial discrimination, and in particular acknowledges the exhausting pain suffered by families who have lost children to racial violence, and who must suffer the humiliation of working with systems of Whiteness to find racial justice. In her book *On Being Included*, Sara Ahmed (2012) reminds us of how tiring it can be to coexist in spaces of Whiteness. She highlights the mental and emotional labour that comes from being different, but crucially *'the political labour it takes to have spaces of relief from Whiteness'* (Ahmed, 2012, pp 36–7).

It should be noted that in the United Kingdom, equality is a not a devolved matter; it remains reserved to parliament at Westminster. However, education and training *are* devolved. The disparity in power causes tensions and contradictions for the social justice agenda in the university sector and in other educational establishments; and inadvertently the gap secures hiding places for those who wish to evade or deny racism in Scotland (Marcus, 2019). This will be explored further in this book.

The living legacies of racialisation

Our understandings of race, racism, racialisation and decolonisation crucially ought to be firmly based in an understanding of colonialism and its continuing insidious impact on the world. Our work responds to this call and encourages readers to consider their own narrative and actions, challenging them to recognise that in Britain we share a history, parts of which have been blotted out or misconstrued over centuries. British colonisation of huge areas around the globe has ensured a continued oppressive and racialised attitude not only towards British identity but also towards its previous and current colonies. Decolonial thinking must embrace the humility to unlearn the dominant discourse on Britishness and move away from the grand narratives of our historiographies. Indeed, Chimamanda Ngozi Adiche (2009) warns of *'the danger of a single story'* and, along with other seminal texts, this book goes some way towards reframing that imbalance.

Tuck and Yang (2021, p 1) remind us that the easy adoption of decolonising and anti-racist discourse in education, academia, schools, research, critical methodologies and ethics can *'decentre'* the *'settler colonist's perspective'* in several ways: ongoing evasions, continued complicity, *'settler moves to innocence'* as a means of dealing with communal guilt. They argue that the experiences of *'settlers'* (Whiteness) are incomparable and *'incommensurate'* with the experiences of *'the settled upon'* (otherness) (Tuck and Yang, 2021, p 1). As co-editors, we would like to emphasise our agreement with this view, and our respect for the distinct narratives of those who have been colonised, racially marked and abused, and racially oppressed in the past and present. Virdee (2019, p 1) contends that *'viewed from the marginalised vantage point, the history of the modern world has been a catastrophe marked by land dispossession, genocide, enslavement, forced migration, structural discrimination, everyday racism and grieving for lives made unlivable'*. Racism 'settles upon' and feeds off the others' land, opportunities, identity, language, culture, history and, of course, physical bodies as property. This book cannot make amends for the irreconcilable loss and damage felt, but it hopes to make room for more meaningful potential alliances for transformation.

And so, six months after George Floyd's killing, the seeds of alliances at our institution were sown at a series of lightning talks on decolonisation held on St Andrew's Day, 30 November 2020. Academics from a range of fields came together to share their experiences, their solidarity with anti-racist movements, their confusion, ignorance and frustrations. The event was organised, endorsed and hosted by our principal, Sir Paul Grice. He publicly acknowledged that *'racism exists on our campuses and in our society*' (Advanced HE, 2020) and urged us to '*stand united against racism*'. Testimonies of racism and anti-racism at this event resulted in networked solidarities across divisions and between colleagues who had not previously worked together. This then translated into a newly formed grouping of students and staff, called Decolonise Research NOW, which continues to meet monthly in a reading group space where systemic racism and continued colonial legacies in our institutions and in our work are discussed and deconstructed. The networks fostered within and from this group are what fed the testimonies that shape the chapters that follow.

Complexities, gaps and the impetus for change

Many of us recognise the complex problems within racist systems and the glacial progress being made by a profession that strives for social justice to have addressed this in any meaningful way. There remains a vast gap between legislation, policy rhetoric and meaningful action that goes beyond a tick-box exercise. Moreover, educators in higher education are in the front row: observing and engaging with the next generation of citizenry, our students. Their lives are embedded in the digital age, and social media provide an essential tool in the spread of both racist and anti-racist activism. This book shows how we can begin to contribute in a meaningful way to the creation of the change we need as we each demonstrate how we work with students to critically reflect on racial injustice in all its forms. The cast of personable and relatable activists encourages readers to consider their own roles in dismantling racism in institutions and communities. The impact of the campaign described in this book is that university lecturers across the board have been called upon to improve their understanding of anti-racist action. This book forms a dynamic and contemporary critique of that direction.

This book, then, tells the story of anti-racist actions staged by academic educators and encourages readers to consider their own options for anti-racist action in higher education. In framing this book as a collection of individual and collective experiences and attempts to come to terms with the role of the educator in the so-called decolonisation of the university as an institution, we envisage a showcase of practice across a small institution, which we hope can inspire other individuals as well as larger institutions across the United Kingdom. We do not argue that these are best practices; rather, each chapter highlights strengths and drawbacks, and illustrates just how problematic it is to take anti-racist action in education. Discipline-specific case studies of anti-racist action indeed illustrate how difficult it is for institutions to move beyond the discourse, yet as a collective of individual attempts to break out of discourse and into action, these cases also illustrate the possibilities available to people as opposed to institutions. As a collective of individual case studies, then, this book is a call to action, which shows what those who are (partly) dependent on the university as an institution can achieve to combat individual and institutional racism. Each case study is written from a subjective perspective and laid out as a specific experience by an academic affiliated with an institution that promotes itself as devoted to social justice. Scholars from diverse backgrounds and at various stages in their careers engage with the question: What is social justice if it becomes a concept on which the identity of an institution hinges? As such, this book not only represents individual occasions that became turning points for educators; it also offers the wider perspective on how we can collectively decolonise the academy from the inside out, as the profession recognises its need to take action against racism, racial prejudice and racialisation.

Challenging the neoliberal agenda

The key role of a university is to educate. Yet the neoliberalisation of the academy has seen the decline of the number of professors teaching. Instead, their responsibilities have shifted towards publications and research projects, bringing prestige and money into university institutes from beyond the education sector. The agenda of movements dedicated to the decolonisation of the university has thus focused most of its attention on research. Large-scale decolonisation projects, where high-ranking professors lead heavily funded and time-restricted events, reports and publications, suffer from the time-consuming nature of research, publication and impact. Changing things in a top-down manner is a slow and sometimes agonising process that does not take into consideration student voices in a way that more effectively and efficiently reviews static situations. That the movement to decolonise the university is a slow process is entirely dependent on the existing structures and a fear of breaking down structures for fear of a collapse. As such, the care and time it takes to make changes feels like stagnation. Where efforts have been made to bring the student experience into the discussions around decolonisation of the university, these efforts continue to be seen as tangential to the structural, prestige-fuelled research and output production. But grassroots efforts to make changes are more visible to students and acknowledge the importance of students in the exchange of knowledge.

The bottom-up approach shows commitment from tutors, lecturers and professors to an implementation not of structural changes but of individual changes at low levels that can be witnessed immediately, even on a smaller scale. These collective efforts can then feed into the larger structural changes needed. As bell hooks (1994) has shown, learning can be revolutionary, nurturing and enabling. In the same vein, Nelson Mandela (2003) said *'education is the most powerful weapon which you can use to change the world'*. To change things without postponing the execution of those changes, we need to start by challenging the young people in the education system to inform us, and indeed guide us as educators, so the changes can be shown to be effective and appreciated. Racism, racist attitudes and bias stem from miseducation.

The stories of activism: learning to love

This book will serve to re-educate educators by reframing our history and understandings of race and ethnicity, showing examples of how to take action as scholars. *'No one is born hating another person because of the colour of his skin, or his background, or his religion. People must learn to hate, and if they can learn to hate, they can be taught to love'* (Mandela, 2004, p 784). Education is the starting point for change and for people to imagine an anti-racist future.

As the chapters in this book deal with individual case studies drawn from the experiences and perspectives of educators in diverse specialisms, the book also tasks readers with questions and considerations that serve to reflect upon their own role in the systemic tolerance of racist structures, both historical and contemporary, and to consider their individual roles in helping to create anti-racist university communities. At the end of each chapter, when the narrative of the case study feeds into a self-reflexive exercise on the part of the author, readers are invited to engage meaningfully with their own experiences through sections of exercises and questions. These questions provoke critical thinking and refer to relevant reading and useful resources that are cross-referenced and included in the reference lists.

Chapter 1 details the author's journey from being one of only a few BAME headteachers in Scotland to a sociologist and teacher-activist in Initial

Teacher Education at three Scottish universities, working with mainly White colleagues and students. Geetha Marcus delineates the strategies she uses to champion anti-racism, the challenges she faces in doing so and approaches to self-care that have helped her to rise above the actions of those who believe we live in a post-racial era, or for whom racism is an uncomfortable conversational taboo. She highlights the work of key Black feminists bell hooks, Audre Lorde (1983), Sara Ahmed and Heidi Mirza, who have taught her that teaching students to understand racial injustice by combining *'reason and emotion'* would benefit more from *'thought and action'*, a more comprehensive approach inspired by what Jane Roland Martin (1986, pp 7, 10) describes as the *'3 Cs of generative love'*: care, concern and connection.

Chapter 2 is framed by Caralyn Blaisdell's question about whose knowledge counts in early childhood education and care. Using her own journey as an early childhood educator as a roadmap, the chapter highlights waypoints where the author's understanding of whose knowledge counts has been disrupted and enhanced. After locating her own positionality in the field, the chapter visits three waypoints: first, young children's rights as enshrined in the UN Convention on the Rights of the Child (UNICEF, 1989); second, the early years pioneers; and third, anti-racist activism in the Scottish early years sector. Each waypoint troubles the Whiteness of whose knowledge counts in early years, and offers different paths where racism and anti-racist practice both become visible.

In Chapter 3, Simon Hoult writes about the role of study visits to the Global South and exposes the consequences of conflicting worldviews. The author reflects on the implications for wider teacher education pedagogy within the anti-racist agenda, drawn from his experiences of leading, teaching and researching study visits of UK-based student teachers to the Global South. Such study visits are contentious, and not feasible for all students to engage in. Hoult's research (eg Hoult, 2018, 2020; Lal and Hoult, 2019), however, identified several pedagogic dimensions within such intercultural engagements. These factors can be drawn upon in wider teacher education practice to examine inequality and privilege, and to expose apparently universal worldviews as eminently Western Eurocentric in their origin.

Chapter 4 highlights the use of critical dialogue to address racism, humanise the 'other' and create solidarity in the classroom. In this chapter, Emma Wood focuses on a case study in which she attempted to develop solidarity between White students in Scotland and poverty-experienced young people from the Global South. It analyses how several Scottish students resented the philosophy behind the project – they were defending young Scots' right to visit Malawi to 'save' the poor and criticising 'them' (the young Malawians) for not being grateful for having jobs done for them by the school pupils, such as having their bedrooms painted. This chapter shows how the Scottish students' views changed when the tutor abandoned the typical tutorial format and instead ran Critical Dialogue Groups with these students.

Chapter 5, by Eurig Scandrett, looks at decolonisation as public sociology practice. He shows that public sociology is a discipline that puts the intellectual resources of sociology in the hands of publics that are struggling to challenge oppression, exploitation and injustice, an engagement with the subaltern counter-public sphere. That is what he teaches his students, what he writes about in his scholarship and what underpins his research. But here he asks: What does that mean for a White, British, academic sociologist in Scotland seeking to challenge racism through public sociology, in which institutional and epistemic racism is embedded in so much of the resources of sociology? This chapter is a reflection on Scandrett's journey of decolonisation as an activist-educator with roots in the environmental movement. It covers his engagement with environmental justice, 'critical race dialogues', postcolonial research in India and solidarity scholarship with the Palestinian anti-colonial struggle, and the impact of his discovery, in besieged Gaza, of the Arabic-Islamic origins of sociology.

Marion Ellison writes in Chapter 6, on the Scottish Centre for Social Justice, that public sociology research and education at Queen Margaret University encourage, facilitate and advance sociological knowledge, which is generated through engagement between academic researchers and key publics involved in social justice issues across Scotland. This includes communities, employer organisations, trade unions, NGOs and policy makers at the local, national and international levels. The main aim of the Scottish Centre for Social Justice is to provide a dynamic platform for collaborative work, co-generated knowledge and action on key social justice issues, and intersectional themes in a post-pandemic Scotland. Facilitating the co-production and co-design of policies with communities affected by them is central to providing a more comprehensive strategy for shared well-being. This chapter charts the rationale for the centre, its aims and its journey in enabling a more socially just and inclusive society.

Chapter 7 challenges dominant narratives about the Global South to address implicit bias and othering. It is based on an interview with Walid Salhab about his experience as an immigrant to Britain and how he learned to be quiet as he felt that people did not want to hear his story, and one with Sandra Ndale about her experience of being mentored by Walid during her time at Queen Margaret University as a student. Walid details how he has subsequently used his lived experience to make films that give a voice to people who are othered as 'immigrants' or 'refugees' in the United Kingdom, and how these are used to generate debate and insight into political and humanitarian issues with students and other publics. Sandra testifies to her experiences in Scotland, both at university and in watching the representation of people from the Global South on TV. With Emma Wood, she critically analyses the process used to secure access to the university for very marginalised people from the Global South. Together, they critically review how young survivors learn to navigate the assumptions made about them so they can make films, which means they can also tell their own stories.

Chapter 8 charts Stefanie Van de Peer's journey as a lecturer in films towards an anti-racist approach to curation and education. She looks at her interrelated roles as a film festival curator and as a lecturer in film studies – both roles she has long considered part of the idea of a feminist and anti-racist 'busting' of the canon. Even so, the process of decolonising her work has required a difficult journey through the paradoxical forces of speaking up and shutting up. The hunger for global cinema among audiences and students remains limited to Eurocentric experiences, where 'different' types of narratives, editing, storytelling techniques and structuring devices are seen to carry low production values, or as plain boring, not related to the students' own lived experiences. The chapter asks what we teach in film studies in Britain, to what extent we see our students as audiences and how we curate our syllabi.

In Chapter 9, Anthony Schrag charts the pedagogical practice informed by more than 15 years' experience as a professional artist in community settings. The chapter is framed by the concept of dialogue to integrate notions of decolonisation within his teaching. In an artistic context, dialogue manifests in a variety of forms, including discussions, talks, events, activities and debates. In a pedagogical context, dialogue underpins Schrag's understanding that education cannot develop without parity of engagement. Relationships based upon dialogic negotiation are therefore essential to his profession, teaching and teaching practice. This chapter discusses two case studies within Schrag's teaching practice where dialogue has both challenged power structures but also proposed new ways of organising educational experiences in line with a decolonising approach.

In Chapter 10, Bianca Mastrominico testifies that White is the colour of her name. As a professional performance maker, scholar and educator, she has inhabited the floating islands of her creativity on journeys across countries and artistic traditions that have challenged her perceptions of culture, diversity and – inevitably – her embodied experiences of racism. As a European woman from Southern Italy meeting non-Western theatre practices, she learnt the value of inner peace, silence and rituals in transcending systemic barriers in human relationships, and confronted bias, stigma and fear of 'otherness' due to her White upbringing. In this chapter, Mastrominico explores the deep value of anti-racist positioning from the perspective of her professional practice, and examines the tools she can create to disentangle herself from patriarchal conditioning surrounding White supremacist thinking and behaviour. In the unrest and upheaval of this historical moment of rebellion, she is interested in how we can collectively break the unnerving silence around racially motivated abuse of power and engender spaces of dialogue, awareness, creative alliances and empowerment for those who are not heard.

Chapter 11 by Anne O'Donnell describes her journey into mad studies and how she grew from activism into a role as an educator at Queen Margaret University. In her role as a lecturer and a PhD candidate, she is navigating the learning experience in a context in Scotland about which she is learning as she teaches it. Mad studies is a new discipline and Queen Margaret University is one of the first institutes to teach it at postgraduate level. In her pioneering role, Anne is designing a curriculum that she needs and wants to be explicitly anti-racist. With roots in Canadian research and based on lived experiences of the learners and teachers in mad studies, the discipline can be seen as fertile ground to explore anti-racist curricula, so this chapter explains what mad studies is and why it is important to decentre Whiteness in this emerging field. It then shows specifically how the learning environment is being decolonised.

In Chapter 12, Arek Dakessian, Georgina Pearson and their students ask us to imagine defragmented university spaces. Along with Anthony Ataekong, Joy Owojuyigbe, Olutayo Burrows, MD Rezaur Rahman and Misbah Haqani, they describe the role of student voices in bringing urgency and momentum to changing a world where academic institutions are slow. The authors draw on areas of activism around anti-racism in academia, along with student participation in industrial action. The marketisation, neoliberalisation and fragmentation in academia result in the 'siloing' of people into 'teacher', 'student', 'researcher' and 'management'. This division fractures and restricts opportunities for coherent political action. It is in this febrile context that student voices are the 'x-factor' in driving anti-racist activism in the academy. As part of their business model, academic institutions value what students say, as they are increasingly being viewed as 'clients'. When students speak up, it therefore moves these institutions much more quickly. The role of students in anti-racist activism in the academy is key to institutions acting with greater speed and efficacy for change.

In Chapter 13, Kavi Jagadamma, Judith Lane and Jane Culpan showcase their critical conversations on decolonising the physiotherapy curriculum. The phrase 'decolonising the curriculum' has become a buzzword across all health disciplines, and inclusivity is at the heart of physiotherapy practice. Indeed, there is a current drive to 'humanise' physiotherapy. However, conversations around humanising physiotherapy fail to acknowledge the discipline's implicit Eurocentric values and principles. In this chapter, the authors discuss a shared journey of exploring the impact of coloniality on the physiotherapy curriculum. They draw on examples from their practice and lived experiences to explore how coloniality manifests in various aspects of learning and practice – including canons of knowledge, epistemic dominance, homogeneity of representation in the profession, and principles and values.

In Chapter 14, Michelle L Elliot and Zaynab Akhtar discuss walking the talk: changing the challenging conversations in occupational therapy education. In response to global movements of anti-racism and decolonisation, they highlight that the profession and practice of occupational therapy have been challenged to speak up, step forward and act against racial injustice. However, there is a growing disconnect between the ethos of the profession and the enactment of its underpinning values. Statements from governing bodies and national organisations may be one way forward, but on-the-ground praxis needs to follow. This chapter reflects some approaches with which the authors have dealt as teachers, learners and practitioners in pre-registration education. A critical gaze is applied to occupational therapy and occupational therapists in professed roles as change agents and the need to examine our own need for change.

The editors conclude the book with a commentary on common themes and a summary on how we can all be anti-racist allies working towards a just and peaceful society in which we appreciate our similarities as human beings and celebrate our differences.

References

Adichie, C N (2009) The Danger of a Single Story. TED Talk. [online] Available at: www.youtube.com/watch?v=D9Ihs241zeg (accessed 12 September 2022).

Advanced HE (2020) We Stand United Against Racism. [online] Available at: www.advance-he.ac.uk/we-stand-united-against-racism (accessed 12 September 2022).

Ahmed, S (2004) Declarations of Whiteness: The Non-Performativity of Anti-Racism. *borderlands*, 3(2). [online] Available at: ww16.borderlands.net.au/vol3no2_2004/ahmed_declarations.htm?sub1=20230220-1052-585e-9053-9019b8750e7a (accessed 20 February 2023).

Ahmed, S (2012) *On Being Included: Racism and Diversity in Institutional Life*. Durham, NC: Duke University Press.

Bhopal, K (2021) The Sewell Report Displays a Basic Misunderstanding of How Racism Works. *The Guardian*, 31 March. [online] Available at: www.theguardian.com/commentisfree/2021/mar/31/sewell-report-racism-government-racial-disparity-uk (accessed 12 September 2022).

Church of England (2022) *First Report of the Archbishop's Commission for Racial Justice*. [online] Available at: www.churchofengland.org/about/archbishops-commissions/racial-justice/first-report-archbishops-commission-racial-justice (accessed 12 September 2022).

Equality and Human Rights Commission's (EHRC) (2016) *Healing a Divided Britain*. [online] Available at: www.equalityhumanrights.com/en/publication-download/healing-divided-britain-need-comprehensive-race-equality-strategy (accessed 12 September 2022).

Equality and Human Rights Commission's (EHRC) (2022) Publications Library: Race. [online] Available at: www.equalityhumanrights.com/en/our-work/publications-library?f%5B0%5D=node%253Afield_discrimination%3A9 (accessed 12 September 2022).

gov.uk (2017) *Race Disparity Audit*. [online] Available at: www.gov.uk/government/publications/race-disparity-audit (accessed 12 September 2022).

gov.uk (2021) *Report of the Commission on Race and Ethnic Disparities*. [online] Available at: www.gov.uk/government/publications/the-report-of-the-commission-on-race-and-ethnic-disparities (accessed 12 September 2022).

hooks, b (1994) *Teaching to Transgress: Education as the Practice of Freedom*. London: Routledge.

Hope Not Hate (2022) *State of Hate Report 2022*. [online] Available at: https://hopenothate.org.uk/2022/03/09/state-of-hate-2022-on-the-march-again/ (accessed 12 September 2022).

Hoult, S (2018) Aspiring to a Postcolonial Pedagogy Through Engagement with the Other: Deepening Intercultural Learning from a South Indian Study Visit. In Jackson, J and Oguro, S (eds) *Intercultural Interventions in Study Abroad* (pp 71–87). London: Routledge.

Hoult, S (2020) Engaging with the Cultural Other: The 'Colonial Signature' and Learning from Intercultural Engagements. *International Journal of Development Education and Global Learning*. [online] Available from https://uclpress.scienceopen.com/hosted-document?doi=10.14324/IJDEGL.12.2.03 (accessed 20 February 2023).

Lal, C A and Hoult, S (2019) What Can Be Gained from Intercultural Engagements? In Hammond, S and Sangster, M (eds) *Perspectives on Educational Practice Around the World*. London: Bloomsbury.

Lavery, H (2021) *Lament for Sheku Bayoh*. Edinburgh: Salamander Street.

Lawrence, S (2021) *Silence is Not an Option: You Can Impact the World for Change*. Jefferson City, MO: Scholastic.

Lorde, A (1983) There is No Hierarchy of Oppressions. *Bulletin: Homophobia and Education*, 14: 1–59.

Mandela, N (2003) Education is the Most Powerful Weapon We Can Use to Change the World. *Address to the Planetarium*. Johannesburg.

Mandela, N (2004) *Long Walk to Freedom: The Autobiography of Nelson Mandela*. London: Abacus.

Marcus, G (2019) *Gypsy and Traveller Girls: Silence, Agency and Power*. London: Springer.

Martin, J R (1986) Redefining the Educated Person: Rethinking the Significance of Gender. *Educational Researcher*, 15: 6–10.

Tuck, E and Yang, K W (2021) Decolonization is not a Metaphor. *Tabula Rasa*, 38: 61–111.

UNICEF (1989) *United Nations Convention on the Rights of the Child*. [online] Available at: www.unicef.org.uk/what-we-do/un-convention-child-rights (accessed 12 September 2022).

Virdee, S (2019) The Racialized Outsider as the Conscience of Modernity. British Sociological Association Conference Keynote Lecture, Glasgow.

CHAPTER 1

'AND STILL I RISE'

Geetha Marcus

Introduction

This first chapter in the book details my journey from being one of a few Black and minority ethnic headteachers in Scotland to becoming a sociologist and teacher-activist in initial teacher education (ITE) at three Scottish universities, working with mainly White colleagues and students. I will try to synthesise the deeply complex aspects of being racialised. The strategies I have attempted to use to champion anti-racism within schools and ITE programmes, and the challenges I have faced in doing so, are delineated for the reader. The chapter highlights approaches to self-care that have helped me to rise above the actions of those who believe we live in a post-racial era or for whom racism is an uncomfortable conversational taboo. I draw on the works of several key Black feminists – bell hooks, Audre Lorde, Sara Ahmed, Heidi Mirza – from whom I have learnt that teaching students to understand racial injustice by combining 'reason and emotion' would be of more benefit than just 'thought and action', a more comprehensive approach inspired by what Jane Roland Martin (1986, pp 7, 10) describes as the '*3 Cs of generative love*': care, concern and connection. I also share the main tenets of culturally responsive pedagogy (CRP), its proven benefits and how to get started as an anti-racist educator using CRP.

My background

Diversity in Singapore

I was raised in a pluralistic world where diversity and intercultural relations were the norm within a largely Chinese population. Although I am ethnically of Indian origin, I am third-generation Singaporean, a product of two sets of aspiring diasporic families who escaped the British Raj in the nineteenth century. I was formally educated in a single-sex Methodist missionary school, as were three generations of women in my family. In colonial Singapore, it was probably seen as a way of bettering oneself, of assimilating into the gold standard of an 'English education'. I witnessed numerous interracial marriages among family and friends – a curious mix of castes, religions and languages. I was brought up as a Hindu and a Christian. Six nations, five of the world's major religions and several caste levels are represented in my family, but as a 'minority ethnic woman', this did not preclude me from experiencing race and gender prejudice throughout my childhood.

'The coloured headteacher'

Marrying a Scot brought me to these shores, and for two decades I integrated and worked with hundreds of young people and their families in Scottish schools, first as a teacher and later as a headteacher (one of only five in 2011, which remains the case today). Similar to my life in Singapore, I experienced instances of racial abuse – both verbal and physical – in Scotland, but it felt much worse. I was once called *'the coloured headteacher'*, and my *'brun'* (brown) skin was often referred to as a mark of identification and difference. Throughout my time working in Scottish primary schools, I was 'othered' and faced everyday racism, which I either did not recognise at the time, or recognised and ignored. Many Black feminists highlight this as the first stage – one of non-recognition, shame and silence (Ahmed, 2012; Marcus, 2019; Mirza, 2009, 2015). I did not have the courage to call it out for what it was. I did not have the language. I resigned.

The immense impact on my mental and physical health led to a nervous breakdown. Sadly, this trauma is not unique. There are countless studies on the harm that is caused, intergenerational trauma even, of lives made unlivable. I hid my shame and trauma well, my home being a refuge and a space of respite. The political becomes personal and private (Ahmed, 2016). It was an incisive moment in my life and provided the catalyst for change. It is perhaps almost unimaginable for 'Whiteness' to comprehend the situatedness of the chaffing effect of being racially othered and the depth of despair to which it can lead.

The colour of scholarship in the ivory tower

I started a master's degree at the University of Edinburgh and then enrolled in a PhD. It transformed me. As a *'non-White, colonial immigrant'* doing intersectional research, I learned about my potential to be *'ideologically co-opted'* by the dominant systems of knowledge that have trained me to think and teach, as Bilge (2014, p 16) warns. As an educator, I recognise how education can also control and confine.

My research has forced me to confront many established assumptions within my own mindset. Pring (2004, p 9) argues that *'there are different views as to what is to be counted as an "educated person", and there is no obvious way that these differences might be resolved'*. The concept of the 'intellectual' – what and whose knowledge counts – can be used by dominant powers to restrict access to education, politics and other arenas of influence. hooks (1994, 2003) argues that formal education systems maintain *'White supremacist patriarchy'*. *'Education is deeply political... at all levels it is shaped by relations of power'* (Benjamin and Emejulu, 2012, p 33).

Haraway's (1988, p 584) thesis on the *'the politics and epistemology of partial perspectives'* guides my work. My personal identity, and racialised and gendered experiences, assumptions and views on racism and gender bias, as well as on education, have impacted my work and life. I acknowledge the limited power and privilege I do have, and use these to challenge and problematise existing *'understandings of power, inequality and difference... firmly supported by the [decolonising] epistemological foundations of intersectionality'* (Inken, 2014, p 266). I am also deeply scarred by the bullying and everyday and institutional racism faced by so many of my colleagues and students of colour, mirroring the cruel dog-whistle politics of our time. The reports cited in the introduction to this book have established that it is rife in academia.

However, not everyone will 'see' this partial perspective. People in positions of power cannot always 'see' – power can be blinding. The dominator cannot easily visualise the perspective of the 'othered' and suppressed. *'Vision is always a question of the power to see and perhaps of the violence implicit in our visualizing practices. With whose blood were my eyes crafted?'* (Haraway, 1988, p 585). These are challenging questions to ask ourselves – hence the conundrum of identity and why it is both personal and political. Yet this does not excuse us from being critically objective in our subjectivity.

Silence, silencing and agency

It is assumed that if you have power, you have agency and a voice. In my experience, this is not always the case. The three do not necessarily coexist neatly. For example, some women (regardless of ethnicity and class) who hold power, and who seem to have broken through the barriers in their careers, use that very same power to silence other women, artfully obstructing their progress. Rather than lifting others up with them, they pull up the ladder, and burn bridges to their compatriots, silencing their own consciences. *'It is unfortunately possible for the subjugated to lust for and even scramble into that [dominator] position and then disappear from view'* (Haraway, 1988, p 587). They become dominators too. This has been my experience (and that of many others) throughout my academic career – White women and women of colour placing themselves as barriers to opportunities in my career path, which I found hurtful and perplexing. I was once advised by a senior female academic that I could never work at a Russell Group university. I have now worked in two. Three years after being awarded my PhD, I was promoted to senior lecturer. *'And still I rise'* (Angelou, 2013).

Figure 1.1: 'And still I rise', Maya Angelou (Source: Teaching Resources)

The Athena Swan initiative, so often the pride and joy of human resources departments and equality and diversity committees, does not represent women like me. It continues to ignore the cries of marginalised staff and students, and cannot 'see' and 'hear' that this project misrepresents the experiences of the essentialised group called 'women' – the non-performativity of institutional attempts to embrace diversity (Ahmed, 2012). Equally, of course, there are women who on the face of it have little power yet use silence and their limited agency in artful ways to negotiate patriarchal terrains within family and community settings. They support each other with matriarchal kindness and compassion, without burning bridges.

Minoritised and marginalised women can become dependent on '*intellectuals*' and possibly '*feminists*' and '*feminist killjoys*' (Ahmed and Bonis, 2012, p 77), like this researcher, who are in positions of privilege, to speak for their condition. Their truth is constructed for them. Spivak (1988) rightly asks whether the subaltern can speak. The point, in fact, is whether she will be heard. In her study *Silence and Concealment in Political Discourse*, Schröter (2013, p 4) points out that '*it is typical for societies to have discourses about minorities in which the minorities themselves are hardly ever heard*'.

I have now been to several conferences about women and feminism, and I would argue that there is a difference in emphasis between those organised by White feminists in the West and those organised by Black feminists. For example, White feminist conferences tend to interrogate the right of women to wear clothes and makeup in a particular way, exploring the gender pay gap, lamenting breaking the glass ceiling or reflecting on the rights of women who are violent. Some do go further, intersecting gender with disability or gender with social class. Black feminists are concerned primarily with the political challenge to White supremacy in feminist politics and feminist social science, and this is reflected in their gatherings (Bilge, 2014; Mirza, 2009). Then again, my Arab friends speak differently about feminism, not only being critical of the colonial, neoliberal capitalist, racist, patriarchal mindset of the superpowers, but also countering the religious practices that oppress women in their communities. They do not separate the fight for the liberation of their bodies, liberation of women and the liberation of their country from colonial rule. They disrupt and call for the re-reading of their histories. And many minoritised and racialised women have paid a heavy price for this stance – shaming, silencing, ostracisation, exile, imprisonment, torture and death.

Ahmed (2016) reminds us that feminism is not always public; it can be deeply private and personal, because 'the personal is political'. It is also about consciousness, choice and change. Consciousness can lead to choice, however limited (hooks, 2015), and eventually lead to change. Countering the patriarchal mindset, as women and feminists, must be done with the utmost care and compassion, and without using what Lorde (2018) would call the *'master's tools'*, because it will not dismantle the master's house. Roland Martin's three Cs of generative love – care, compassion and connection (1986, pp 7, 10) – are necessary for us to *'rise'* together (Angelou, 2013).

Complain and rest

Being silent does not help to change the status quo, but speaking up about these problems ends up being perceived as a complaint by those in power. Complaints cause unhappiness – and indeed, as Ahmed (2021) argues, the 'complainer' becomes the problem. At the institutional level, well-meaning policies are then dusted off and duly applied as the complaint and the complainer necessitates investigation. Inquiries about racist behaviour towards a colleague or student of colour are more likely to be investigated by a White person – who, of course, cannot possibly have the experience of being racialised – personally, professionally and by the systems we live in.

'Causing unhappiness' (Ahmed, 2016, p 53) does not sit comfortably with me, and doing it can place you in the firing line. Yet causing unhappiness is necessary for this uncomfortable work. As women and feminists, we can live in hope – even if it is an irrational hope that the system will slowly but surely be disrupted and transformed over time. But just how one does this, without considerable harm to one's spirit, remains a continuing struggle for me. It is a conundrum faced by most activists. And so the key point is to take time to rest, to take a step back. Learn to share the brave space with others, and recognise that the fight is a communal effort. As I have discovered, much to my own detriment, the emotional and political labour cannot be pursued relentlessly. Rest and self-care are crucial to being an anti-racist, educator, activist and killjoy (Ahmed and Bonis, 2012).

I write here very much from the perspective of minoritised and marginalised women, and so my thoughts necessarily interrogate racialised and gendered patriarchal systems, which of course exists in universities. I am a Black feminist and use this framework to understand the world in which we live:

> Black feminist methodology or intersectionality allows us to see [people] in their particular context, without minimizing the effects of differences between different forms of subjugations or concealing one form in another. Rather, each form of oppression informs the other.
>
> (Marcus, 2019, p 113)

It is only by attention to situated localised accounts of *'marginalised lives'* that we can reveal the ways of *'being and becoming' ... [it] valorises situated experience which is at the heart of Black feminist epistemology'* (Mirza, 2015, p 4). Being an anti-racist and feminist must involve understanding and respecting the lived experiences of the individual in our midst. And herein, I argue, lies the power of Black feminism and what it has to offer the rest of the world.

Now I turn to one possible solution or way forward, which I have tried to implement in my ITE classrooms. It does require some understanding of the complexity of key terms such as 'culture' and 'cultural relativism' as contested concepts, and the nature of culturally responsive pedagogies.

What are culture and cultural relativism?

Definitions of culture have developed over time and continue to change. Social anthropologists in the nineteenth century viewed civilisation and culture as intertwined. Culture was defined broadly as a complex canon of *'knowledge, belief, art, morals, law, and custom'*, which is learned by those who belong to it (Scott, 2014, p 147). Superior cultures have higher moral values, which *'enabled the Victorian mind to construct a hierarchy of cultures or civilizations that provided a rationale for colonial activities by apparently higher-order Western civilizations'* (Scott, 2014, p 147). Cultures were – and still are – ranked.

However, cultural relativists argue that concepts are socially constructed and differ cross-culturally. These concepts may include such basic ideas as what is considered to be the truth or morally sound, and what constitutes knowledge or even reality itself. They tend to view culture formation as primarily being linked to language and discourse. Scott (2014, p 144) asserts that this

> has major implications for the study of non-Western societies [or communities]. If importing a Western rationalist approach is ethnocentric, then we must understand cultural patterns in their own terms, adopting an insider's view of culture.

Feyerabend (cited in Scott, 2014, p 144) argues that there are *'cultures so different from the West that they are incomprehensible to outsiders, who therefore cannot translate them into their own terms'*. Yet, to this day, cultures are pitted against one another, stratified and measured against the high European standard. Eurocentrism is embedded globally. Sociologists, ethnographers and anthropologists have variously attempted to define and describe cultures: culture is arguably not a description, but an explanation. As anti-racist educators, the challenge for us is to unlearn the patronising, patriarchal ranking, and objectively understand how cultures explain themselves.

Culturally responsive and sustaining pedagogies: learning to love

Culturally responsive pedagogy (CRP) *'empowers students to maintain cultural integrity, while succeeding academically'* (Ladson-Billings, 1995, p 476). The term has its roots with instruction of African American students in the United States (Ladson-Billings, 1994), and Indigenous children in Canada and Australia (Curwin Doige, 2003). It has been proven to be an effective form of pedagogy for students of all racial and ethnic backgrounds. By making education culturally relevant, CRP is thought to improve academic achievement. It urges collective action grounded in cultural understanding, experiences and ways of knowing the world. Gay (2018, p 8) expanded the traditional view of culture beyond race and ethnicity: *'Even without being consciously aware of it, culture determines how we think, believe, and behave.'*

Students bring a wealth of knowledge and experiences to their classes, and CRP honours this uniqueness. Using a research-based approach, teachers and scholars can draw from their students' languages, culture and life experiences to build a curriculum that resonates with their class on a deeper level. It is a constructivist approach, as it recognises multiple cultural viewpoints. It is also a social, not a deficit, model (Gewirtz, 1998). This approach is especially important for students of colour and diverse students, whose experiences do not often get the spotlight they need in the classroom. By embracing culturally responsive teaching, it is possible to create learning environments that are multicultural and more supportive of each student's ability to learn, while empowering them and helping them develop stronger academic skills.

Gay (2018, p 53) argues that CRP has five proven main benefits for students and colleagues:

- validating and affirming;
- multidimensional;
- empowering;
- liberating;
- transformative.

Culturally relevant pedagogy also extends to being culturally sustaining (CSP) (Paris, 2012; Paris and Alim, 2014). *'CSP seeks to perpetuate and foster – to sustain linguistic, literate, and cultural pluralism as part of the democratic project of schooling and as a needed response to demographic and social change*' (Paris and Alim, 2014, p 88). It aims to sustain pluralism through and with education in order to bring about racially just societies (Paris and Alim, 2014, p 88). Like CRP, it is socio-political and seeks to challenge power structures embedded in the dominant knowledge system, to ask '*What would education and pedagogies look like if we embraced other knowledges?*'

Getting started

Three cultural landscapes and functional dimensions

In order to effect change, three cultural landscapes, or functional dimensions, need to be understood, challenged and potentially reformed.

- The personal refers to the process by which educators learn to become culturally responsive.
- The institutional emphasises the need for reform of the cultural factors affecting the organisation of educational institutions such as universities, their policies and procedures and community involvement.
- The instructional refers to practices and challenges associated with implementing cultural responsiveness in the classroom (Richards et al, 2007).

The internal audit (personal dimension)

There is no one way of practising CRP. The first step is to do an internal audit of yourself, which is not easy. Haraway (1988, p 585) asserts that *'we are not immediately present to ourselves. Self-knowledge requires a semiotic-material technology to link meanings and bodies. Self-identity [can be] a bad visual system'*. The experiences you have had along your journey in life have formed stereotypes, which have then turned into implicit and explicit biases. These unintentional, unconscious attitudes impact how you relate to your students and colleagues, and how you design and plan courses and assess learning. Once you have conducted an internal self-audit, your curriculum will need one as well. The processes necessary for preparing to teach in a culturally responsive manner can be broken down into three general categories:

- exploring one's own culture and biases;
- learning about other cultures and diversities;
- learning about students' cultures and diversities.

Being aware of the status quo (institutional dimension)

As mentioned above, the institutional dimension requires you to be aware of the socio-political context within which universities operate and to dare to go against that status quo. You ought to understand the system that is working around us in educational settings. You ought not to avoid talking about the tough subjects that may not be addressed in our universities. Challenging fixed assumptions, expectations and habits may involve discomfort, so it takes courage (Arao and Clemens, 2013). It can be a form of 'crisis learning' – or even be quite inspirational for some people.

Conditions for creating a culturally responsive learning environment (instructional dimension)

Here are some ideas that have been proven to work (Ladson-Billings, 1994, 1995).

- Be reflective and encourage reflection in your seminars.
- Develop positive attitudes.

- Be attentive to the 'symbolic curriculum', or visuals displayed on PowerPoint slides.
- Establish meaningful inclusion practices.
- Try reciprocal teaching.
- Use cooperative learning techniques.

Being an anti-racist educator and activist requires a certain mindset:

- lifelong learning – being a lifelong learner oneself, and promoting it for students through curriculum and pedagogy;
- being reflexive;
- recognising that you are an agent for change;
- being prepared to be transformative.

Transformative learning transforms and challenges fixed assumptions, expectations and habits to make learners more open, reflective and emotionally able to change (Mezirow, 2000). It involves challenges and threats to existing beliefs and ideas, which may involve discomfort and resistance (Sterling, 2011). Moreover, it requires what I call an 'essential heart-set':

- having emotional literacy – ' care, concern and connection'. These are referred to as the *'three Cs of generative love'* by Martin (1986, p 7). She explains that teaching ought to combine *'reason and emotion'*, *'thought and action'*, and argues that this would be a more holistic approach. She therefore calls for education to be *'restructured'* along these lines (Martin, 1986, p 10);
- connecting to patterns of suffering in other social injustices;
- having emotional preparedness, humility and courage.

Much of this is about basic respect and acknowledgement of our common (and diverse) humanity. In other words, being an anti-racist, culturally responsive educator is fundamentally about exercising our integrity as humane professionals. Integrity is an individual mindset and heart-set, crucial to being a transformative agent for change in a racially just world. In a sense, education as a meaningful undertaking ought not to be for social justice, but rather ought to be an innate part of it. Education and social justice ought to be hardwired, symbiotic constituents – one and the same thing.

Conclusion

This chapter has detailed my journey from being one of a few Black and minority ethnic headteachers in Scotland to becoming a sociologist and teacher-activist in ITE. Having synthesised the deeply complex aspects of being racialised and gendered, I delineated the strategies I have used to champion anti-racism within schools and ITE programmes. The challenges you will face require courage to act within safe and many unsafe spaces. As I experienced, your reputation, chances of promotion and even your job (through constructive dismissal tactics) may be at risk. The chapter highlighted approaches to self-care and the importance of rest. Drawing on the works of several key Black feminists – bell hooks, Audre Lorde, Sara Ahmed and Heidi Mirza – I exposed some of the challenges faced by people of colour and argued that combining 'reason and emotion' with 'thought and action' is a more comprehensive approach, highlighting the need for care, concern, connection and integrity. I followed Lorde's (2018) argument that anti-racists ought to think outside of the box and avoid the normalised 'master's tools' to try new approaches. I shared the main tenets of CRP, its proven benefits and how to get started in practical terms as an anti-racist educator using these principles.

> *No one is born hating another person because of the colour of his skin, or his background, or his religion. People must learn to hate, and if they can learn to hate, they can be taught to love.*
>
> (Mandela, 2004, p 784)

I believe anti-racist education is fundamentally about sharing compassion, respecting difference and teaching people to love. It is not about being objective and uncritical of diverse ways of being and knowing. I offer a gentle reminder that self-identity, our view of ourselves, is not perfect – but it is important. Like my colleagues and friends who have shared their stories in this book, I believe that education is the kernel for peaceful resolution of differences and conflict; a site where we re-frame and re-balance our collective knowledges and experiences for better understanding. I argue we ought to embrace critical subjectivity and objectivity, in order for people to imagine an anti-racist future. It has enabled me to rise despite the discrimination and hatred I have faced, to continue to hope for a reconciled future.

Reflective questions

- How do you 'unlearn' what has been taught?
- How do you embrace the full narrative, which includes your own history and culture? Is this possible?
- How would you get started as an anti-racist educator?

Recommended reading

- Ahmed, S (2004) Declarations of Whiteness: The Non-Performativity of Anti-Racism. *borderlands*, 3(2). [online] Available at: ww16.borderlands.net.au/vol3no2_2004/ahmed_declarations.htm?sub1=20230220-1052-585e-9053-9019b8750e7a (accessed 20 February 2023).
- Ahmed, S (2012) *On Being Included: Racism and Diversity in Institutional Life.* Durham, NC: Duke University Press.
- Gay, G (2018) *Culturally Responsive Teaching: Theory, Research, and Practice.* New York: Teachers College Press.

References

Ahmed, S (2012) *On Being Included: Racism and Diversity in Institutional Life.* Durham, NC: Duke University Press.

Ahmed, S (2016) *Living a Feminist Life.* Durham, NC: Duke University Press.

Ahmed, S (2021) *Complaint!* Durham, NC: Duke University Press.

Ahmed, S and Bonis, O (2012) Feminist Killjoys (and Other Willful Subjects). *Cahiers du Genre*, 53: 77–98.

Angelou, M (2013) *And Still I Rise.* London: Hachette.

Arao, B and Clemens, K (2013) From Safe Spaces to Brave Spaces: A New Way to Frame Dialogue Around Diversity and Social Justice. In Landreman

L M (ed) *The Art of Effective Facilitation: Reflection from Social Justice Educators* (pp 135–50). Sterling: Stylus.

Benjamin, S and Emejulu, A (2012) Social Justice: Learning About Concepts, Terminology and Theories. In Arshad, R, Pratt, L and Wrigley, T (eds) *Social Justice Re-examined* (pp 22–47). Stoke-on-Trent: Trentham Books.

Bilge, S (2014) Whitening Intersectionality. *Racism and Sociology*, 5: 175.

Curwin Doige, L A (2003) A Missing Link: Between Traditional Aboriginal Education and the Western System of Education. *Canadian Journal of Native Education*, 27(2): 144–60.

Gay, G (2018) *Culturally Responsive Teaching: Theory, Research, and Practice*. New York: Teachers College Press.

Gewirtz, S (1998) Conceptualizing Social Justice in Education: Mapping the Territory. *Journal of Education Policy*, 13: 469–84.

Haraway, D (1988) Situated Knowledges: The Science Question in Feminism and the Privilege of Partial Perspective. *Feminist Studies*, 14: 575–99.

hooks, b (1994) *Teaching to Transgress: Education as the Practice of Freedom*. London: Routledge.

hooks, b (2003) *Teaching Community: A Pedagogy of Hope*. London: Routledge.

hooks, b (2015) *Feminist Theory: From Margin to Center*. London: Routledge.

Inken C E (2014) Connecting Intersectionality and Reflexivity: Methodological Approaches to Social Positionalities. *Erkunde*, 68: 265–76.

Ladson-Billings, G (1994) *The Dreamkeepers: Successful Teaching for African-American Students*. San Francisco: Jossey-Bass.

Ladson-Billings, G (1995) Toward a Theory of Culturally Relevant Pedagogy. *American Educational Research Journal*, 32(3): 465–91.

Lorde, A (2018) *The Master's Tools Will Never Dismantle the Master's House*. London: Penguin Modern.

Mandela, N (2004) *Long Walk to Freedom: The Autobiography of Nelson Mandela*. London: Abacus.

Marcus, G (2019) *Gypsy and Traveller Girls: Silence, Agency and Power*. London: Springer.

Mezirow, J (2000) *Learning as Transformation: Critical Perspectives on a Theory in Progress*. San Francisco: Jossey-Bass.

Mirza, H S (2009) Plotting a History: Black and Postcolonial Feminisms in 'New Times'. *Race Ethnicity and Education*, 12: 1–10.

Mirza, H S (2015) Harvesting our Collective Intelligence: Black British Feminism in Post-race Times. *Women's Studies International Forum*, 51: 1–9.

Paris, D (2012), Culturally Sustaining Pedagogy: A Needed Change in Stance, Terminology, and Practice. *Educational Researcher*, 41(3): 93–7.

Paris, D and Alim, H S (2014) What are We Seeking to Sustain Through Culturally Sustaining Pedagogy? A Loving Critique Forward. *Harvard Educational Review*, 84(1): 85–100.

Pring, R (2004) *Philosophy of Educational Research* (2nd ed). London: Continuum.

Richards, H V, Brown, A F and Forde, T B (2007) Addressing Diversity in Schools: Culturally Responsive Pedagogy. *Teaching Exceptional Children*, 39: 64–8.

Schröter, M (2013) *Silence and Concealment in Political Discourse*. Amsterdam: John Benjamins.

Scott, J (2014) *The Oxford Dictionary of Sociology* (4th ed). Oxford: Oxford University Press.

Spivak, G (1988) Can the Subaltern Speak? In Nelson, C and Grossberg, L (eds) *Marxism and the Interpretation of Culture* (pp 271–316). Urbana, IL: University of Illinois Press.

Sterling, S (2011) Transformative Learning and Sustainability: Sketching the Conceptual Ground. *Learning and Teaching in Higher Education*, 5: 17–33.

CHAPTER 2

WHOSE KNOWLEDGE COUNTS IN EARLY CHILDHOOD EDUCATION AND CARE?

Caralyn Blaisdell

Introduction

This chapter deals with anti-racism in early years research, policy and practice, with the early years being widely accepted as including children from birth to eight years of age. In a short chapter, it is impossible to cover all ground on the matter of anti-racism in the early years, and I have focused on weaving particular personal reflections together with some aspects of research, policy and practice that have helped me, as a White early years practitioner, to think differently about racism and anti-racism in the early years. These ideas will not be new to many, including many people of colour working in early years education.

The chapter begins with a short reflective biography, in which I locate some of the positions from which I view and experience the early years sector. As Haraway (1988) argues, the creation of knowledge is situated and partial; as a White, cisgender, straight, non-disabled middle-class American woman working in early years, my understandings come from those positions in mainly dominant groups, as well as from my learning from differently positioned others. The chapter then borrows Gallacher's (2020) concept of wayfaring in early childhood development to visit certain points in my own development, growth and change. First, the chapter visits the concept of young children's rights as enshrined in the UN Convention on the Rights of the Child (UNICEF, 1989), connecting this to children's right to non-discrimination and asking who is listening to young Black and Brown children in Scotland. Second, the chapter visits Black feminist and abolitionist perspectives on early years, particularly questioning the 'early years pioneers'. The final waypoint in the chapter looks at anti-racist activism among practitioners and researchers in the early years sector in Scotland. Each waypoint troubles the issue of whose knowledge counts in the early years, with an eye toward anti-racism, and attempts to challenge predetermined paths and landmarks in early years education.

Wayfaring: a short reflexive biography

I began working in the early years sector in 1999 during my undergraduate degree in the United States. There was an early years centre on campus, and I enjoyed seeing the children playing outside as I walked to class. At the time, I was studying chemistry, biology and neuroscience classes, with the aim of going to medical school and becoming a paediatrician, so I knew I wanted to work with children. I joined the early years centre part time as my work/study job, which is a financial aid programme in the United States providing work for students in financial need. Although I loved working at the early years centre, it took several years for me to let go of the idea of going to medical school (which I dreaded) and instead pursue a career in early childhood education (which I loved and enjoyed). This period of denial was partly because of the gap in prestige conferred by these professions.

During my career as an early years educator in the United States, there were clear racialised and classed patterns regarding who occupied which roles in the settings where I worked. Working-class people, particularly Black and Brown women, were persistently in lower-paid 'assistant' roles, while middle to upper middle-class White people, myself included, tended to be hired into better-paid 'lead teacher' roles or to be promoted into them quickly. Although these patterns were obvious and I discussed them often with friends, I was depoliticised and not engaged with larger solidarities or workplace activism that could have raised these issues and pressured managers to repair the injustices in these settings.

As these aspects of my professional journey illustrate, early childhood education is not neutral. My experiences demonstrate how the sector is intertwined with aspects of identity, power, personal and professional social positioning, and broader social, political and economic relations. Having moved from early childhood practice to doctoral study, to teaching about early years in higher education, there may seem to be a linear trajectory to my career and professional identity. However, as Gallacher (2020) argues, human development is less like a linear path and more like a process of movement and perception in the landscapes people inhabit. In the next sections of the chapter, I will visit three waypoints in my own landscape, where new possibilities emerged for making anti-racist early years practice more visible.

Waypoint 1: young children's right to be heard

The first waypoint, when considering whose knowledge counts in early years, relates to children's own knowledge and their right to be heard. The UN Convention on the Rights of the Child (UNICEF, 1989) enshrines a variety of rights for children into international law. The UNCRC is the most widely and rapidly ratified treaty in UN history; all countries save the United States of America have ratified it (Together, 2022). Two aspects of the UNCRC are particularly relevant for this chapter. First, children's right to be heard (Article 12) states that:

1. *States Parties shall assure to the child who is capable of forming his or her own views the right to express those views freely in all matters affecting the child, the views of the child being given due weight in accordance with the age and maturity of the child.*

2. *For this purpose, the child shall in particular be provided the opportunity to be heard in any judicial and administrative proceedings affecting the child, either directly, or through a representative or an appropriate body, in a manner consistent with the procedural rules of national law.*

Article 12 is one of a cluster of 'participation rights' which enshrine certain civil rights and freedoms for children (UN Committee on the Rights of the Child, 2009). Crucially, young children are holders of participation rights, just like their older counterparts; for the purposes of the UNCRC, a child means every human being below the age of 18 years unless, under the law applicable to the child, majority is attained earlier (Article 1).

The second relevant aspect of the UNCRC for this chapter is young children's right to non-discrimination (Article 2). This article ensures the full suite of UNCRC rights are available to children irrespective of their or their parents' or legal guardian's *'race, colour, sex, language, religion, political or other opinion, national, ethnic or social origin, property, disability, birth or other status'* (paragraph 1). Both the right to be heard and the right to non-discrimination are considered general principles of the UNCRC, which means they should be given particular attention when implementing the full suite of children's rights.

Perhaps because the United States has not ratified the UNCRC, young children's right to be heard was not an explicit part of my teacher education nor my practice before I came to Scotland. However, it has since had a deep and meaningful impact on my educational practice and my understanding of children and childhood. For many people – including me – participation rights require a rethink of the assumption that young children are too young, too innocent and too immature to form valid views, and that adults should therefore be in control. Young children's participation rights often require respect for non-verbal or not entirely verbal forms of communication, including how children express themselves through their ways of *'being and doing'* (Alderson, 2008, p 80). To exercise participation rights, and to have those rights recognised, can be understood as young children having a presence in life and society (Moosa-Mitha, 2005). To deny young children that presence is a form of silencing and oppression.

Exemplifying this, in a research project conducted during the Covid-19 pandemic, children of colour in Scotland were clear that Black and Brown children should be heard more by people in power (Blaisdell et al, 2021). They wanted investment in public services, childcare and parks to enable their communities to thrive. One young child (age seven, Chinese-British) expressed his views about his right not to experience discrimination – in this case, racism. He described his experiences.

> *My classmates told me that I was not invited to their birthday party because I was Chinese. I asked them why and they told me that their mothers told them so.*
>
> *I was walking through the park with my mum and people shouted horrible names at us for being Chinese.*

I wish some people would stop thinking that we have Covid because we are Chinese.

(Blaisdell et al, 2021)

The incident is portrayed in visual form in Figure 2.1.

Figure 2.1: Children should not experience racism (reproduced from Daramy et al, 2022)

Importantly, this young participant also had ideas for how people in power could help his and others' situation. He wished for *'teachers to teach kids about unkind behaviour (due to Covid-19) in the playground'* and for *'politicians to explain to people that Chinese doesn't equal Covid'*. His knowledge counts – but who is listening? Young children and children from marginalised groups are less likely to have their participation rights recognised (UN Committee on the Rights of the Child, 2009), leading to an intersection of identities that means young, racially minoritised children are less likely to be heard, particularly in majority White countries such as Scotland. This silencing can be compounded further by intersections with disability and gender, among other overlapping facets of identity (eg UN Committee on the Rights of the Child, 2009).

Waypoint 2: the early years pioneers

The second waypoint of the chapter visits the idea of early years pioneers. Those working in the early years sector will be familiar with many of 'the pioneers', a group of theorists and educators whose work has influenced, and continues to influence, early years practice today. The list of pioneers is flexible and not fixed, but often includes Piaget, Vygotsky, Pestalozzi, Froebel, Montessori, Malaguzzi and Steiner, among others (eg Nutbrown and Clough, 2014; Saracho and Evans, 2021). Crucially, the people whose ideas circulate widely and are legitimised with the title of 'pioneering' tend to be from White, Western European and North American backgrounds. The early years pioneers are so frequently named that they begin to seem inevitable, calling to mind Ahmed's (2013a) work on disciplinary paths. She argues that paths are a paradox: they are created by being followed and are then followed because they have been created. Thinking about the question of whose knowledge counts, creating a disciplinary path involves citation of particular (White, male) scholars and reproduction of their ideas; this leads to restriction and screening out of others. In early years, the ubiquity of White, European and American early years pioneers creates a well-trodden path that is hard to escape. The pioneers screen out the existence of other thinkers.

However, Ahmed (2013a, 2013b) argues that there is a certain pleasure when something derails you from the path; being derailed can put a spring in your step. In early years education, Pérez (2017) has put a spring in my step by pushing me off the well-trodden path of the early years pioneers. In her work, she describes how a light bulb went on for her when she realised that early years theory and practice is a field founded on White patriarchy (including the historical White pioneers). She notes that the work of the pioneers is replicated by teacher education programmes and teaching licensing exams, and that her choice not to cite the pioneers is perceived as neglect. However, Pérez (2017) prefers to turn her focus to scholars who are women of colour, particularly those working with Black feminist thought:

> *For early childhood, theorizing lived experiences with Black feminist thought (rather than White patriarchal viewpoints) challenges and broadens past and contemporary constructions of childhood/s and calls for research, policies, and pedagogies to centralize the perspectives of women of color and other oppressed peoples.*
>
> (Pérez, 2017, p 54)

By derailing her readers off the path of the pioneers, Pérez connects directly to the question of whose knowledge counts in early years education. She insists that despite historical erasure of the perspectives of women of colour in early childhood theorising, Black feminist thought is essential in early childhood (Pérez, 2017). In her view, this is because Black feminist thought centres perspectives from the margins, affirms the presence of women of colour as early childhood educators and explicitly politicises children and educators' understanding of social inequalities.

By derailing me from the usual path, Pérez's work opened up a new space for theorising and understanding early childhood, and particularly what anti-racist early childhood practice could look like. From this, I have connected with other work such as the abolitionist Akiea Gross (they/them), founder of Woke Kindergarten, who also disrupts normative White patriarchal early years discourses. Gross (2023) creates practical resources to support young children and adults to imagine more just futures together, with a specific focus on healing, liberation and resistance for young Black and Brown children. Here, rather than assume young children do not understand, or should be sheltered from thinking or learning about social inequality, Gross draws on Black feminist thought to assert that these issues are already affecting Black and Brown children. Gross frames young children as equal participants in critical conversations about social life. For example, they offer frameworks for considering issues such as police abolition, erasing borders and unschooling (Woke Kindergarten). Their work resonates with other abolitionist work in early childhood, which offers space for re-envisioning worlds where Black children's aliveness and *'ways of being in the world are nurtured'* (Nxumalo and Pacini-Ketchabaw, 2022, p 4).

Waypoint 3: Anti-Racist Early Years Collective

The final waypoint in this chapter is the Anti-Racist Early Years Collective (AREYC), which is a group of academics, practitioners and grassroots activists, founded in Scotland in 2020, of which I am a member. The Anti-Racist Early Years Collective is a group led by women of colour, which has an intersectional ethos. At the time the group was founded, anti-racist protests and uprisings were happening around the world, with activists speaking out against racism, police brutality and the ongoing legacies of European colonialism. During this time of social uprising, there was little to be heard from majority White early years scholars and policy-makers in Scotland, and it was difficult to reconcile Scottish policy rhetoric on inclusion and well-being with a silence on racism. AREYC was founded to highlight the grassroots anti-racist activism, research and practice that was already going on in the Scottish early years sector and to challenge racism, collaborate with other groups and push for change.

It has been in some ways easy and in most ways difficult to approach this work in Scottish early years education. By easy I mean that many organisations initially seemed interested in AREYC's work. By difficult – among other things – I mean that organisations wanted us to work for free and to have women of colour do consulting work without compensation. This work takes an emotional toll on people of colour, which was rarely recognised. Members of the group would have long, usually unpaid, meetings with organisations, after which things seemed to quickly 'snap back' to the more well-trodden path of Scottish early years policy in terms of dominant discourses around generic well-being and universal 'needs' of children, rather than naming racism (and other inequalities) and holding it as a central concern in the long term.

Working with the group has triggered many reflections for me about my own early years practice – particularly now that I work in higher education – and how often I 'snap back' to the generic path. There can be a culture of (White) cosiness and comfort (eg Palmer, 2021) in the early years sector that smothers sharper, more uncomfortable and more political discussions of inequalities in the sector. Another aspect that has triggered reflection for me has been the 'newness' of anti-racism as a concern for many majority-White organisations, and the sense that both racism and anti-racism only came into existence in the summer of 2020. Along with my colleagues, I have witnessed White responses to discussions about anti-racism, including defensiveness, racist harassment online, silence and expecting spoon-fed solutions to racism during a two-hour training session. These responses are directed at the women of colour in the group; the White members of the group do not experience them. A final aspect has been my own fragility and discomfort with disagreement and tension that has sometimes arisen in the group, and my instinct to swoop in, propose solutions and try to smooth things out; as a White person I perhaps expect to play a central role and control the dynamics, and feel entitled to do so.

Returning to the question of whose knowledge counts in early years education, there are early years educators and activists in Scotland and elsewhere in the United Kingdom, many of whom are people of colour, who are campaigning, consulting, writing, researching and practising anti-racism in early years. I would like to close this section by highlighting four pieces of publicly accessible work that have particularly resonated with me regarding the Scottish context and that may be useful for other (White) early years educators. The first is Shaddai Tembo's (2021) chapter in the recent book *Play is the Way*. In this chapter, Tembo names the silences in Scotland around racism, linking this to other inequalities around gender and heteronormativity, and identifying the potential of resisting normative, limiting discourses around difference in early years. The second is activist Pavithra Sarma's (2020) essay 'Just Listen … Please', published on her personal blog, in which she describes the *'malaise coupled with extreme denial'* that she experiences from White people when she talks about the racist experiences she and her family have had in Scotland. Sarma implores White readers to listen and see the power dynamics at play across the broad early years sector. Third, Caroline Wagstaff (2020) describes how her experiences as a woman of Scottish-Ghanaian heritage have led to solidarity with other groups who have had to fight to have their voices heard, such as LGBTQ+ and disabled communities. Finally, Khadija Mohammed (2022) argues that anti-racism must become everyone's concern in Scottish education, including in schools where children are from a White ethnic identity background. These four pieces of writing all explore different nuances and positions within anti-racist education in Scottish early years, but they share two key themes: the perniciousness of silences about racism and the powerful potential of building solidarities in the struggle against racism.

Conclusion

This chapter has explored three waypoints in my particular journey as a White educator learning about anti-racism in the early years sector, particularly with regard to higher education. Each waypoint troubles the Whiteness of whose knowledge counts in the early years, and offers different paths where racism and anti-racist practice become visible. The chapter ended with the concept of silences and solidarity, and highlighted work by people of colour working in Scottish early years education. There are many other resources online and in print to help (White) early childhood educators understand and trouble the racialised patterns of the profession. By stepping off the beaten path, early childhood educators can build solidarity across difference, realising the potential to end silences on racism and intersecting inequalities.

Reflective questions

- Whose knowledge counts in your early years (or other educational) practice?
- Whose work do you read, share and learn from?
- Who are you working in solidarity with, in order to develop anti-racist practices and resist the 'cosiness' of White comfort in your educational practice?

Recommended reading

- Sarma, P (2020) 'Just Listen ... Please!' [online] Available at: https://funningandallthat.blogspot.com/2020/07/is-scottish-education-system-racist.html (accessed 14 November 2022).
- Tembo, S (2021) More Work to Do: Thinking Through Equalities with Young Children in Scotland. In Palmer, S (ed) *Play is the Way: Child Development, Early Years and the Future of Scottish Education* (pp 187–95). Paisley: Postcards from Scotland. [online] Available at: https://postcardsfromscotland.co.uk/play-is-the-way (accessed 14 November 2022).

References

Ahmed, S (2013a) Creating Feminist Paths. *feministkilljoys*. [online] Available at: https://feministkilljoys.com/2013/08/27/creating-feminist-paths (accessed 9 December 2022).

Ahmed, S (2013b) Making Feminist Points. *feministkilljoys*. [online] Available at: https://feministkilljoys.com/2013/09/11/making-feminist-points (accessed 9 December 2022).

Alderson, P (2008) *Young Children's Rights: Exploring Beliefs, Principles and Practice* (2nd ed). London: Jessica Kingsley.

Blaisdell, C, Daramy, F and Sarma, P (2021) Impact of COVID-19 on Children of Colour in Scotland. QMU Research. [online] Available at: www.qmu.ac.uk/research-and-knowledge-exchange/qmu-research/covid-19/impact-of-covid-19-on-children-of-colour-in-scotland (accessed 9 December 2022).

Daramy, F, Blaisdell, C, Sarma, P and New Africa Comics (2022) *The Impact of the COVID-19 Pandemic on Children of Colour in Scotland: Visions for Change*. [online] Available at: www.qmu.ac.uk/media/cpkogqqd/impact-of-covid-comic-compressed.pdf (accessed 9 December 2022).

Gallacher, L (2020) *From Milestones to Wayfaring: Geographic Metaphors and Iconography of Embodied Growth and Change in Infancy and Early Childhood*. Newcastle-upon-Tyne: Northumbria University. [online] Available at: https://researchportal.northumbria.ac.uk/ws/portalfiles/portal/39899705/Revised_GeoHumanities_Submission_Body_for_PP0566.pdf (accessed 20 February 2023).

Gross, A (2023) Woke Wonderings: Unconventional Questions Rooted in Liberatory Thought. *Woke Kindergarten*. [online] Available at: www.wokekindergarten.org/woke-wonderings (accessed 8 July 2022).

Haraway, D (1988) Situated Knowledges: The Science Question in Feminism and the Privilege of Partial Perspective. *Feminist Studies*, 14(3): 575–99.

Mohammed, K (2022) Taking Action on Racism. *Teaching Scotland*. [online] Available at: https://readymag.com/4009612 (accessed 9 December 2022).

Moosa-Mitha, M (2005) A Difference-Centred Alternative to Theorization of Children's Citizenship Rights. *Citizenship Studies*, 9(4): 369–88.

Nutbrown, C and Clough, P (2014) *Early Childhood Education: History, Philosophy and Experience* (2nd ed). London: Sage.

Nxumalo, F and Pacini-Ketchabaw, V (2022) Centering Black Life in Canadian Early Childhood Education. *Gender & Education*, 35(2): 186–98.

Palmer, S (2021) Preface to the Second Edition. In Palmer, S (ed) *Play is the Way* (2nd ed) (p 1). Paisley: Postcards from Scotland.

Perez, M S (2017) Black Feminist Thought in Early Childhood Studies: (Re)Centering Marginalized Feminist Perspectives. In Smith, K, Alexander, K and Campbell, S (eds) *Feminism(s) in Early Childhood: Using Feminist Theories in Research and Practice* (pp 49–62). Singapore: Springer.

Saracho, O and Evans, R (2021) The Metamorphosis of Early Childhood Theorists and Pioneers. *Early Child Development and Care*, 191(7–8): 991–2.

Sarma, P (2020) 'Just Listen … Please!' [online] Available at: https://funningandallthat.blogspot.com/2020/07/is-scottish-education-system-racist.html (accessed 14 November 2022).

Tembo, S (2021) More Work to Do: Thinking Through Equalities with Young Children in Scotland. In Palmer, S (ed) *Play is the Way* (pp 186–95). Paisley: Postcards from Scotland.

Together (2022) UN Convention on the Rights of the Child. [online] Available at: www.togetherscotland.org.uk/about-childrens-rights/un-convention-on-the-rights-of-the-child (accessed 9 December 2022).

UN Committee on the Rights of the Child (2009) General Comment No. 12: The Right of the Child to be Heard. Office of the UN High Commissioner for Human Rights. [online] Available at: http://tbinternet.ohchr.org/_layouts/treatybodyexternal/TBSearch.aspx?Lang=en&TreatyID=5&DocTypeID=11 (accessed 9 December 2022).

UNICEF (1989) *United Nations Convention on the Rights of the Child.* [online] Available at: www.unicef.org.uk/what-we-do/un-convention-child-rights (accessed 12 September 2022).

Wagstaff, C (2020) Black Lives Matter: Caroline Wagstaff Shares Her Personal Story. *NewsBeat Edinburgh Council*. [online] Available at: https://newsbeat-edinburgh.tfemagazine.co.uk/summer-2020/latest-news/black-lives-matter-caroline-wagstaff-shares-her-personal-story (accessed 9 December 2022).

CHAPTER 3

CHANGING WORLDVIEWS THROUGH STUDY VISITS

Simon Hoult

Introduction

Over the first part of this century, there has been a considerable national focus on the internationalisation of higher education within a neoliberal agenda (Harris, 2008). One significant aspect of such a development has been the inclusion of international study visits in school and university teaching programmes. Such visits are controversial matters, however, and there is a growing body of literature reviewing the influence of study visits on participants' thinking, which often shows limited exposure of the global powerbase on which these thoughts were constructed (eg Martin and Griffiths, 2012; Martin and Wyness, 2013; Weeden and Hayter, 1996). The enormity of any experience to effect such an ontological and epistemological change by overcoming Eurocentric beliefs formed over a lifetime is significant and fraught with the possibility of failure (Finney and Orr, 1995). As a leader of study visits for university education students, however, to me their limited outcomes were a provocation to potentially challenge students' worldviews and expand their global awareness.

In this chapter, I reflect on the implications of 'study abroad' for anti-racist activism from my experiences of leading, teaching and researching study visits of UK-based student teachers to South India. My research (eg Hoult, 2018, 2020; Lal and Hoult, 2019) identified a number of pedagogic dimensions within such intercultural engagements where there was demonstrable change in participants' worldviews through a focus on understanding the process of their intercultural engagement using careful and negotiated reflection and reflexivity. I reflect here that such a change in worldview is an important element to help develop anti-racism activism through the examination of inequality and privilege and an awakening of the falsity of apparently universal thinking that are then exposed as Eurocentric in their nature.

The study visit

The study visits on which I base these reflections are framed within an elective master's module called 'Intercultural Learning: A South India Study Visit'. It involved participants' attendance at three days of teaching before the visit, the completion of an intercultural learning journal during the module and re-immersion into the participants' placement school upon their return home. The participants were then required to write a reflection about their intercultural learning. Through careful local negotiation, the visit focused on a broad range of schools as well as higher educational engagement. My attempts to aspire to greater equitability between hosts and visitors were advanced by growing the interaction between the participants and their Indian peers in sharing experiences as student teachers in supportive but unstructured situations. A focus on relationship-building and mutual learning did not disregard the economic disparity between the two groups, but through this focus I aimed to avoid the imbalance that Burr (2008, p 6) noted during a Ghanaian study visit, where a local teacher said *'when you come to us you are a visitor, when we come to you we are a resource'*.

To aid mutual learning, a conference was organised that focused on education, language and culture, jointly sponsored by my institution and the local university. Local student teachers, English master's students and the visit participants were able to speak about their research projects at the conference and, through joint university funding, an edited book was published containing many of the speakers' papers (Hoult and Lal, 2015). In this way, the project strived for equity that focused on the professional and academic relationship between Indian and UK-based student teachers, notwithstanding their economic differentials and the reality that Eurocentric approaches to research are globally privileged.

My teaching was informed by my scholarly endeavours associated with understanding the intercultural processes at work. In articulating a positioning where I considered that we were written through the colonial and that its powers were such that this needed exposure, I took the pedagogically political decision, supported by Martin and Griffiths (2012), to expose the participants to postcolonial theory. This potentially provided them with a lens through which to consider their experiences and illustrated that my pedagogy was no neutral act, but rather politically charged.

In my pre-visit teaching, I argued that the influences on our perceptions of India were also not neutral. I shared my own influences and asked the participants to create their own montages of conscious influences. I introduced ideas of Orientalism (Said, 2003), illustrated through contemporary film and advertising as well as nineteenth-century narrative art, and asked the participants to critique these artefacts. From the ideas of the artist having control of the narrative, up to the point of a painting's completion at least, I introduced the idea of voice and of representation, showing Adichie's (2009) TED Talk on the dangers of the single story. Using these ideas of representation and postcolonialism, we critiqued the intercultural learning of the three brothers in Wes Anderson's film *The Darjeeling Limited* (2007) regarding film as a safe space to articulate colonially infused actions or expressions of privilege.

For my research, I interviewed participants after their module concluded and, with their permission, analysed their assignments and journals as well as my own research journal. The richness and diversity that emerged from the participants' learning narratives provided idiosyncratic stories about intercultural learning that revealed an array of provocations to my thinking. The emergent themes were grouped broadly around challenging pre-assumptions about India and the influence of place; power and colonial triggers; intercultural learning processes; changing perceptions of India and home; and personal and professional change. It was in this last theme that participants' activism particularly emerged, provoked by their thinking and responses to other themes.

The crossing of cultural boundaries by returning 'home' was an important dimension to deepening intercultural learning, although it initially generated bewilderment for some, especially those who thought reflexively about their experiences. It further revealed the socio-cultural construction of society and challenged a reconsideration of the self for some, and eventually resulted in change and related actions for many.

Agency was an important idiosyncratic outcome in many narratives that, in almost all cases, emerged after returning 'home'. The early intangible nature of learning illustrated the cultural translation required to consider one's learning, and agency only seemed able to develop once learning became tangible. Such learning became explicit through reflection over varied timescales prompted by the academic reflection and interviews. Agency also emerged later due to the cultural, economic and professional capital being predominantly home-based. Some of the narratives suggested the participants became agents of change from within the 'centre'. They were aware of the power dynamics about representation and marginalisation and strove to change matters through third-sector engagement, changing their approach to teaching about race and place, and shifting their focus of future employment to work in more racially diverse parts of the country.

I do not intend to consider further the outcomes of my research here, but provide these themes to illustrate the potential of such study visits to challenge worldviews and expose the apparent universality of Western forms of thinking as Eurocentric. I turn now to reflect on the theoretical and pedagogical influences that helped to develop my thinking and approach to study abroad. In doing so, I deliberately attempt to draw on literature that may be used as part of an anti-racist agenda.

Theoretical influences

I should start by explaining why I chose to underpin my thinking with postcolonial theory. It was provoked by my curiosity and some discomfort in experiencing the ways in which me and my students were treated in South India. This not only extended to high-profile welcomes at schools in huge assemblies and the student teachers given celebrity status by the pupils, but also in the way well-respected educationalists sought the pedagogical expertise from student teachers, who had been on an initial training programme for a little over three months! Such experiences made me wonder whether there was something more to these experiences than the undoubted evident kindness and hospitality. The following thus provides some insight into how my thinking developed from such provocations.

To some degree, we live in political, and to a lesser extent economic, postcolonial times; however, as Wa Thiong'o (1986) says, *'decolonising the mind'* for us all is an ongoing struggle. Understanding postcolonial theory, drawing on feminist Orientalism (Yeğonoğlu, 1998), helped me to explore intercultural learning, potentially to expose and transcend hidden colonial dimensions to our thinking in aspiring to a postcolonial engagement with the Other. Theoretically as well as experientially, it is clear that study visits are potentially fraught with neocolonial difficulties relating to power, voice, language and stereotyping, as well as unreciprocated plundering of local 'knowledge'. Postcolonial theory therefore potentially provides a critique to consider not just intercultural learning, but the pedagogic processes and nature of such visits.

Our social actions and decisions happen in complex situations where their outcomes are uncertain, but often have global determining factors (Delanty, 2009); however, our psychosocial interpretations of these factors mean that we all consider matters differently – albeit within dominant cultural paradigms. A cosmopolitan orientation towards our social actions and decision-making provides a means to express and interpret our world experiences, which connects theories of globalisation to those of social and political theory (Delanty, 2009). The cosmopolitan experience and interpretation of the Other through the reinterpretation of the self is called the '*cosmopolitan imagination*'; it is provoked during '*moments of openness*' to develop a new relationship between self and Other in a world setting (Delanty, 2009, p 53).

A cosmopolitan imagination has the potential to provide a base from which to consider our changing views about self and Other in the context of intercultural learning as well as indicating a means by which transformative learning takes place; one's ability to imagine other viewpoints is a significant dimension of transformative learning (Mezirow, 2000).

Delanty (2009, p 7) identifies four social orientations that enable a cosmopolitan imagination to be developed, which:

1. stresses cultural difference and pluralisation;
2. occurs in the context of global-local relations;
3. thinks beyond established borders;
4. involves the reinvention of political community around global ethics.

There is considerable resonance between the dimensions of cosmopolitan imagination, intercultural learning and associated pedagogy, and theories of transformative learning. The cosmopolitan orientation recognises the importance of plurality, fluid boundaries and an openness to change associated with open *'dispositions towards difference'* (Andreotti, 2013) and progressive views of place and its global connectedness (Massey, 2005). Delanty's fourth dimension highlights the significance of pedagogy in challenging us to expose hidden ideologies and reorientate our thinking towards the political community and global ethics; pedagogy is never a neutral act and nor are its outcomes.

What is clear from the literature I have drawn upon is that the space where imagining the self and Other relationship happens is one of fluidity and provisionality of thought. Such metaphysical spaces are called *'liminality'* by Land et al (2008); I rename them 'liminal places' to reflect the influence of physical location within study abroad. These spaces/places are the antithesis of the fixed thinking associated with a certainty of knowing, which Sterling (2001, p 15) calls *'first order thinking'*. It is only when learners develop an awareness of their own and others' *'tacit assumptions'* (Mezirow, 2000, p 4), and how these inform interpretations of the world, that learners develop an understanding of their own learning processes, or *'second order learning'* (Sterling, 2001, p 15). This exposure of our assumptions provides the foundation for learning to become potentially transformative. Transformative learning changes *'how we know'* (Kegan, 2000, p 50), and it occurs through the exposure and critique of our epistemology. Transformative learning is a form of third-order learning in that it provides us with a deep understanding of an *'alternative worldview'* (Sterling, 2001, p 15). This is not a simple rejection, or even reforming, of existing knowledge in favour of something new, but an *'evolutionary'* way of thinking that arises from the *'subordination of once-ruling capacities to the dominion of more complex capacities'* (Kegan, 2000, p 60).

The seven 'learning spaces' developed by Andreotti (2010) help illustrate how different approaches to global learning may be used to understand the spaces inhabited by learners as a response to a stimulus. The first learning space is akin to Sterling's first-order thinking, reflecting singular, certain and fixed approaches to learning without the conditions for a cosmopolitan imagination to emerge and suggesting a 'concrete' worldview where the development of knowledge would focus on content.

The second and third learning spaces first recognise the contradictory nature of our thinking, which may be likened to Meyer and Land's (2003) 'troublesome knowledge', and recognise the lens(es) through which we form our worldview based on our epistemological assumptions. An epistemological exposure provides the platform for reflection akin to a liminal place and suggests a plurality of thinking not seen earlier. Multiple perspectives build on this plurality and emerge along with their underpinning assumptions in the fifth learning space. It is here that the potential for transformative learning and a cosmopolitan imagination emerge, associated with fluidity and a lack of fixed boundaries, which also highlights where the learner begins to identify different solutions to issues in different contexts – in other words, learning becomes contextualised. Contextualised learning that highlights a plurality of thinking suggests an ability to read issues in terms of local to global relationships, and to begin to read issues with more fluid boundaries akin to cosmopolitan imagination.

The sixth and seventh spaces are indicative of learners being able to embrace complexity and conflicting opinion, and understanding that our responses are highly contextualised and change as situations alter. Andreotti (2010, p 16) emphasises the social construction of *provisional meaning* and the deepening of analysis that occurs. These learning spaces seem to concur with her epistemological position where *'knowledge, learning, reality and identities [are] socially constructed, fluid, open to negotiation and always provisional'* (Andreotti, 2010, p 6).

The transformative potential of learning about global issues to alter one's way of life personally and/or professionally was observed by Rogers and Tough (1992). These authors note, however, that the potential for transformation is only realised if certain cognitive and emotional barriers to learning are overcome. Rogers (1998) identifies five distinct but frequently interlinked dimensions to her students' global learning: cognitive, affective, existential, empowerment and action. This suggests that a precursor for activism is a significant change in thinking and a sense of agency.

The significance of the affective domain is signalled by Hicks (2006) as an often-neglected dimension of global pedagogy; however, to separate it from the cognitive dimension, despite the recognition of their interconnectedness, still seems to over-simplify the holistic and deeply personal learning identified by Hicks. This is echoed by Scoffham and Barnes (2009), who applaud the recognition of feelings in the learning process, but challenge the suggested sequential nature of the five dimensions and indicate that it is the emotional trigger of the experience that is the apparent learning stimulus rather than an initial cognate response. The emotional dimension within transformative learning is also highlighted by Mezirow (2000), who argues that it is not only the assumptions supporting our thinking that are exposed in such learning, but also those that are the foundation for our emotions.

A cyclical 'three awakenings' model to learning about global issues was developed by Rogers and Tough (1992), which indicates a deepening of learning from the initial engagement to developing further knowledge (the *'awakening of the mind'*), to a more empathetic position for global learning (*'awakening of the heart'*), which lead through one's growing duty and allegiance to the Other to an *'awakening of the soul'* (Hicks, 2006, p 102). Mezirow (2000, p 6) explains that *'learning through soul'* is where the *'socioemotional'* and *'intellectual'* converge. In the 'three awakenings' model, learning becomes potentially deeper and possibly transformative. The existential dimension to learning leads potentially to personal action through a *'personal sense of power and hope'* (Hicks, 2006, p 102). The cyclical nature of this model perhaps implies that the outcomes of actions and hope lead to further engagement with learning and activism over the longer term – or, in other words, is sustainable and enduring.

A fundamental dimension of intercultural learning that is informed by postcolonial theory is the recognition of the power and privilege of the 'centre'. To expose such a 'centre', and thus illustrate privilege, is itself a political act. In interpreting Spivak's postcolonial theories for education, Andreotti's (2011, p 230) four-point conceptual framework provides a basis on which to construct a radical pedagogy for activism.

1. *'Learning to unlearn'*: stemming from an initial realisation that our worldview of what is 'right' comes from a positioning that is a construction of our social, historical and cultural world and that we carry certain 'cultural baggage' that shapes our learning.

2. *'Learning to listen'*: enables us to recognise the influences our 'centre' thinking has upon the world and to be open to new interpretations of worldviews while still thinking about how our 'cultural baggage' shapes our thinking and how our engagement with the Other shapes our sense of self.

3. *'Learning to learn'*: the process by which we enable new perspectives to influence our worldview and to recognise what we do not know. It enables new perspectives to develop through *'seeing through other eyes'* (Andreotti, 2011, p 230) without trying to appropriate the Other within oneself or vice versa. Through crossing cultural boundaries and engaging with new cultural experiences, we may allow our 'cultural baggage' to be reshaped.

4. *'Learning to reach out'*: we are able to incorporate our learning into our own context and in our relationship with the Other while still reflecting on *'ways of being, thinking, doing, knowing and relating'* (Andreotti, 2011, p 230). The outcomes of our engagement with the Other are unpredictable through the mutual teaching and learning potentially brought by this contact with difference. Our learning comes from reaching out with *'respect and accountability in the complex and uncomfortable intercultural space where identities, power and ideas are negotiated'*

The four dimensions are regarded by Andreotti to be cyclical with our initial 'learning to unlearn' exposing our worldviews, leading to opportunities to listen and then learn before reframing our worldviews through an adjusted view of the relationship between self and Other. Such a developmental process is perhaps visualised better as a spiral of ever-deepening understanding of Self/Other and the significance of reflexivity is not to be under-estimated in this process, including the recognition and subsequent dropping of 'cultural baggage' should we successfully 'learn to unlearn'. Such an action chimes with Bhaba's (2004) 'third space', which exists between the cultures of the self and Other in a process of 'hybridity'. Martin and Griffiths (2012, p 922) argue that such learning becomes possible if we are troubled by existing worldviews that *'disrupt and resist: the notion of a single story; essential ideas about self and identity; forms of colonialism and imperialism; and neo-liberal conceptualisations of care'*. Moreover, they argue that pedagogic approaches should enable such spaces to emerge to help avoid any disavowal of experiences due to a paralysis in learning.

Towards a decolonial pedagogy?

While the exploration of postcolonial theories underpinned my approach to study visits, they remain a lens through which to view the world. They do not inherently change practice unless consequential actions arise. As an account of ethical attempts to provoke a response in my participants (as well as myself) it was therefore important to consider the pedagogical dimensions used, which were theoretically infused with postcolonialism to enable students to be in a position to reimagine themselves in a global context – in effect, a decolonial pedagogy.

A curriculum that explicitly identifies the *'cultural violence'* of Eurocentric power, which promotes *'coexistence'* and *'kindredness'* through a *'pedagogy of lovingness'*, is argued for by De Lissovoy (2010, p 279). Such a pedagogy rails against cultural domination through an anti-colonial agenda that draws on postcolonial theory extending into ways of knowing and being – in short, a transformative intercultural pedagogy. De Lissovoy's pedagogy places high regard on relationships with the Other, which he argues to be matters of our ontology. In this way, he concurs with the significance of the encounter portrayed by Levinas (2006). In a similar manner, Martin and Griffiths (2012, p 921) argue that intercultural experiences should not be seen as an *'encounter'* with the Other, but rather *'a postcolonial space for learning that focuses on negotiation and discussion and in which participants think dialogically rather than dually'*. Relationships form through our recognition of the interconnected and interdependent world in which we live, which is encouraged through processes such as globalisation and time–space compression. Our interconnectedness does not mean a simple recognition of difference; this is used to imagine a relationship starting from an *'ethical, political, and spiritual foundation for a genuine opening'* built less on an *'egalitarian reciprocity'* and more on a *'radical receptivity of being'* (De Lissovoy, 2010, p 284). In this way, relationships can aspire to transcend 'centre' supremacy by realising the Eurocentric and oppressive nature of its thinking. The relationship is similar to Freire's ideas whereby, through hope, *'alliances across difference can be forged'* (Darder, 2002, p 30) and we begin to expose the extent to which the 'centre' is written through with the colonial.

A porosity between self and Other opens up the potential for an open relationship beyond the privileges that Andreotti (2011) warns we must unlearn. An ethically based relationship respects difference in the Other, and is the precursor to kindredness, which develops from a cosmopolitan orientation (Delanty, 2009). De Lissovoy (2010), drawing on Apiah (2007), argues that cosmopolitanism highlights the need for the *'negotiation of differences within this global multiculturalism [which] should reject a priori judgements about essential and universal human truths*' (De Lissovoy, 2010, p 281). In this way, difference is treated with respect and becomes a key dimension of our relationship with the Other, a matter echoed by Martin and Griffiths (2012, p 923), who argue *'it is possible to feel connected through difference when one aims not to resolve those differences, but to understand them'*.

In recognising difference, and in developing a critical pedagogy with a focus on global commonalities as a form of community, De Lissovoy (2010) reminds us that we should acknowledge the cultural violence of the Eurocentric colonial project, including the way this constructs and positions us from the 'centre' and why places are politically and culturally construed as either 'peripheral' or 'central'. In doing so, our pedagogy challenges the sources of power implicit in the 'centre' and recognises history and culture from the 'periphery', which is incorporated in the curriculum. Such a project is far more than teaching about distant places and cultures, or even changing our views about such places; it means destabilising the dominant history and reveals Bhabha's (2004) notion that the coloniser is a product of the colonial project. A decolonial pedagogy does not reject such a history, but uses it to decentre its supremacy, building a pedagogic relationship through difference that is articulated through our humility and built upon relationships and interconnectedness.

Conclusion

I am cautious about suggesting general points from reflections and related research, but in concluding this chapter I draw on the following five points made elsewhere (Hoult, 2018, p 85) in identifying some useful points to support the anti-racist agenda in higher education.

1. A pedagogy that does not pretend to be neutral, but rather is explicit in its aims to expose the significant hidden power dynamics that underpin Eurocentric thinking, is powerful in unlocking assumptions that are built over a lifetime.

2. Deeper learning is supported through a pedagogy that provides learners with a theoretical language to articulate their learning and provokes their thinking about their experiences theoretically, including local/global power dynamics.

3. A pedagogy that supports the need for reflexive approaches to learning helps to expose the positioning of students and the Eurocentric assumptions we make.

4. There is a need for liminal places within which learners can articulate their emerging ideas without being judged or conclusions being demanded.

5. Relationships with the Other are important to deepening intercultural learning and are augmented through a mutual endeavour.

My empirical research in conjunction with associated critical reading, analysis and reflexivity related to study visits to India challenged my thinking in various ways and led me to read the world differently. It has been personally and professionally transformative, permitting me to learn in different ways. My intercultural learning exposed apparent universalities as Eurocentric and a reflexive approach that recognised the global context of learning in local places provoked me further to aspire to a postcolonial engagement not only with the Other, but through a continued reflexive reconsideration of myself as a teacher educator.

Reflective questions

- In what ways and where do we engage interculturally on a regular basis?
- What are the ethics of educational provocation and how do teachers do this while including their students?
- What stories are missing from our practice? What does this tell us about privilege and how might these 'missing' stories be drawn upon to disrupt dominant histories and geographies to provide a richer cultural awareness and understanding of self and Other?

Recommended reading

- Andreotti, V (2011) *Actionable Postcolonial Theory in Education*. New York: Palgrave Macmillan.
- Bhabha, H K (2004 [1994]) *The Location of Culture*. London: Routledge.
- De Lissovoy, N (2010) Decolonial Pedagogy and the Ethics of the Global. *Discourse Studies in the Cultural Politics of Education*, 31(3): 279–93.

References

Adichie, C (2009) The Danger of a Single Story. TED Talk. [online] Available at: www.ted.com/talks/chimamanda_ngozi_adichie_the_danger_of_a_single_story/comments (accessed 12 December 2022).

Andreotti, V (2010) Global Education in the 21st Century: Two Different Perspectives on the 'Post-' of Postmodernism. *International Journal of Development Education and Global Learning*, 2(2): 5–22.

Andreotti, V (2011) *Actionable Postcolonial Theory in Education*. New York: Palgrave Macmillan.

Andreotti, V (2013) Taking Minds to Other Places. *Primary Geographer*, 80: 12–13.

Apiah, K A (2007) *Cosmopolitanism: Ethics in a World of Strangers*. New York: W W Norton.

Bhabha, H K (2004 [1994]) *The Location of Culture*. London: Routledge.

Burr, M (2008) Thinking About Linking? DEA Thinkpiece. [online] Available at: www.dea.org.uk/thinkpieces (accessed 20 February 2023).

Darder, A (2002) *Reinventing Paulo Freire: A Pedagogy of Love*. Boulder, CO: Westview Press.

The Darjeeling Limited (2007) Directed by Wes Anderson (DVD). USA: Twentieth Century Fox.

De Lissovoy, N (2010) Decolonial Pedagogy and the Ethics of the Global. *Discourse Studies in the Cultural Politics of Education*, 31(3): 279–93.

Delanty, G (2009) *The Cosmopolitan Imagination: The Renewal of Critical Social Theory*. Cambridge: Cambridge University Press.

Finney, S and Orr, J (1995) 'I've Really Learned a Lot, but ...': Cross-cultural Understanding and Teacher Education in a Racist Society. *Journal of Teacher Education*, 46(5): 327–33.

Harris, S (2008) Internationalising the University. *Educational Philosophy and Theory: Incorporating ACCESS*, 40(2): 346–57.

Hicks, D (2006) *Lessons for the Future: The Missing Dimension in Education.* Oxford: Trafford.

Hoult, S (2018) Aspiring to a Postcolonial Pedagogy Through Engagement with the Other: Deepening Intercultural Learning from a South Indian Study Visit. In Jackson, J and Oguro, S (eds) *Intercultural Interventions in Study Abroad* (pp 71–87). London: Routledge.

Hoult, S (2020) Engaging with the Cultural Other: The 'Colonial Signature' and Learning from Intercultural Engagements. *International Journal of Development Education and Global Learning*, 12(2): 106–20.

Hoult, S and Lal, C A (eds) (2015) *Bridging the Gaps: Critical Reflections on Intercultural Learning.* Trivandrum: Bodhi Tree Books.

Kegan, R (2000) What 'Form' Transforms? A Constructive-Developmental Approach to Transformative Learning. In Mezirow, J (ed) *Learning as Transformation: Critical Perspectives on a Theory in Progress* (pp 35–70). San Francisco: Jossey-Bass.

Lal, C A and Hoult, S (2019) What Can Be Gained from Intercultural Engagements? In Hammond, S and Sangster, M (eds) *Perspectives on Educational Practice Around the World* (pp 177–82). London, Bloomsbury.

Land, J, Meyer, R and Smith J (eds) (2008) *Threshold Concepts Within the Disciplines.* Rotterdam: Sense.

Levinas, E (2006 [1972]) *Humanism of the Other.* Urbana, IL: University of Illinois Press.

Martin, F and Griffiths, H (2012) Power and Representation: A Postcolonial Reading of Global Partnerships and Teacher Development Through North–South Study Visits. *British Educational Research Journal*, 38(6): 907–27.

Martin, F and Wyness, L (2013) Global Partnerships as Sites for Mutual Learning. *Policy and Practice: A Development Education Review*, 16: 13–40.

Massey, D (1994) *A Global Sense of Place.* Minneapolis, MN: University of Minnesota Press.

Meyer, J and Land, R (2003) *Threshold Concepts and Troublesome Knowledge: Linkages to Ways of Thinking and Practising Within the Disciplines.* Edinburgh: University of Edinburgh.

Mezirow, J (2000) *Learning as Transformation: Critical Perspectives on a Theory in Progress*. San Francisco: Jossey Bass.

Rogers, M (1998) Student Responses to Learning About Futures. In Hicks, D and Slaughter, R (eds) *Futures Education: The World Yearbook of Education 1998* (pp 203–16). London: Kogan Page.

Rogers, M and Tough, A (1992) What Happens When Students Face the Future? *Futures Research Quarterly*, 8(4): 9–18.

Said, E (2003 [1978]) *Orientalism*. Harmondsworth: Penguin.

Scoffham, S and Barnes, J (2009) Transformational Experiences and Deep Learning: The Impact of an Intercultural Study Visit to India on UK Initial Teacher Education Students. *Journal of Education for Teaching: International Research and Pedagogy*, 35(3): 257–70.

Sterling, S (2001) *Sustainable Education: Re-visioning Learning and Change*. Totnes: Green Books.

Wa Thiong'o, N (1986) *Decolonising the Mind: The Politics of Language in African Literature*. Oxford: James Curry.

Weeden, P and Hayter, R J (1996) PGCE Student Visit to the Gambia: 'Learning Experience of a Lifetime' or 'Just More Savannah'? In Claxton, G, Atkinson, T, Osborn, M and Wallace, M (eds) *Liberating the Learner: Lessons for Professional Development in Education* (pp 108–23). London: Routledge.

Yeğonoğlu, M (1998) *Colonial Fantasies: Towards a Feminist Reading of Orientalism*. Cambridge: Cambridge University Press.

CHAPTER 4

USING CRITICAL DIALOGUE TO ADDRESS RACISM, HUMANISE THE OTHER AND CREATE SOLIDARITY AND PRAXIS IN THE CLASSROOM

Emma Wood

Introduction

This chapter describes a case where I asked my public relations students to focus on Malawian charity STEKA, a children's home established in 2007 by Godknows Maseko and his wife Helen that has provided a safe home for around 100 children and young adults in Blantyre, Malawi. For full disclosure, I should also point out that I am chair of a related charity, STEKAskills, located in Scotland, which works with STEKA in Malawi to develop a vocational skills centre so that older STEKA residents and local people can earn the skills they need to work their way out of poverty. The charity was presented as a 'client' for public relations (PR) students, who were tasked with creating a campaign to raise awareness of the charity's Youth Solidarity Critical Dialogue Groups, developed in partnership with STEKA's young residents. These Critical Dialogue Groups were developed as an alternative experience for Scottish pupils who travel to Malawi on school trips. Many of these school trips follow an aid-framed approach, which denies Malawians agency. The visiting Scottish pupils do voluntary work, which they often describe as '*making a difference*' to poor communities. When White people visited the STEKA home, for example, they would often paint walls, play with the children and take selfies with them to post on social media, seemingly denying the Malawian children agency. In contrast, the award-winning Critical Dialogue Groups are run by the young poverty-experienced Malawian residents of the home and the Scottish pupils pay for the privilege to participate.

In the PR classroom, my expectation was that using this case would not just teach my students how to create a campaign for a client, but would also teach them about global citizenship, how to represent people in the Global South with dignity and to understand the rights-based approach to international development that many governments (including the Scottish Government) now advocate. In practice, though, many students seemed to reject the philosophy behind the Critical Dialogue Group approach, with some saying that 'they' (the young Malawian STEKA residents) should be grateful for Scottish students doing things for them and not expect agency over what happens in their care home.

The atmosphere within the Queen Margaret University student group became so tense and negative that I decided to suspend the usual tutorials/seminars that followed lectures and hold Critical Dialogue Groups instead. This enabled us to critically reflect on what was happening by setting up a so-called 'brave space' with Gift Thompson, a resident of the Malawian STEKA care home who was studying at the university at that time. This chapter explores what happened and reflects on the value of using critical dialogue – or, more specifically, my previously designed and published Critical Dialogue for Youth Solidarity model (Wood, 2020a).

Context

Malawi is one of the poorest countries in the world, and Scotland (as part of the United Kingdom) is among the richest, but the governments of both countries have a 'special relationship' dating from the time when the Scottish explorer David Livingstone went to Malawi in 1867. In the context of that 'special relationship', a number of Scottish schools organise trips to Malawi, where they visit a variety of projects, schools and initiatives. Indeed, voluntourism trips, where people from the Global North travel on holiday to 'poor' countries to 'make a difference', is a growing sector for many countries in the Global South (see Atkins and Thompson, 2012; Mostafanezhad, 2014; Wearing and McGehee, 2013). In an introductory lecture, I taught my PR students that current voluntourist models typically involve young people from the Global North travelling as volunteer-tourists to visit poor people in Global South countries, taking selfies with their babies for social media and then doing jobs that the local people would actually prefer to be paid to do themselves (for example, painting walls or digging wells). These voluntourists may describe their trips as them '*making a difference*' to poor, helpless Global South people.

The visitors may then often distribute donations, which they feel Malawians need, but which actually have a detrimental effect on the local economy – for example, through the donation of clothes, which deprives local tailors of business. To illustrate this in the lecture, I used examples of visits I had witnessed to STEKA when visitors distributed novelty items bought at significant expense at a local South African-owned supermarket to some of the 95 children there who did not need or want them. Instead, STEKA needs money to pay for the children's school fees and food. Sandra Ndale, a resident of the STEKA home, describes her perspective of this as follows:

> Before we started doing the Dialogue Groups, Scottish schools would visit us and listen to Godknows' story and then play with the children. They would bring gifts which they would distribute to who they liked the best and the rest of us did not benefit. And often these gifts were things we did not need. They did not talk to the older residents who are the same age as them, they just gave toys to the youngest children and took pictures and put them up on Facebook without asking us. I hated their attitudes towards us. I hated them for that. We tried to tell them what to do and not do, but they did not listen and just did what they liked.
> (Quoted in Wood, 2020a, p 4)

In my lecture, I acknowledged that voluntourism is an important and growing source of aid (Kennedy and Dornan, 2009) and that small grassroots charities such as STEKA depended on them. However, I cited evidence showing that the particular approach described above can be seen to reinforce stereotypes and aid-framed agendas instead of focusing on human rights and structural inequality (Freidus, 2016; Mostafanezhad, 2014). Given the resources, local people know perfectly well how to bring about their own change (Crewe and Harrison, 1998; Georgeou, 2012; McGloin and Georgeou, 2016; Simpson, 2004) so these aid-framed agendas actually perpetuate a racist narrative of development (Freidus, 2016; Pailey, 2020). I shared growing criticism of voluntourism in the literature as well as explanations of why voluntourists with this mindset are often disparagingly called 'White saviours'. They are seen as consuming the experience of saving poor people by communicating about their trip on social networking sites through selfies, often with babies or children, instead of learning about structural inequalities or standing in solidarity with their Global South peers to campaign for social change (Germann Molz, 2016; McGloin and Georgeou, 2016; Vodopivec and Jaffe, 2011).

So the 'product' my students had to promote, the Critical Dialogue Groups for Youth Solidarity, was an alternative experience for the Scottish schools that visit Malawi and the STEKA home. Instead of volunteering, the visitors pay to take part in a Malawian-led experience designed to create mutual understanding of and deep insight into life in Malawi and Scotland, and into the reality of the UN Sustainability Development Goals (SDGs).

Figure 4.1: The UN Sustainability Development Goals (SDGs)

Through their lived experience, the STEKA residents have expert knowledge about issues such as hunger, poverty, access to education, the impact of gender inequality and climate change, and in particular the structural causes of, and barriers to overcoming, them. The Critical Dialogue Group experience involves Scottish school pupils being led through the three stages of the model of critical dialogue (Wood, 2020b) as follows:

- *Stage 1: Problematisation.* In Scotland, pupils examine motivations for their trip. In Malawi, the Dialogue Groups begin with a session aimed at exposing and disrupting assumptions made about narratives of aid, development, and people living in poverty and inequality. This session resembles the lecture delivered to my Scottish students, described above.

- *Stages 2 and 3: Conscientisation and humanisation.* In Malawi, the students in the young STEKA Dialogue team form three groups with their Scottish peers in the

STEKA garden. Those in the STEKA team lead in-depth Critical Dialogue Groups focused on telling their life stories (no adults are involved). The stories model the resilience of young Malawians and illustrate the reality of SDG topics such as the impact of climate change and of gender inequality. The format means the young STEKA dialoguers share stories reflecting their lived experience and pose questions to allow all the young people to learn from each other as equals and without judgement. For example, following stories of some girls being forced to take part in initiation camps, the Scots mentioned the UK phone service Childline, and the Malawians were intrigued. The Scots saw the consequences of gender inequality in new ways.

- *Stage 4: Praxis.* Young people develop a clearer understanding of concepts such as rights and equality, global citizenship, the human reality of SDG challenges, inclusive ways of two-way learning and achieving international development (or perhaps de-development in the Global North). They have learned how to be more resilient, built relationships and learned how to communicate differently. Most Scots are committed to bringing about change in solidarity with their allies at STEKA.

Students' responses to criticism of voluntourism

Co-producing this initiative with the young STEKA team took two years – getting to a point where some of the world's most marginalised young people could take power and lead groups for White visitors took time. It was achieved using the above model of critical dialogue, which operationalises Freire's (2017) pedagogy of the oppressed (Wood 2020a, 2020b). The Dialogue Project attracted Scottish Government international development funding and has since won an award for the charity STEKAskills and is deemed to be of international significance and leading the world in the UK Government's Research Excellence Framework 2021. But the initiative was only at the prototype stage of development at the time of this case-study.

As mentioned above, far from embracing this task, a few weeks into the semester my class seemed antagonistic and adopted what I interpreted as a defensive and individualist stance in relation to the philosophy behind the Critical Dialogue Groups. They did not want to accept criticism of voluntourism and seemed critical of the STEKA team for expecting more agency in relation to visits to their home. Rather than dismissing this as racism, however, I think it is important to consider what triggered this response from my approach to teaching the module, and in particular from the lecture that had intended to contextualise and problematise voluntourism.

Race

In Freirian (Freire, 2000) terms, to help my students 'problematise' voluntourism, I referred to a number of contemporary publications that I felt offered a useful insight into White people's power and defensiveness in relation to discussions about race, which makes it easier for voluntourists to do things for people in the Global South instead of engaging with structural issues. The first was Eddo-Lodge's (2017) *Why I'm No Longer Talking to White People About Race*. Her experience is that White people have never had to think about what it means, in power terms, to be White – so any time they are vaguely reminded of this fact, they interpret it as an affront. The journey towards understanding structural racism still requires people of colour to prioritise White feelings. *'Their eyes glaze over in boredom or widen in indignation. Their mouths start twitching as they get defensive. Their throats open up as they try to interrupt, itching to talk over you but not really listening, because they need to let you know that you've got it wrong'* (Eddo-Lodge, 2017, p x).

Ironically, although the purpose of citing this source was to help my students understand the context that the Critical Dialogue Groups sought to address, there was a real resistance to it. Seen through this lens, Eddo-Lodge (2017) could have been describing exactly the response I witnessed from the students in the class to the ideas I presented in my lecture. I also pointed to DiAngelo's (2018) stance on 'White fragility' causing White people to find it so hard to talk about race. DiAngelo is uncompromising in her insistence that wanting to jump over the hard, personal work and get to 'solutions' is what she calls a foundation of White fragility, and that *'People of color don't need to twist themselves into knots trying to navigate us as painlessly as possible'* (Di Angelo, 2018, p 152). Instead, she wants White people to focus on identifying and challenging their own White privilege. Again, perhaps this term 'White fragility' was a trigger for the students' defensiveness in relation to the challenges I delivered in my approach and lecture.

Decolonisation

Ideas about de-centering the White gaze (eg see Toni Morrison, 2019 and other sources) and the concept of decolonisation were another useful way to disrupt my students' social norms and assumptions about their accepted paradigm of 'development'. I drew on sources such as Neajai Pailey (2020), who refers to development as a racist discipline in theory and practice:

> *The White gaze of development is measuring Black, brown and non-White people against the standard of Northern Whiteness, and taking their political, economic and social processes as a norm… Development uses that standard of Northern Whiteness to measure economic, political and social processes of people in the so-called 'Global South'.*
>
> (Pailey, 2020)

I was unapologetic about challenging their worldview in this way, using Pailey's statement. I suggested that:

> *Decolonization is not a new phenomenon… But with the 21st century version of this has become very apolitical… without linking it to the everyday dilemmas that people in the global South face: fighting autocracy, homophobia, ecological damage, racism, patriarchy. Those are the real issues that people face. And I think that decolonization as an academic pursuit is one that misses out on those linkages… Decolonization is political, it's violent, it's disruptive, it's not about maintaining the status quo.*
>
> (Pailey, 2020)

The pedagogical problem

My approach used critical literature consciously selected to disrupt my students' social norms about development and poor (oppressed) people in the Global South. This literature on decolonisation and anti-racism explicitly does not present solutions, nor does it enable *'a set of evasions, or "settler moves to innocence", that problematically attempt to reconcile settler guilt and complicity, and rescue settler futurity'* (Tuck and Yang, 2012, p 9). While my personal view might be that people should do the work and we should not tolerate fragility as an excuse, in my professional capacity as a teacher, and in light of my students' response, I did not feel comfortable pursuing an antagonistic relationship with them. I needed to address the polarisation between my own and my students' attitude to STEKA. I needed to build productive and professional relationships between my Scottish students and the residents of the STEKA home, and at the very least facilitate a space in which the students could work effectively for their client to develop a strategy to promote the Youth Solidarity Critical Dialogue Groups. Several sources helped inform my attempts to achieve this.

The dehumanising condescension of White fragility

First, McWhorter's (2020) blog on the dehumanising condescension of *White Fragility* is helpful in trying to understand how the idea of white fragility might inhibit solidarity and activism. It is highly critical of DiAngelo's views on White fragility, not least because of the author's ridiculing of attempts to build solutions to the racism inherent in White society. McWhorter deems DiAngelo's book to be *'a racist tract... few books about race have more openly infantilized Black people than this supposedly authoritative tome. Or simply dehumanized us... I see no connection between DiAngelo's brand of re-education and vigorous, constructive activism in the real world on issues of import to the Black community'*. His focus on humanisation and activism particularly resonates with the philosophy of critical dialogue based on Freire and Buber's ideas of humanisation – and Freire's ideas about building solidarity to bring about praxis (the very basis of the model of critical dialogue that my students were supposed to promote). Consequently, I choose to interpret McWhorter's call for humanisation and constructive activism as a validation of my decision to abandon the usual seminar model for my students and instead organise a critical dialogue session to humanise Malawians and hopefully solve the seeming schism experienced by the Scottish students.

Ubuntu/Umunthu

The focus on humanisation can usefully be elucidated by the African philosophy of *Ubuntu* (referred to as *Umunthu* in Malawi). This philosophy had a very important influence on the co-production of the critical dialogue model used by the STEKA team in Malawi with their Scottish visitors, which I also decided to use with the students in this case of misunderstanding of voluntourism. Ubuntu is helpful in deepening the understanding that White fragility dehumanises Black people. Desmond Tutu illuminated the concept: *'In Africa we have a word, Ubuntu, which is difficult to render in Western languages. It speaks about the essence of being human: that my humanity is caught up in your humanity because we say a person is a person through other persons'* (Tutu, 1999, p ix, quoted in Kayange, 2018, p 220). Space precludes an in-depth analysis of this African philosophy, which is complex and nuanced; however, the way in which it was introduced to me by Godknows and the young people at STEKA (and the way in which it subsequently influenced our critical dialogue approach) is encapsulated by the Malawian scholar Kayange (2018), who explains that:

> *When Chichewa language speakers are using the word Umunthu... it may be used in communitarianism when an individual chooses to explain moral correctness in relation to respect of moral or intellectual communitarian virtues such as solidarity, respect, mutual trust and collegiality.*
>
> (Kayange, 2018, p 129)

I had seen *Umunthu* in action through the Critical Dialogue Groups in Malawi. Just as my Scottish students found it difficult to think in a collegiate way about their Malawian peers, before we ran our dialogue groups in Malawi, some of the STEKA team had also been wary of their impending Scottish visitors. Sandra Ndale explains:

> *With the Dialogues a lot of things changed. Now we have the power to tell them what they can and cannot do, and they listen... Now, I like the Scots. We have a few hours to converse, and we only concentrate on the dialogue until the very end when we teach each other games and dances. I like them.*
>
> (Wood, 2020b)

So, just as the Malawians' views of their White visitors had changed through critical dialogue, my hope was that my Scottish students' views of the Malawians would also shift – and they too would see themselves in the communitarian sense of *Umunthu*.

The impact of critical dialogue for youth solidarity

Upon reflection, battering my students' assumptions about development and leaving them to make sense of how to move forward in solidarity with their client was too difficult for them. Tavernaro-Haidarian's (2018) premise that efforts to decolonise can deepen coloniality, and that the African philosophy of *Ubuntu* can help, is deeply significant to this case. She explains:

> Efforts to decolonise societies... have frequently been framed in terms of 'dismantling' strategies [deriving] from a realism of 'normative adversarialism', where power is negotiated conflictually and contests, struggles, and protests are seen as natural and inevitable strategies of social organisation. Such approaches are unattractive, as they effectively deepen coloniality rather than unravelling it. The African moral philosophy of ubuntu provides a very different realism, where processes of decolonisation can be framed as evolutionary, developmental, and integrative.

Through the lens of ubuntu, decolonisation can be reimagined as a constructive process. She continues:

> This integrative approach is constructive in its orientation, as it builds on, combines, enhances, matures, evolves, and brings together in mutual dialogue various traditions and wisdoms. It is resilient in the way that it transcends the narrow confines of normative adversarialism, colonialism, and coloniality that have thus far prevailed and that would continue to motivate a reactionary approach. It requires those interested in the project to step outside of their current worldview, to broaden their horizons, and to look towards the wealth that can be created when we mine and combine the gems that lie hidden in the repositories of the world's peoples and cultures. Decolonisation as constructive resilience takes into account '[t]he wealth of a common global culture [which] will then be expressed in the particularities of our different languages and cultures very much like a universal garden of many-colored flowers' (McLaren 1998: 390). It is an invitational approach that offers a remedy rather than aggression in the face of existing injustices.
>
> (Tavernaro-Haidarian, 2018)

The positive and ambitious approach referred to by Tavernaro-Haidarian (2018) very closely resembles the spirit of the Malawian STEKA team's ambitions for their Critical Dialogue Groups. As Sandra Ndale says:

> I have learnt that my role is to change Malawi. To take it to another level. Like the issue of street kids. Maybe if we can just stand together, we will not have street kids in town. If we can come together, we can change the world.
>
> (Wood, 2020b, p 3)

This was echoed in the comments from the young Scottish pupils who participated in their Malawian dialogue groups – for example, *'The strength and courage they [the STEKA team] showed was inspiring. We are lucky to have such a strong relationship as we can learn a lot from them and help spread awareness to fight inequality'* (Wood, 2020b, p 3). My task was to help my students in Scotland to move beyond their defensiveness and instead tempt them into McLaren's *'universal garden of many-colored flowers'* (Tavernaro-Haidarian, 2018).

Critical Dialogue Groups as an alternative to the seminar format

A very basic tenet of our Youth Solidarity Critical Dialogue Groups is that they are confidential. No one takes notes and they are not recorded. As Kelly (2013, p 55) explains:

> *Dialogue, by its nature, is a type of conversation that challenges people to enhance their understanding of themselves and others by sharing and reflecting on deeply held beliefs and values. This, perhaps, is what differentiates dialogue from debate most clearly. For this to become possible, participants need to be able to trust in the process, and to feel that their attempts to articulate what can be very personal thoughts and feelings will be respected as what they often are – tentative and uncertain expressions of thoughts-in-progress rather than fully formulated views.*

I am unable to betray that trust by relating what happened in detail. In general terms, however, our dialogue focused on the fact that a number of the students in the class were themselves poverty-experienced and felt they were being personally diminished by the views cited in my lecture. In our Critical Dialogue Group, we were able to devote time and energy to hearing about that. And Gift and I also had space to talk about our personal feelings.

As such, we all learned that it is vital to acknowledge, and empathise with, lived experience of poverty in Scotland as well as Malawi. In addition, perhaps the Scottish students began to understand the meaning and impact of intersectionality. For example, being poverty experienced, Black and female, and living in a country where less than 11 per cent of the population can complete primary school, very few women have access to education and may have to endure sexual initiation at a young age, is different from being a White poverty-experienced Scot.

Hearing Gift tell the stories of his brothers and sisters at STEKA helped our students to understand the human dimension of that reality. Seeing what they had in common, but also the different scale of the challenges they faced, helped to build understanding and solidarity. The key is that one group experiencing marginalisation or oppression does not preclude another from feeling that too – in fact, a shared experience can enhance two-way understanding. And everyone learned that dialogue is not about creating consensus: it is perfectly acceptable to *'hold one's own position while being profoundly open to the other'* (Pearce and Pearce, 2000, p 168). Indeed, the dialogue could be seen to move the students towards the collective, communitarian view seen in conceptualisations of *Umunthu*. It helped to create a human dimension, also understood as 'love' by Buber and others (see Pearce and Pearce, 2000, p 162). I certainly witnessed this through some long-lasting bonds created between some of the students and Gift. Importantly, some of the students who had been most resistant to my views showed huge maturity in remaining behind after the Dialogue Group to share their changed perception and the profound impact the experience had had on them.

What I learned

Adapting to the situation and using the principles and format of critical dialogue instead of the usual seminar format enabled me to deal with the pedagogical problem, and the students went on to produce some amazing work and learned a great deal about dealing with a client. My own key learning was not to polarise issues in the classroom and learn how to walk the tightrope between creating a chasm that would be too difficult for young people to breach and ensuring that I did not dilute issues such as racism and decolonisation to make them easy for my students to engage with. Bringing the dialogic values of humanisation and love into my teaching and understanding the journey my students needed to make in relation to development narratives and race was really helpful.

I relied heavily on Kyle 'Guante' Tran Myhre's (2018) poem to guide me with this, especially his view that *'White supremacy is not the shark; it's the water.'* This taught me that the trick is to not be too immersed in my own position and to be true to the central tenets of dialogue – not just problematisation, conscientisation and humanisation, but the dialogic value of being brave. I want to continue to be brave in terms of overtly addressing racism and other attendant issues that students find difficult by continuing to use this Malawian client in my teaching. By pushing my students into viewing the world through a dialogic social justice lens, I know that, although many will dislike me for it in the short term, in the long term some will understand the value of what they have learned beyond achieving 'module outcomes'. Over the years, I have been contacted by former students who found my approach in the classroom challenging; they now say that they believe this teaching has informed the way they practise professionally from an inclusive, socially just perspective. Gift and I were lucky enough to receive the following email from a student following our introductory lecture, delivered the year after the case outlined in this chapter.

> *I just wanted to personally thank you for such an eye-opening, raw and important lecture. What particularly stood out for me was the resilience of all the people at STEKA. I will admit that I often find it uncomfortable talking about race for fear of coming across wrong. I'm never quite sure if it's my place to have opinions on oppression that I am passively benefitting from. However, after today I feel completely different. By you being unapologetic and real about the reality of the White saviour complex and seeing all the nods of agreement around the room I feel so much more comfortable in the way that I feel. Today you were a model for how to speak about it respectfully and I feel like I can take everything I've learned and put it to good use. I want to be an ally and you've inspired me to do more.*
>
> (Wood, 2020b, p 18)

Finally, I would like to acknowledge that my dual role as lecturer and client is challenging for my students, and I want to pay tribute to them for rising to that challenge and sticking with me. The *Umunthu* philosophy is most definitely pertinent here – working like this over the years with my various dialogue projects as a client, generations of Queen Margaret University students have devoted their energies to helping critique, refine, develop and improve what is now the Youth Solidarity model – I am who I am through them.

Reflective questions

- According to Nagda and Roper (2019, p 117), *'the critique-and-imagination of social reality... must occur in contexts and interactions that are not just replications of the unjust social reality'*. What methods can you use to disrupt the normal teaching mode to help students focus on inequalities (including race) and intersectionality?
- Could you use a critical dialogue approach to reveal and address issues such as White privilege and power imbalances between global citizens?
- Can you find a case similar to that of STEKAskills for your students to focus on in their learning and assessment?

Recommended reading

- Pailey, R N (2020) De-centring the 'White Gaze' of Development. Keynote, Development Studies Association Conference, June 2019. In Faciolince, M, Does Development Have a Problem with Racism? [online] Available at: https://frompoverty.oxfam.org.uk/does-development-have-a-problem-with-racism (accessed 12 December 2022).
- Tavernaro-Haidaria, L (2018) Why Efforts to Decolonise Can Deepen Coloniality and What *Ubuntu* Can Do to Help. *Critical Arts*, 32(5–6): 104–18.

References

Atkins, S G and Thompson, L F (2012) Online Volunteers and Smart Aid. In Carr, S C et al (eds) *Humanitarian Work Psychology* (pp 266–92). New York: Springer.

Crewe, E and Harrison, E (1998) *Whose Development? An Ethnography of Aid.* London: Bloomsbury.

DiAngelo, R (2018) *White Fragility.* Boston, MA: Beacon Press.

Eddo-Lodge, R (2017) *Why I'm No Longer Talking to White People About Race.* London: Bloomsbury.

Freidus, A L (2016) Unanticipated Outcomes of Voluntourism Among Malawi's Orphans. *Journal of Sustainable Tourism*, 16(5): 530–43.

Freire, P (2000 [1968]) *Pedagogy of the Oppressed.* New York: Continuum.

Georgeou, N (2012) *Neoliberalism, Development, and Aid.* New York: Routledge.

Germann Molz, J (2016) Making a Difference Together: Discourses of Transformation in Family Voluntourism. *Journal of Sustainable Tourism,* 24(6): 805–23.

Kayange, G M (2018) *Meaning and Truth in African Philosophy: Doing African Philosophy with Language.* Cham: Springer.

Kelly, U (2013) Studying Dialogue: Some Reflections. *Journal of Dialogue Studies*, 1(1): 51–62.

Kennedy, K and Dornan, D (2009) An Overview: Tourism Non-governmental Organizations and Poverty Reduction in Developing Countries. *Asia-Pacific Journal of Tourism Research*, 14(2): 183–200.

McGloin, C and Georgeou, N (2016) 'Looks Good on Your CV': The Sociology of Voluntourism Recruitment in Higher Education. *Journal of Sociology*, 52(2): 403–17.

McWhorter, J (2020) The Dehumanizing Condescension of *White Fragility*. *The Atlantic*, July. [online] Available at: www.theatlantic.com/ideas/archive/2020/07/dehumanizing-condescension-white-fragility/614146 (accessed 20 February 2023).

Morrison, T (2019) *Toni Morrison: The Pieces I Am*. Documentary. Dir. Timothy Greenfield-Sanders.

Mostafanezhad, M (2014) *Volunteer Tourism: Popular Humanitarianism in Neoliberal Times.* London: Routledge.

Myhre, K T (2018) How to Explain White Supremacy to a White Supremacist. In *A Love Song, a Death Rattle, a Battle Cry* (pp 36–7). Minneapolis, MN: Button Poetry.

Nagda, B A and Roper, L D (2019) Reimagining Leadership Development for Social Change Through Critical Dialogue Practices. *New Directions for Student Leadership*, 163: 117–36.

Pailey, R N (2020) De-centring the 'White Gaze' of Development. Keynote, Development Studies Association Conference, June 2019. In Faciolince, M, Does Development Have a Problem with Racism? [online] Available at: https://frompoverty.oxfam.org.uk/does-development-have-a-problem-with-racism (accessed 12 December 2022).

Pearce, W B and Pearce, K A (2000) Combining Passions and Abilities: Toward Dialogic Virtuosity. *Southern Communication Journal*, 65: 161–75.

Tavernaro-Haidaria, L (2018) Why Efforts to Decolonise Can Deepen Coloniality and What *Ubuntu* Can Do to Help. *Critical Arts*, 32(5–6): 104–18.

Tuck, E and Yang, K W (2012) Decolonization is Not a Metaphor. *Decolonization: Indigeneity, Education & Society*, 1(1): 1–40.

Vodopivec, B and Jaffe, R (2011) Save the World in a Week: Volunteer Tourism, Development and Difference. *The European Journal of Development Research*, 23(1): 111–28.

Wearing, S and McGehee, N G (2013) Volunteer Tourism: A Review. *Tourism Management*, 38, 120–30.

Wood, E (2020a) Young People, Alcohol, Dialogical Methods. In Scandrett, E (ed) *Public Sociology as Educational Practice: Challenges, Dialogues and Counter-Publics* (pp 153–70). Bristol: Bristol University Press.

Wood, E (2020b) An Alternative to Voluntourism: How Youth Solidarity Groups in Malawi Empower Young Malawians and Scots. *STEKAskills*. [online] Available at: www.stekaskills.com/international-school-workshops (accessed 12 December 2022).

CHAPTER 5

DECOLONISATION AS PUBLIC SOCIOLOGY PRACTICE

Eurig Scandrett

Introduction

The methodology I have adopted in this chapter is to reflect on key experiences of engaging with the influence of critical race analysis and decolonisation in my work in education, research and solidarity scholarship: how I have sought to respond and then to reflect, dialectically, on the limitations, contradictions and countervailing forces to these responses. This has led to a progression of sorts, both in my understanding of anti-racist and decolonising practice in academia and in my discipline of sociology, particularly public sociology. My thinking has developed from educational responses to the needs of anti-racism through to a recognition that anti-racism in academia requires a commitment to decolonising education, research and scholarship. Moreover, decolonisation requires acting in solidarity with current, active anti-colonial struggles as well as responding to the impacts of colonialism in the past. This needs to recognise the particular role of colonial countries and the distinctive histories of colonial practices, including both imperial and settler colonialism. Decolonisation involves live and contentious politics, which involves professional risk. There continue to be powerful defenders and deniers of colonialism, and they need to be confronted.

Education: critical race dialogues

My entry to full-time academic work at the age of 45, after a career change from the biological sciences and 15 years in adult and community education, was facilitated by a collaboration between Queen Margaret University and Friends of the Earth Scotland. The university and the environmental NGO had jointly run an educational programme for activists on environmental justice, 'Agents for Environmental Justice' (Wilkinson and Scandrett, 2003). The idea of environmental justice has its roots in the US movement against environmental racism. Some high-profile campaigns against toxic dumps in the 1970s and 1980s led to research across the United States, which revealed that African American, Hispanic and Native American communities are disproportionately exposed to environmentally hazardous sites (Bullard, 1990; Commission for Racial Justice, 1987). Building on the work of the Civil Rights movement, the First People of Color Environmental Leadership Summit took place in Washington, DC in 1991; from it, the environmental justice movement emerged to challenge environmental racism. While environmental justice has become a broader analysis of how environmental destruction correlates with various social injustices across the globe, our Agents for Environmental Justice student group (majority White) – all activists fighting environmental injustices in their own communities – learned that some of the roots of their analysis lay in US anti-racism struggles.

My early work at the university continued to develop the pedagogical model of working in partnership with civil society organisations with central roles in social movements in Scotland. The partnership with Friends of the Earth Scotland on environmental justice was followed by a collaboration with Scottish Women's Aid on gender justice (Orr and Whiting, 2020). Seeking an exploration of how this educational model could support anti-racism in Scotland, me and my colleagues looked for a social movement organisation fighting racism across Scotland. We were unaware of any ongoing or previous institutional relationships with anti-racist organisations, nor did there appear to be an obvious, core Scottish racial justice organisation to work with that was comparable with Friends of the Earth for environmental justice or Women's Aid for gender justice.

There appeared to be a heightened public need for an educational response to racial injustice, with which popular educators needed to engage, particularly university-based public sociologists. The year 2005 was also when the

Danish newspaper *Jyllands-Posten* printed cartoons depicting the Prophet Mohammad, which offended many Muslims and led to worldwide protests including violence. Thus, within five years of the 9/11 attacks on New York's World Trade Center by militants in the name of Islam, and ten years after the publication of Samuel P Huntington's (1996) often quoted *Clash of Civilisations* in the context of the increasing influence of explicitly racist political parties and a growth of racist policies in Western countries for many academics, as well as community workers and activists, there seemed to be an urgent need to understand the phenomena of racism, the Muslim experience, free speech, White privilege, Islamism, Eurocentrism, colonial histories, migration, populist xenophobia and so much more. From Queen Margaret University's experience of working with civil society campaigners, this demanded a pedagogical response. Rather than establish a formal collaborative programme, Queen Margaret University partnered with the journal *Concept* (of community education practice and theory) to offer a series of structured, non-formal critical race dialogues.

It is fair to say that the Dialogues met the need for the White academics and community workers to explore these issues in a relatively safe space. What it did not seem to meet were the needs of the Black activists who attended; they reported that they were constantly having to explain 'the basics'. Not having been part of all the conversations in the structured small group discussions or the informal chats in the coffee breaks, I cannot report exactly what these basics are, but this certainly seemed to be a shared experience of many Black and minority ethnic participants. The workshops were not a disaster, but this felt like a serious bump in my journey as an anti-racist scholar. Something different was needed.

Things have certainly moved on. I am writing this nearly 20 years later, following the protests at the murder of George Floyd and many other Black people in the United States, the United Kingdom and elsewhere, the popular dethroning of the Edward Colston statue in Bristol and the rise of Black Lives Matter. But with the ongoing legacy of slavery and colonialism so blatantly clear, are we still only having the basics explained?

Research: postcolonial India

As a new-old academic with a background in environmentalism and community education, my research interest very quickly developed into environmental justice movements and their role in informal and non-formal learning. Almost by accident, I stumbled into an iconic environmental justice movement that threw up challenges for academic literature on social movement learning: the survivors of the 1984 Bhopal gas disaster. At a time when social movement scholarship was emphasising the role of movement activists (as distinct from academics) in generating theory, here was a movement that predominantly comprised poorly educated and non-literate women who had sustained an ambitious movement challenging the Indian state, a US transnational corporation and global toxic capital.

My memory of the disaster itself was acute. In 1984 I was in the middle of a PhD in botany, peripherally active in the science for people movement and developing an interest in the social studies of science; at this time the 'science wars' were taking place in the United Kingdom in the arena of Margaret Thatcher's neoliberal policy interventions, the promotion of 'near market research' and science for business. Bhopal – thousands killed and tens of thousands injured – is what happens when science is used in the interests of the market – a racialised market in which the health, safety and lives of Indian workers are valued less than that of the White-dominated US boardrooms of transnational corporations making investment decisions. Twenty years later, I met some of the Bhopal activists in Mumbai as part of a Friends of the Earth international group at the World Social Forum, and I became a supporter of the survivors' movement. Two years after that, during a visiting scholarship at the University of Delhi, I decided to visit Bhopal, which led to the Bhopal Survivors' Movement Study.

For a White British person to conduct research in postcolonial India, a decolonising approach to methodology is a priority. Drawing on my background in adult and community education, I based my research methodology on Freirean pedagogy and activist ethnography: a 'video dialogue' method of semi-structured interviews and a commitment to reflective activism alongside and in solidarity with the survivors' movement. A research team was put together comprising a Delhi-based Indian academic and two Indian research assistants, all of whom had experience of solidarity activism with Bhopal or related campaigns. Funds were raised through research grants supplemented by a personal contribution amounting to the difference between my salary and that of a similar-grade academic in India, minus housing costs. Details of the methodology are provided elsewhere (Mukherjee et al, 2011), but these were based on the principle that power over the data, its interpretation and use should reside with the survivors' movement and outputs should remain accountable to the movement.

This led to extensive discussions within the team, and with some of the Bhopal-based activists. Since I do not speak Hindi, these discussions took place largely in English or sometimes through interpretation. Issues that became a focus of these discussions on accountability and decolonialisation included:

- the researchers' dual responsibility to academic integrity and partisan solidarity;
- how to maintain solidarity with the movement without aligning with factions within it;
- how to report critically on research findings without risking public criticism of the movement;
- the tendency of research ethics to be based on the informed consent of individual participants with anonymity by default; the culture of social movement activism in India is for collective consent and maximising publicity;
- how publications should be authored when research is co-produced;
- how accountability can be assured for written publications in English resulting from co-produced research with non-literate people with no English;
- the benefits to the careers of the researchers – especially those of us employed as academics – from publications, conference presentations and the like, based on co-produced research.

One issue of particular concern, which arose a considerable time after the research team had disbanded, was the Research Excellence Framework (REF). As with all UK universities, Queen Margaret University was required to submit to the REF2021, and sought to make use of my Bhopal research as an impact case study. Public research funding to the university is based on a ranking of the outcome of the university's submission to the REF comprising research outputs, research environment and impact case studies. Such impact case studies were based on a research model in which evidence was required of impacts based on pathways from underpinning research. To what extent was it legitimate to offer the Bhopal research, designed as dialogical co-generation accountable to the movement, as a case study of how my research at Queen Margaret University led to an impact in the lives of the Bhopal movement? It is notoriously difficult to assess the contribution of any impact of social movement activity, especially when facing such powerful adversaries as US-based transnational corporations, an Indian state committed to neoliberalisation and, more generally, the forces of capital. Any benefits at all are rarely conceded by the powerful and are often claimed, with justification, by multiple activist groups. For a sociology researcher interested in learning in social movements and committed to accountability to the movement, what can legitimately be claimed with integrity? The REF impact case study, in its structural assumptions of academic privilege, serves to reproduce the colonisation of those who are 'impacted'.

Anti-colonial solidarity scholarship

Decolonisation is an ongoing praxis with its roots in the historical reality of colonisation. As a sociologist, understanding colonisation is essential to applying the sociological imagination to the current social reality that constitutes the central subjects of our discipline: class, identity, inequality, race and racism, divisions of labour, communication, globalisation, migration, resource distribution, the built and natural environments and so on. That necessarily requires a historical sensibility. The European empires are no more. The age of colonisation was primarily between the seventeenth and twentieth centuries. Most of Britain's imperial colonies had achieved independent nation status through anti-colonial struggles in the mid-twentieth century. Meanwhile, most British settler colonies (the United States, Canada, Australia, New Zealand) had formed more or less stable independent regimes in earlier centuries through the settler colonial logic of ethnic cleansing: the annihilation or extreme marginalisation of Indigenous populations (Wolfe, 2006). One notable exception, at least in its timeframe, is the Zionist colonisation of Palestine, a settler colonisation project engineered by the British Colonial Office that continues as a project of eviction of the Palestinian population and annihilation of its culture – with a vibrant Palestinian anti-colonial resistance movement and a network of international solidarity.

Under the British Mandate, which de facto existed from the collapse of the Ottoman Empire until 1948, much of Palestine was settled, as an explicit

Mandate policy, not by exiles from Britain (as the North American and antipodean settler colonies) but by Jews from across Europe. The initial European Jewish settlers who formed the political infrastructure of colonisation were driven by the nationalist ideology of Zionism. These settlers subsequently were joined by refugees from antisemitic violence in Russia and Europe, and the Middle East. The Zionist settler colonisation of Palestine, and the accompanying attempts to annihilate, expel or repress the Indigenous population, which was facilitated by British colonial policy during the Mandate, continues to this day. An active, ongoing anti-colonial struggle also continues through a variety of means. A compelling option in anti-colonial academic praxis is therefore active engagement in solidarity work with the Palestinian anti-colonial struggle.

In 2010 I had the opportunity to start my process of learning anti-colonial struggle. The World Education Forum was being held in Palestine, with events organised across the land of Palestine segregated by Zionism (West Bank, Gaza Strip, the State of Israel), as well as in some of the Palestinian refugee camps in neighbouring Arab countries. I attended events in the West Bank (my first visit to the occupied territory) and learned about a wide range of radical, popular and political education from across the world, particularly in Palestine: schools rehearsing Palestinian traditional culture in resistance to Zionist attempts to eliminate it; structured political and vocational education organised by Palestinian political prisoners in Israeli prisons; environmental education for young people to protect the Palestinian environment threatened by occupation; decolonisation actions of the Frantz Fanon Foundation. This led to a period of learning, scholarship and solidarity concerning the history and current reality of Palestine that enriched my understanding of decolonisation as public sociology practice.

After my initial visit, I sought out further opportunities to learn and to engage in solidarity. With my academic and political interest in environmentalism, in late 2010 I joined a study tour in the State of Israel and the Occupied Territory on the Jewish National Fund (JNF), organised by the Scottish Palestine Solidarity Campaign. JNF was formed in 1901 by the World Zionist Congress to acquire land in Palestine for Jewish settlement, but from the middle of the twentieth century it branded itself an environmental NGO, with branches in many countries, including Scotland. Uncovering and exposing the colonial purposes of the JNF beneath the greenwash became a part of my scholar-activism, including building a case against the JNF in Scotland (KKL Scotland) (eg Scandrett, 2021).

Due to my engagement with environmentalism, I was invited to participate in an observer mission to Palestine in 2012 on behalf of Friends of the Earth International and co-authored its report, *Environmental Nakba: Environmental Injustice and Violations of the Israeli Occupation of Palestine* (al-Butmeh et al, 2012). My engagement with Palestinian anti-colonialism has been as an academic and as a citizen, which is consistent with the practice of public sociology. As an activist, I have since participated in a range of protest activities both in the United Kingdom and in Palestine, and as an academic I have conducted research, given public presentations and written articles: the co-generation of academic papers with anti-colonial activists has become an important component of my anti-racist scholarship (al-Butmeh et al, 2019; al-Shalalafeh et al, 2018; Scandrett et al, 2020).

Through education, research and activism, decolonising scholarship requires naming and taking a stand against current Zionist settler-colonising practice. This is particularly significant in higher education institutions in Europe and the English-speaking established settler colonies (especially the United States), where Zionist propaganda is aggressively seeking to prevent decolonising scholarship and anti-colonial solidarity on campuses, including the corporate capture of institutions, victimisation of academics, interfering with curricula and silencing academic and student activities. In many cases, this has been facilitated institutionally by what has become known as the International Holocaust Remembrance Alliance (IHRA) definition of antisemitism.

The use of 'IHRA definition of antisemitism' as a means of undermining decolonising scholarship and anti-colonial solidarity has been influential, and it is worth addressing this as an illustration of the ideological forces in support of active colonisation that decolonisers need to recognise. The American Jewish Committee (2004) put together a draft *'working definition of antisemitism'* that, in the words of its lead author, Kenneth Stern (2019), *'was created primarily so that European data collectors could know what to include and exclude. That way antisemitism could be monitored better over time and across borders.'* The working definition contained examples of where antisemitism may emerge, including in the context of discussions of the State of Israel, which identifies itself as a 'Jewish State'. Leaving aside the effectiveness of the working definition for its original function, its subsequent capture by Zionists to silence anti-colonial scholarship has been profound. After several Zionist attempts to upgrade the working definition of antisemitism, in 2016 it was adopted by the International Holocaust Remembrance Alliance, and the working definition subsequently became known as the 'IHRA definition of antisemitism'. With that status, Zionist groups promoted, with considerable success, the adoption of the 'IHRA definition' by states, public bodies and civil society organisations, including many universities. Indeed, the UK Government threatened sanctions against universities in England that did not adopt the 'IHRA definition'.

The impact of this activity is significant, including in universities. A (flawed) 'working definition' designed to assist data collection on antisemitism has become a tool to promote colonial practice and to silence anti-colonial solidarity and distort scholarship. Individual academics have been victimised, including being subject to disciplinary proceedings and even dismissed for alleged antisemitism. Solidarity events by student organisations and university premises booked by external organisations have been banned by university leadership. A culture of fear has developed among some academics concerning researching, teaching or even discussing Israel and Palestine, thereby undermining anti-colonial scholarship. In the words of Kenneth Stern, the *'working definition of antisemitism' 'was never intended to be a campus hate speech code'* (Stern, 2019). Zionist weaponisation of the 'definition' has also undermined attempts to challenge genuine antisemitism. In response to this, a group of scholars have since developed the Jerusalem Declaration on Antisemitism (JDA, 2020), which more clearly distinguishes antisemitism from anti-colonial critiques of Zionism and the State of Israel.

Indeed, it is widely believed that the promotion by Zionist groups of the 'IHRA definition' was specifically prompted by the success of the campaign for Boycott, Divestment and Sanctions (BDS) against Israel, called for by Palestinian civil society in 2005. While BDS demands are limited to Israel adhering to international law (to end the occupation, abolish apartheid laws and honour the right of return of Palestinian refugees), the campaign is compatible with, and has also been supported and adopted as part of, wider anti-colonial solidarity. Anti-colonial scholarship does not explicitly require support for BDS, but is inevitably affected by the Zionist reaction to it. To practise anti-colonial scholarship means standing up to and challenging the powerful Zionist lobby and other forces that defend or deny colonisation and its legacy.

Decolonising the curriculum

During a visit to Gaza in 2014–15 as part of activism with the Scottish Palestine Solidarity Campaign, our local organiser's family invited us to dinner. Having introduced myself as a lecturer in sociology, I was asked by one of the family whether I was aware that the discipline of sociology was originally developed in the fourteenth century by the Muslim Arab Ibn Khaldûn. I admitted that I did not know this, and said I was keen to learn. I was not surprised that all the sociology textbooks that I drew on did not seem to know it either. After a little research, I started introducing Ibn Khaldûn into my teaching.

Standard textbooks in sociology usually locate the discipline's origins to nineteenth-century European scholars such as Comte, Marx, Durkheim and Spencer, although it is now recognised that Ibn Khaldûn's (2015) *Muqaddimah*, published in Arabic in 1377, was the earliest known text to regard the study of society as an academic discipline. Ibn Khaldûn developed a rigorous methodology that distinguished the 'science of human social organisation' from mythical and religious explanations. With this science, he analysed the historical development of, and dynamic relationship between nomadic and settled societies through kinship, class structure, governance, authority, productive relations and social solidarity (the latter being his central concept of *asabiyyah*). Rather than rewrite the canonical version of the origins of sociology in our courses, Ibn Khaldûn's work is introduced to students after two years of study to demonstrate the Eurocentrism of sociology.

This illustrates a wider issue. Decolonisation is not a process of airbrushing out the legacy of colonialism. The public debate over statues, street names and other means of social honouring of slave owners, colonisers and others who have perpetrated racism from which (largely White) sections of modern society has economically benefited has focused attention on the necessity of neither celebrating nor obliterating Europe's colonial history. We cannot, in our scholarship, banish colonialism. Decolonisation requires academics to find ways to be explicit about our colonial history and ongoing complicity in colonial, settler-colonial, neocolonial and postcolonial racist exploitation; its impact on the knowledge content and methodologies of our education, research and scholarship; and from this position of honesty explore ways to value the knowledge of the colonised that has been generated in anti-colonial struggles.

Wolfe (2006) declared that settler-colonisation is a structure and not an event. Decolonisation involves deconstruction, a process in which academics have a role. Starting where we are, with the legacy of colonial racism, means that our attempts at decolonisation will be tentative and contingent. We will make mistakes, and come up against barriers and limitations in our efforts. Decolonisation is therefore a reflexive process in which we are engaged collectively, requiring self-critique and humility, and facing many challenges. But as products of colonial exploitation, the task of decolonisation is necessary. Decolonisation involves challenging the apologists, deniers and defenders of colonisation, and standing in explicit solidarity with those on the front lines of anti-colonial struggles. This can involve some professional risk. But this is a process that those of us committed to anti-colonial, anti-racist, humanist and emancipatory academic practice are engaged in collectively.

Reflective questions

- How can we consider anti-racism and decolonisation as ongoing processes?
- What are the limitations, contradictions and countervailing forces to anti-racist and decolonising practices in academia, and what can we learn from them?
- How can sociology – or indeed any academic discipline – combine political solidarity with intellectual rigour?

Recommended reading

- Bhopal Survivors' Movement Study (2009) *Bhopal Survivors Speak: Emergent Voices from a People's Movement.* Edinburgh: Word Power Books.
- Bullard, R D (1990) *Dumping on Dixie: Race, Class and Environmental Quality.* New York: Routledge.
- Masalha, N (2010) *The Palestine Nakba: Decolonising History, Narrating the Subaltern, Reclaiming Memory.* London: Zed Books.
- Scandrett, E (ed) (2020) *Public Sociology as Educational Practice: Challenges, Dialogues and Counter-Publics.* Bristol: Bristol University Press.

References

al-Butmeh, A, Peek, B and Scandrett, E (2012) *Environmental Nakba: Environmental Injustice and Violations of the Israeli Occupation of Palestine.* Amsterdam: Friends of the Earth International.

al-Butmeh, A, al-Shalalfeh, Z and Zwahre, M with Scandrett, E (2019) The Environment as a Site of Struggle Against Settler-colonisation in Palestine. In Harley, A and Scandrett, E (eds) *Environmental Justice, Popular Struggle and Community Development* (pp 1–14). Bristol: Policy Press.

al-Shalalfeh, Z, Napier, F and Scandrett, E (2018) Water Nakba in Palestine: Sustainable Development Goal 6 versus Israeli Hydro-hegemony. *Local Environment*, 23(1): 117–24.

American Jewish Committee (2004) The Working Definition of Antisemitism. [online] Available at: www.ajc.org/the-working-definition-of-antisemitism (accessed 21 February 2023).

Bullard, R D (1990) *Dumping on Dixie: Race, Class and Environmental Quality.* New York: Routledge.

Commission for Racial Justice (1987) *Toxic Wastes and Race in the United States.* New York: United Church of Christ.

Huntington, S P (1996) *The Clash of Civilisations and the Remaking of World Order.* New York: Simon and Schuster.

Ibn Khaldûn, I (2015 [1377]). *The Muqaddimah: An Introduction to History*. Princeton, NJ: Princeton University Press.

JDA (2020) *Jerusalem Declaration on Antisemitism*. [online] Available at: https://jerusalemdeclaration.org (accessed 21 February 2023).

Mukherjee, S, Scandrett, E, Sen, T and Shah, D (2011) Generating Theory in the Bhopal Survivors' Movement. In Motta, S C and Nilsen, A G (eds) *Social Movements in the Global South: Dispossession, Development and Resistance* (pp 150–77). Basingstoke: Palgrave Macmillan.

Scandrett, E (2021) Decolonising the Environmental Movement: Break with the JNF. *Transactions of the Jewish National Fund: a Journal of Environmental Colonialism*, 1: 34–44.

Scandrett, E, Soliman, M and Stone, P (2020) Cultural Resistance in Occupied Palestine and the Use of Creative International Solidarity through Song. *Journal of Arts and Communities*, 12(1): 41–56.

Orr, L and Whiting, N (2020) 'Seeing Things Differently': Gender Justice and Counter-Hegemony in Higher Education'. In Scandrett, E (ed) *Public Sociology as Educational Practice: Challenges, Dialogues and Counter-Publics* (pp 37–51). Bristol: Bristol University Press.

Stern, K (2019) I drafted the definition of antisemitism. Rightwing Jews are weaponizing it. *The Guardian*, 13 December. [online] Available at: www.theguardian.com/commentisfree/2019/dec/13/antisemitism-executive-order-trump-chilling-effect (accessed 20 March 2023).

Wilkinson, M and Scandrett, E (2003) A Popular Education Approach to Tackling Environmental Injustice and Widening Participation. *Concept*, 13 (1/2): 11–16.

Wolfe, P (2006) Settler Colonialism and the Elimination of the Native. *Journal of Genocide Research*, 8(4): 387–409.

CHAPTER 6

THE SCOTTISH CENTRE FOR SOCIAL JUSTICE

Marion Ellison

Introduction and background

> *I look forward to the days ahead when this Chamber will sound with debate, argument, and passion. When men and women from all over Scotland will meet to work together for a future built from the first principles of social justice.*
>
> (Donald Dewar's opening of the Scottish Parliament, 1 July 1999, p 2)

The current cost of living crisis has exacerbated pre-existing inequalities in Scotland, as it has across many societies globally in the post-Covid-19 era. The extent and depth of poverty in Scotland are evidenced by a recent survey conducted by the Joseph Rowntree Foundation (2022), which describes the situation as a *'national emergency'*, with around 65 per cent of people surveyed stating that they have cut back on essential items and 26 per cent of families cutting back on food or childcare. Moreover, 18 per cent of households have missed or reduced the size of meals and turned their heating off due to the cost-of-living crisis (Joseph Rowntree Foundation, 2022). Recent evidence also reveals the extent of relative poverty in Scotland. Between 2017 and 2020, 24 per cent of children in Scotland were living in relative poverty, with 32 per cent of families with three or more children living in relative poverty during this period and 38 per cent of single-parent families experiencing relative poverty during this period (Joseph Rowntree Foundation, 2022).

Critically, findings also reveal that some groups are more at risk of relative poverty than others. For example, 44 per cent of people from minority ethnic backgrounds are living in relative poverty, equating to two in every five people from this group compared with 18 per cent of White people in Scotland, which is less than one in every five.

The lived experiences of poverty and deprivation emerge from multiple inequalities across intersecting life domains, including work and income, health, environment, education and housing. There is also clear evidence that place matters, with recent epidemiological evidence revealing that healthy life expectancy is significantly lower for those living in the most deprived areas than for those living in the least deprived areas of Scotland. In 2017–19, males in the most deprived areas were, on average, expected to live 26.0 fewer years in good health than those in the least deprived areas of Scotland (47.0 years vs 73.0 years). Females in the most deprived areas were, on average, expected to live 22.1 fewer years in good health than those in the least deprived areas of Scotland (49.5 years versus 71.6 years).

During the Covid-19 pandemic, people living in the most deprived areas of Scotland were disproportionately more likely to be infected by the Covid-19 virus and experience long-term Covid-19 symptoms (Scottish Government, 2021b). Data also revealed that people living in deprived areas of Scotland were 2.3 times more likely to die from the disease as those living in the least deprived areas of Scotland (National Records of Scotland, 2021). Life chances were also significantly impacted by Covid-19 and lockdown measures, with some communities and groups more likely to experience negative effects in employment, educational opportunities, social outcomes, and health and well-being (Beattie et al, 2022; Couper-Kenney and Riddell, 2021; McGhee and Roesch-Marsh, 2020; McLennan et al, 2020).

Recognising the profound economic, social and environmental challenges faced by people and communities living in poverty and deprivation across Scotland, the Scottish Government created the Social Renewal Board on 9 June 2020. Adopting a human-rights based approach with a focus on equality, the central aim of the Board is to emerge from the pandemic while reducing poverty and disadvantage by building on *'the shifts in policy and practice that took place as a result of working across portfolios and in partnership with frontline service deliverers in local government, the third sector and communities*' (Scottish Government, 2020b). To further this aim, the Scottish Government Equality Unit, working in conjunction with CEMVO Scotland, developed strategic partnerships with a number of third-sector organisations and community groups across Scotland. Exemplifying this, Our Rights, Our Communities is a community-based project that advances and promotes equality and human rights of New Scots Women (refugees, asylum seekers and migrants). Focusing on co-generating understandings of the lived experiences of intersectional oppressions suffered by asylum seekers, refugees and migrant women, the project has enabled the co-creation of collective and accessible resources relevant to New Scots Women across Glasgow. Community organisations involved in the project include the Milk Café, a social enterprise led by refugee and migrant women, which provides a safe community space for local groups, classes and workshops.

More broadly, the Scottish Government has identified a range of policy areas for strategic partnerships. Policy circles identified include age and disability, addressing low income, community-led and place-based renewal, cross-cutting delivery, financial security, food, the housing system, the third sector and volunteering. The final report, *If Not Now, When?* (Scottish Government, 2021c, p 12) contains 20 calls to action structured around three themes.

1. Money and Work – everyone should have a basic level of income from employment and social security.
2. People, Rights and Advancing Equality – everyone should see their rights realised and have access to a range of basic rights, goods and services.
3. Communities and Collective Endeavour – ensuring that more power is given to people, communities and frontline teams.

The response of the Scottish Government to entrenched inequalities across Scotland is characterised by a 'human-rights approach with a focus on equality' and a recognition that working in partnership between local government, the third sector and local communities is critical to this approach. The Scottish Centre for Social Justice reflects this commitment by working with publics and organisations across Scotland to co-generate knowledge and action on key social justice issues and intersectional themes, including homelessness, income inequalities, racial justice, work and welfare, educational inequalities, gender justice, public health and the environment, social security, and child and youth justice within Scotland. These key social justice issues and intersectional themes have driven my work as an educator and researcher within higher education settings over the last 30 years. As an educator, I have always sought to facilitate mutual learning and critical thinking as a collective experience within seminar discussions by inviting students to connect their pre-existing experiences with empirical research relating to social justice issues and intersectional themes in Scotland, the United Kingdom more broadly and at a global level. Illustrating this, a student recently conveyed the lived experiences of a friend who was subject to the UK-wide policy No Recourse to Public Funds (NRPF), due to their immigration status. The lived experiences of destitution and homelessness conveyed by the student revealed the harsh and brutal realties of destitution and homelessness that lay behind the statistics. Racial injustice and related destitution are among the most conspicuous injustices in Scotland, the United Kingdom generally and across societies globally. The next section explores the impact of the policy of NRPF on the lives of people in Scotland and the rest of the United Kingdom.

Racial injustice and destitution in Scotland and the rest of the United Kingdom

We are people. They look at us as though we are just a piece of paper. We are not paper.

(Scottish Government, 2021a, p 26)

As the above quote illustrates, for people in Scotland who are prevented from accessing all public money or support due to their immigration status, the impact of 'interconnected oppressions', including stigma, prejudice and discrimination, can be devastating. The NRPF rule applies to people who are subject to UK immigration rules, which effectively prevent access to Universal Credit, child benefits, payments from the Scottish Welfare Fund, and housing and homeless services provided by local authorities. Recent research has evidenced the ways in which the NRPF rule has exacerbated interconnected oppressions, including stigma, prejudice and discrimination (Allen, 2018; Bansal et al, 2022; Farmer, 2017; Jolly et al, 2022; Scottish Government 2021a; Smith et al, 2021). Here, NRPF has been revealed as leading to a heightened risk of racial discrimination when people come into contact with public services or apply for entitlements. This increased risk is triggered by assumptions regarding immigration status and entitlement to public support. In this sense,

NRPF may be regarded as reflecting what Geetha Marcus (2015, p 19) describes as follows: *'multiple voices reflect multiple realities influenced by long-standing institutional, structural, political and cultural agendas'*. People who may be subjected to NRPF include international students; people with work visas; British overseas citizens; dependent spouses or family members of people on student or work visas; a person seeking asylum; a child of non-UK nationals born in the United Kingdom; a person with limited leave to remain on a route to settlement; a child in the care of a local authority who was born outside the United Kingdom; European Economic Area (EEA) nationals without status under the EUSS scheme; and stateless people.

Recent evidence has shown that people with NRPF are more likely to experience destitution, homelessness and financial insecurity (Farmer, 2017; Jolly et al, 2022; Scottish Government, 2021b; Smith et al, 2021). Destitution is defined as and is most likely to occur when there is a sudden and unexpected change to employment or income. For people with NRPF, there is also a real danger of entering exploitative working relationships in order to survive. There are an estimated 388,000 non-UK nationals living in Scotland, or about 7.2 per cent of the population, and 154,000 non-UK nationals including non-EU nationals, representing nearly 3 per cent of the population.

While it is the case that most people with NRPF are eventually granted access to public funds by the UK Government and have their right to be in the United Kingdom recognised, it is also the case that long-term hidden destitution pervades the lives of those with NRPF who are not granted access to public funds or the right to remain in the United Kingdom (Farmer, 2017; Jolly et al, 2022; Smith et al, 2021). Community-based organisations and third-sector organisations support destitute people with NRPF. However, insufficient funding and time-limited projects mean that these organisations are often unable to solve the cause of destitution and underlying status issues (Jolly et al, 2022; Smith et al, 2021).

The stark reality of the impact of NRPF on complex inequalities is revealed by recent research undertaken by the citizens advice bureau in the United Kingdom. NRPF makes people fall behind on bills and sink into debt. Without access to Universal Credit, tax credits and other benefits intended to top up low income or replace income when claimants are out of work, people with NRPF find themselves struggling to afford essential services. This has significant impacts. Some 81 per cent of people with NRPF are behind on at least one bill. This compares with one in five people (20 per cent) in the United Kingdom more generally (Smith et al, 2021).

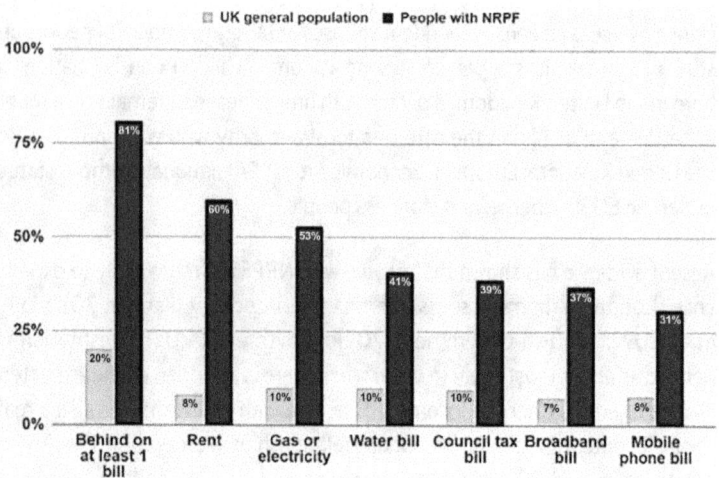

Figure 6.1: People at risk of falling behind on bills in the UK. Source: Smith et al, 2021

Health inequalities and racial injustice

Recent research has highlighted the detrimental impact of NRPF on mental health, with over 83 per cent of people with NRPF reporting that the regulation has had a negative impact and 50 per cent reporting that NRPF has had a very negative impact (Smith et al, 2021). Responding to the overwhelming evidence of the deleterious impact of NRPF on social, psychological and material well-being, the Scottish Government has provided a clear policy position on NRPF, declaring that, *'No one is forced into destitution, and everyone has their human rights protected, regardless of their immigration status'* (Scottish Government, 2021a). The operationalisation of this principle is clearly articulated in the Ending Homelessness Together action plan (Scottish Government, 2020a).

> *We will contribute to the ambition of ending homelessness and specifically support actions relating to people with NRPF and destitute asylum seekers, as set out in the Ending Homelessness Together action plan.*

This includes work to support the development of a five-year delivery plan by the Everyone Home Collective on the 'route-map' to end destitution. This work, which is led by a partnership of third sector and academic organisations across Scotland, will seek to scale-up community-based accommodation provision and holistic support to meet the needs of an estimated 300–500 people with NRPF who are not entitled to local authority housing or homelessness services.

Rationale for the Scottish Centre for Social Justice at Queen Margaret University

The Scottish Centre for Social Justice at Queen Margaret University is situated within the discipline of public sociology. Research and education at QMU encourage, facilitate and advance sociological knowledge, which is generated through engagement between academic researchers and key publics involved in social justice issues across Scotland. This includes communities, employer organisations, trade unions, NGOs and policy-makers at the local, national and international levels. Directly addressing the 'calls to action' identified by the Social Renewal Advisory Board, the Scottish Centre for Social Justice is uniquely placed to provide a dynamic platform for collaborative work, co-generated knowledge and action on key social justice issues and intersectional themes, including homelessness, income inequalities, work and welfare, educational inequalities, public health and the environment, social security, child and youth justice, racial justice and gender justice within a post-pandemic Scotland.

Facilitating the co-production and co-design of policies with communities affected by them is central to providing a more comprehensive strategy for shared well-being at the local level. Exemplifying this, local responses to challenges emerging from the Covid-19 pandemic led to the growth of new social and community enterprises and indigenous community groups across Scotland. Here, recent research has revealed the effectiveness of innovative approaches and new organisational forms at the local level, such as social enterprise ownership at community level, community development corporations, community development financial institutions, and employee stock ownership plans (ESOP). New social and community enterprises and indigenous groups formed at the local level during the Covid-19 pandemic also play a key role in informing post-Covid-19 policy and implementation strategies at national level (Ellison, 2021). The central aims of the Scottish Centre for Social Justice are as follows.

1. To facilitate and advance knowledge which is generated through engagement between academic researchers and key publics involved in social justice issues. This includes communities, employer organisations, trade unions, NGOs and policy makers at local, national and international level.
2. To provide a web-based platform for learning and knowledge exchange on key social justice issues and intersectional themes in Scotland.
3. To inform the post-Covid policy and implementation agenda in Scotland.
4. To disseminate peer-reviewed research relating to social justice issues and intersectional themes in Scotland.

Conclusion

As this chapter has shown, the impact of increasing and deepening levels of poverty and interconnected oppressions including stigma, prejudice and discrimination on both physical and mental health is significant (Allen, 2018; Bansal et al, 2022; Farmer, 2017; Jolly et al, 2022; Scottish Government, 2021a; Smith et al, 2021). Here, the multi-dimensional and interacting relationship between social and environmental determinants of health and health inequalities significantly impacts infancy, childhood development, employment, environment and ageing. As exemplified by the social, economic and cultural injustices arising from the imposition of the NRPF rule, social injustices are forged within broader economic and political systems and forces. Collaborative work within the Scottish Centre for Social Justice at Queen Margaret University is driven by a central aim to work with publics and organisations to co-generate knowledge and action on key social justice issues and intersectional themes, including racial justice, gender justice, homelessness, income inequalities, work and welfare, educational inequalities, public health and the environment, social security, and child and youth justice within a post-pandemic Scotland. The Scottish Centre for Social Justice seeks to enable a more socially just and inclusive society by facilitating the co-production and co-design of policies with publics and communities affected by them to provide a more comprehensive strategy for shared well-being at the local level.

Reflective questions

- In what ways can the Scottish Centre for Social Justice collaborate with 'hidden publics' experiencing social injustice, particularly within the context of 'interconnected oppressions' including stigma, prejudice and discrimination?
- In what ways can the Scottish Centre for Social Justice enable reflective practice within collaborative working?

Recommended reading

- Dickson, E and Rosen, R (2021) 'Punishing Those Who Do the Wrong Thing': Enforcing Destitution and Debt Through the UK's Family Migration Rules. *Critical Social Policy*, 41(4): 545–65.
- Jolly, A and Gupta, A (2022) Children and Families with No Recourse to Public Funds: Learning From Case Reviews. *Children and Society*. [online] Available at: https://onlinelibrary.wiley.com/doi/pdf/10.1111/chso.12646 (accessed 9 December 2022).
- Odumade, V and Graham, P (2019) Everyday Experiences of Migrant Families with No Recourse to Public Funds. *British Psychological Society North-East Branch Bulletin*, 10: 31–42. [online] Available at: https://nrl.northumbria.ac.uk/id/eprint/40461/1/Odumade,%20Graham%20-%20Everyday%20experiences%20of%20migrant%20families%20with%20No%20Recourse%20to%20Public%20Funds%20AAM.pdf (accessed 9 December 2022).

References

Allen, K (2018) Whose Crisis Counts? Intersectionality, Austerity, and the Politics of Survival. *Ethnic and Racial Studies*, 41(13): 2301–9.

Bansal, N, Karlsen, S, Sashidharan, S P, Cohen, R, Chew-Graham, C A and Malpass, A (2022) Understanding Ethnic Inequalities in Mental Healthcare in the UK: A Meta-ethnography. *pLoS Medicine*, 19(12): e1004139.

Beattie, M, Wilson, C and Hendry, G (2022) Learning from Lockdown: Examining Scottish Primary Teachers' Experiences of Emergency Remote Teaching. *British Journal of Educational Studies*, 70(2): 217–34.

Cebula, C, Birt, C, Hay, D and Evans, J (2022). *Poverty in Scotland 2022*. Joseph Rowntree Foundation.

Couper-Kenney, F and Riddell, S (2021) The Impact of Covid-19 on Children with Additional Support Needs and Disabilities in Scotland. *European Journal of Special Needs Education*, 36(1): 20–34.

Ellison, M (2021) Introduction: Healing the Divisions – Restoring the Foundations for a 'Social Europe'. In Bertin, G, Ellison, M and Moro, G (eds) *The European Social Model and an Economy of Well-being: Repairing the Social Fabric of European Societies* (pp 1–16). Cheltenham: Edward Elgar.

Farmer, N J (2017) 'No Recourse to Public Funds': Insecure Immigration Status and Destitution – the Role of Social Work? *Critical and Radical Social Work*, 5(3): 357–67.

Jolly, A, Singh, J and Lobo, S (2022) No Recourse to Public Funds: A Qualitative Evidence Synthesis. *International Journal of Migration, Health, and Social Care*, 18(1). [online] Available at: www.emerald.com/insight/content/doi/10.1108/IJMHSC-11-2021-0107/full/html (accessed 21 February 2023).

Marcus, G (2015) Marginalisation and the Voices of Gypsy/Traveller Girls. *Cambridge Open-Review Educational Research e-Journal*, 1(2). [online] Available at: www.corerj.educ.cam.ac.uk (accessed 21 February 2023).

McGhee, K and Roesch-Marsh, A (2020) *Bridging the Digital Divide for Care Experienced Young People in Scotland: If Not Now, When?* Edinburgh: ELCIS/Scottish Care Leavers Covenant. [online] Available at: www.celcis.org/application/files/5615/9541/7476/Inform_Briefing_-_Bridging_the_digital_divide_for_Care_Leavers_in_Scotland__July_2020.pdf (accessed 20 February 2023).

McLennan, C, Mercieca, D and Mercieca, D (2020) What Can I Do? Teachers, Students, and Families in Relationship during Covid-19 Lockdown in Scotland. *Malta Review of Educational Research*, 14(2): 163–81.

National Records of Scotland (2021) Deaths Involving Coronavirus (COVID-19) in Scotland (4 May to 10 May 2020). [online] Available at: www.nrscotland.gov.uk/statistics-and-data/statistics/statistics-by-theme/vital-events/general-publications/weekly-and-monthly-data-on-births-and-deaths/deaths-involving-coronavirus-covid-19-in-scotland (accessed 12 January 2023).

Scottish Government (2020) *Poverty and Income Inequality in Scotland: 2016–2019*. [online] Available at: www.gov.scot/publications/poverty-income-inequality-scotland-2016-19 (accessed 20 February 2023).

Scottish Government (2021a). *Ending Destitution Together: Strategy. A Strategy to Improve Support for People with No Recourse to Public Funds (NRPF) Living in Scotland*. Edinburgh: Scottish Government.

Scottish Government (2021b) *Long-term Monitoring of Health Inequalities: January 2021 Report*. Edinburgh: Scottish Government. [online] Available at: www.gov.scot/publications/long-term-monitoring-health-inequalities-january-2021-report/pages/4 (accessed 20 February 2023).

Scottish Government (2021c) *If Not Now, When?* Edinburgh: Scottish Government. [online] Available at: www.gov.scot/publications/not-now-social-renewal-advisory-board-report-january-2021(accessed 20 February 2023).

Smith, C, O'Reilly, P, Rumpel, R and White, R (2021) *How Do I Survive Now? The Impact of Living with No Recourse to Public Funds*. Citizens Advice Bureau. [online] Available at: www.citizensadvice.org.uk/Global/Citizens Advice/welfare%20publications/How%20do%20I%20survive%20now_%20November%202021.pdf

CHAPTER 7

CHALLENGING DOMINANT NARRATIVES ABOUT THE GLOBAL SOUTH TO ADDRESS IMPLICIT BIAS AND OTHERING

Walid Salhab, Sandra Ndale and Emma Wood

Introduction

Queen Margaret University (QMU) prides itself on being a university without borders, stating that it *is an outward looking university, engaging with local, national and international communities. [The University welcomes] students from all around the world and [works] with partners in many different countries'* (QMU, 2023). QMU has a formal agreement (Memorandum of Understanding) with the Malawian care home STEKA and with the Scottish-based charity STEKAskills. This MoU aims to advance the cause of social justice through the development of innovative projects, services and learning opportunities. In this chapter, we explore the journey of several poverty-experienced young people from the STEKA home who studied at Queen Margaret University to develop learning and skills. Three young residents of the STEKA home, Sandra Ndale, Gift Thompson and Abigail Maseko, have now studied at Queen Margaret University. In this chapter, we focus particularly on Sandra Ndale, who developed her talents to get people's voices heard through film-making. What was expected to be an enriching and valuable learning experience for all the students involved, both Scottish and Malawian, turned out to be much more complex. This chapter reflects on Sandra's experience, what it taught her tutors and the impact on both Sandra and on Queen Margaret University.

STEKA (Step Kids' Awareness) is a grassroots Malawian NGO that creates sustainable futures for homeless and vulnerable children and young people. It is led by activist and social entrepreneur Godknows Maseko, an ex-'street kid' and survivor of human trafficking, who campaigns for children's rights and gender equality, and against early marriage. For over 10 years, he and his wife Hellen have developed a model for creating sustainable futures for young survivors and street children, establishing a family home for more than 100 very vulnerable young people and supporting many more in their own homes and communities. STEKA is working with partners, including the Scottish charity STEKAskills based at Queen Margaret University, to develop a STEKA Centre for Vocational Skills and Community Enterprise, which will train vulnerable older teenagers to develop the resilience and skills needed to access carefully targeted and locally relevant employment. STEKAskills is an award-winning charity aimed at building solidarity between communities in Scotland and Malawi. Its dialogue work, discussed in Chapter 4, has been commended by the Scottish Government and the Scotland Malawi Partnership.

The authors

Walid Salhab and Emma Wood

Walid and Emma are both lecturers at Queen Margaret University. They have been colleagues for many years and have worked together on several projects, including the development of an MSc in Digital Campaigning and Content Creation, with our colleague Graham Drysdale. Walid Salhab is a multi-award-winning filmmaker and lecturer in media practice. He was born and brought up in Lebanon, spent time in Iraq as a child refugee and, having experienced significant trauma, came to the United Kingdom as a student. He has lived in Scotland for more than 40 years, but his work is heavily influenced by his early experiences as a refugee, and his desire to affect current discourse about refugees and migrants and their right to sanctuary. His short films foreground the voices of the marginalised and dispossessed, and have won accolades at film festivals worldwide. His specific lived experience played a significant role in the decision to bring two young women from the STEKA home in Malawi to Queen Margaret University to develop their skills to tell their stories through film. As he explains:

> *When I first moved to the UK as a 17-year-old, having experienced trauma in Lebanon, I thought people here would want to hear my*

story and offer me support. But I found out that people were not actually interested in what I had to say. So I quickly learned that to fit in I should stop talking about my difficult experiences and instead talk about Scottish popular culture – sports, TV programmes, bands, things like that. When I met Sandra and Abigail, I knew exactly how they were feeling because I had gone through the same thing. Sometimes all you want is for people to listen to you and to say they understand what you are going through. But that is hard to do face to face. I saw myself in them, which motivated me to help them articulate their stories and be listened to. As a filmmaker and as someone with my own experiences of trauma and migration, I know that people who go through trauma need a mechanism to express what they have been through. Film is a way in which this can happen. Sharing experiences with people in the West helps to make the West understand what is really happening in other countries – especially those in the Global South, where people often do not get to speak for themselves but have their experiences interpreted through a White lens. Authentic films made by people living the experience they are reporting on makes situations more real.

When he first moved to the United Kingdom, Walid also felt that the BBC's representation of what was going on in the Arab world was unfair. In his opinion, it did not represent local experiences. He found the way in which the region was represented to be degrading. He believes that people with lived experiences of the trauma of refugeedom and migration must inform the reporting of that experience and on their communities, instead of correspondents catering to the tastes and sensibilities of White people in the West. That way, he feels the understanding of complex issues and experiences will be fairer, and community perspectives will be valued and respected by wider audiences. Teaching the technical skills and storytelling techniques to those with lived experience will enable them to utilise the power to structure and tell their own stories themselves, in a way that will engage universal audiences. That is what being a university without boundaries means, and why, as a filmmaker and tutor, Walid has worked hard alongside Emma to equip some of the STEKA residents to be able to tell their stories through film. This has also led to the inauguration of a media training centre at the STEKA vocational skills centre in Malawi so that more poverty-experienced young people can develop the skills they need to get their voices heard.

Emma Wood's research and practice focus on the ways in which critical dialogue can be utilised in the emancipation of marginalised groups, through an understanding of their lived experience as expertise. They learn to organise and communicate their views, and take action to challenge oppressive social norms. She is chair of the Scottish charity STEKAskills, which aims to connect Scottish communities with their contemporaries in Malawi to bring about social change. She works in close partnership with the grassroots Malawian NGO STEKA, which creates sustainable futures for young survivors of human trafficking.

Sandra Ndale speaks for herself

I was born in Malawi, one of the world's most poverty-experienced countries, in 1994, the last born in a family of five. I grew up with my mother and siblings, since I lost my father when I was nine months old. When I was ten years old, my sister (who grew up with my uncle in Blantyre, Malawi's second city) and brother in-law, Hellen and Godknows Maseko who are the founders of STEKA, came to visit us in my rural village. When they were leaving, I cried so much and said they should take me with them, and my wish was granted. I went to live with them and the other children at the STEKA home. I tried to work very hard at school until I finished my primary studies and was so pleased at being selected to go to secondary school. In secondary school, I worked hard until I finished my studies and passed with good grades. When I was done with my secondary studies, I went on to study journalism and TV production at college, with the support of Godknows and Hellen.

The case

As part of QMU's relationship with STEKA, a camera was loaned to Sandra while she was at college in Blantyre, to make a film about Godknows' vision for a vocational skills training centre in Malawi and the impact it would make on people's lives there. Sandra filmed footage and interviews that would be added to interviews filmed by students in Scotland about QMU's support for the project. When Emma and Walid looked at the footage, they saw that Sandra had also sent a copy of a documentary she had made about the lived experience of her brothers and sisters at the STEKA home as 'street kids'. Walid spotted Sandra's talent based on what she managed to produce despite the huge limitations within which she was working. He explains:

> Sandra is a very talented storyteller with a clear understanding and strong opinions about how her community could lead important social change in Malawi. Her film felt unique because instead of the usual interpretation of events by a White correspondent, she showed poverty-experienced people speaking for themselves: not saying what they think powerful people want to hear but saying what they wanted to say. It is so unusual to see — I thought she should develop more advanced filmmaking skills so that she could express herself more effectively and reach wider audiences.

The film Sandra made in partnership with Scottish QMU students had a big impact. In addition to making a case for a vocational training centre, it helped viewers of the film (particularly in Malawi) to stop judging street kids as lazy, dangerous or criminal (Wood, 2020). It also enhanced their view of street kids, revealing their humanity and the difference structural issues can make – for example, having a safe place to live and loving parents.

Instead of being seen as Others, as objects of pity or thugs to be feared, these young people were shown by Sandra to be victims of structural inequalities. Walid then lobbied for Sandra to come to Scotland to study filmmaking at Queen Margaret University, due to her exceptional talent in using film to tell stories about her poverty-experienced peers in Malawi. The plan was that she would spend one semester with media production students and also contribute to classes focusing on STEKA-related projects with public relations students. It was our assumption that the Scottish students would jump at the chance to make the most of such an intercultural experience with a Malawian student and be as enthusiastic as we were about this unique opportunity to share perspectives. Happily, some did, and warm connections were made; unfortunately, however, we also witnessed some very difficult situations, in particular with some students not wanting Sandra in their groups for assessment, speaking over her (instead of to her) in breakout discussion groups and excluding her entirely from a group assessment, choosing to hold meetings without her and to make a submission that didn't include her. From her perspective, Sandra explains:

> Before I went to Scotland, I was very excited to because it was my first time to go outside my country, and, of course, the continent of Africa. When I thought of flying in an aeroplane I was very happy since we just saw them when flying in the air. I was also happy because I knew I would

learn more things. When I arrived in Scotland, everything was different, including food, weather, people, buildings, culture and everything. Life in Scotland should not have been very hard although some situations made it hard. Starting with life at home. I was staying with the family of Emma Wood. The family was very caring and they accepted me to be part of their family. We were doing things together and this really made me not miss my family back in Africa. Let me appreciate Emma Wood who acted the role of being a mother to me for six months. I really enjoyed her company because almost every day we were together, when I went to school, for the shopping, to walk the dogs, watch films and she even used to accompany me to church. I don't take this for granted. People within the community, more especially adults, were also very friendly and helpful. Let me also give thanks to St John's Catholic Parish in Portobello. These people are so amazing in terms of Christianity. I did not miss my home because of them. I was very happy because they allowed me to join the Saint John's choir and the singing was so awesome.

When I was about to go to the university, I was very happy because this is what I went to Scotland for, and I was expecting that the students and lecturers will treat me the way how the family and the church treated me. There at school the lectures were good, and the lecturers had a heart to assist each and every student without looking at the race and this made me feel good. Nevertheless, somehow life wasn't easy – some classes were tough due to the treatment I was getting from other students. They excluded me from a group assessment. To say the truth, I cried in my bedroom due to the situation. This gave me a bad picture of some students at the university. Although this happened, I still thank Walid Sahab, who made me not feel lonely at university by giving me space in the editing studio to practise things. In addition to that, I would like also to thank Year 3 students in 2017, who acted so nice to me.

Analysis

As they wanted to fully respect their students, Emma and Walid chose not to interpret the difficult behaviour Sandra experienced as overt racism, but rather attributed it to students making assumptions about Sandra's competence according to the aid narrative they had always consumed about people from her background. They found it painful to witness the Scottish students' awkwardness in not understanding how to open a constructive dialogue with someone who seemed to be very different from them. And Sandra's lack of confidence to lead conversations with White people was equally surprising after seeing the film she had made and knowing her tremendous resilience and academic record. (Despite her gender and background, she was part of only 1 per cent that make it on to further education in Malawi.)

Emma and Walid saw Sandra as a powerful young woman who had defied all the odds to become an educated and talented filmmaker. Nevertheless, despite these achievements, Sandra was a Black, poverty-experienced woman and this, as they saw, meant she faced barriers, which merits discussion here. On reflection, then, they were perhaps naive in not appreciating the complexities of intersectionality and how this could have been addressed in advance to help circumnavigate some of the problems Sandra experienced. The following section shows how Walid and Emma worked together with Sandra while she navigated a challenging six months and what they learned in order to improve subsequent experiences for future visiting students.

Establishing a safe space

A safe space is a metaphorical and sometimes physical space in which oppressed or marginalised people can be safe with people who are like themselves. The concept has been seen as a way in which minority groups can feel safe enough to talk about issues that affect them without fear of judgement or attack. The efficacy of creating safe spaces in educational settings is contested owing to the necessary suppression of critical perspectives and opinions within them (Flensner and Von der Lippe, 2019; Stengel and Weems, 2010). Whatever our opinions, however, it is difficult to see how we could have achieved this for Sandra within our university setting. Happily, though, Blessings Kachale, a Malawian researcher who had studied at QMU (whose PhD research focuses on young poverty-experienced Malawian women) was able to step in. She is a member of a large Malawian diaspora group based in Scotland, and she invited Sandra to regular meetings with the Malawian group and was happy to talk to Sandra about her experiences in their language, Chichewa. Blessings was therefore able to provide a safe space for Sandra, making it possible for her to express herself and talk about the experiences of being a young Malawian in Scotland. For Emma, as Sandra's lecturer and host, it was impossible to be involved in this safe space for obvious reasons: she is White, not poverty-experienced, privileged and powerful in terms of providing a Scottish home for Sandra to live in while she studied at the university where Emma works. The role of Blessings and the diaspora group in creating a safe space for Sandra was crucial for her to start to feel safe and valued as a member of the community.

Family and community

The lack of confidence that can come from being a poverty-experienced woman of colour is combatted to an extent in Malawi for Sandra and her peers by having strong family and community support at STEKA. The difficulty in replicating this for Sandra when she was visiting a culture that is very far removed from her home was ameliorated by contact with the Malawian diaspora group, but also by a strong connection with Emma's family, with whom Sandra lived while in Scotland. They tried to create a brave space for Sandra, where they discussed in depth what was happening in her university life. The key for Emma was that Sandra should not accept her experience as inevitable (which seemed to be happening) but rather would problematise it. Together, Emma and Sandra watched Chimamanda Ngozi Adichie's (2009) TED Talk, *The Danger of a Single Story*, which focuses on the misguided assumptions people make about poverty-experienced people of colour. This type of critical reflection continued as Sandra and Emma also watched *Comic Relief* – a television programme that made Sandra see how poverty-experienced people in the Global South are routinely represented in the Global North.

The White gaze: media representations of the Global South

In 2017, the *Comic Relief* programme was a media event whereby mainly White celebrities travelled to the Global North to show people there experiencing poverty. The films of the celebrities showcasing and explaining their experiences mainly in Africa were shown over several hours on a particular evening in order to motivate people in the United Kingdom to donate money to aid charities. The way the celebrities speak on behalf of the people on whom they are reporting and how they interpret their experience for a UK audience seem to be perfect examples of what Pulitzer Prize winning author Toni Morrison (2019) criticises because it signifies: 'Our lives have no meaning, no depth without the White gaze. And I have spent my entire writing life trying to make sure that the White gaze was not the dominant one in any of my books.' Sandra explains her response to the programme.

> Sometimes when we had time as a family, we used to watch TV and there was this day we were watching a programme called Comic Relief, whereby it shows poor people in Africa to people from the North so that they can send donations. By the time I was watching the programme, I cried to see the way how Africa was represented. It made me angry to continue watching the programme, so I left and I went to my room.

The episode of the programme watched by Sandra included a now infamous (in some circles) section where musician Ed Sheeran offered to pay hotel costs for street children in Liberia. It was later deemed as verging on *'poverty tourism'* (*Guardian*, 2017). *Comic Relief* continues a familiar genre of celebrity aid that started with the Band Aid concert in 1984, where celebrities released a song to raise money to alleviate the famine in Ethiopia. This culturally familiar programming may well have influenced Queen Margaret University students' views of the African continent by leading them to believe that problems there can only be solved by 'White saviours' from the Global North.

Although this movement emanated from benevolent intentions, through the choice of the Band Aid song-lyrics, the images displayed, and the comments and decisions made regarding the concert events, the movement served to 'other' people from the Global South. Thus, Band Aid and Live Aid contributed to, and compounded, problematic truths suggesting that the Global North is superior to the Global South (Grant, 2015, p 310).

Sandra explains her personal analysis of the impact of this type of media representation.

> Africa was represented in a negative way as if everything in Africa is bad, as if we are all poor and dirty. So this makes people from the North think that Africans are very poor people. They look dirty and I linked this with the way I was treated by the students at the university; maybe they thought I am stupid and I cannot contribute anything

because of programmes like this. They think 'how can an African girl who is coming from a dirty and poor country tell us anything?' Once, when I was chatting with a Scottish student, they asked me, 'Where did you learn how to speak English because you are speaking very good English'. Maybe she was thinking that we are not educated – that is what Chimamanda Ngozi Adichie called the single story. It made me determined to challenge it by making films where people like me have their own voice and by taking charge of visits from White people to our home in Malawi by running Critical Dialogue Groups.

(See Chapter 4 in this book and Wood, 2020.)

Brave space, critical race theory and counter-spaces

Reflecting on her experience in a brave space in Emma's home and with the Malawian diaspora was an important part of Sandra building her resilience and motivating her to counter the invisible narrative that impacts how people in the Global North construct stereotypes of people living in Africa. On reflection, it would have been useful to extend the brave space beyond the home and community environment into the university to specifically address what was happening to Sandra with other students involved. This is shown to have been effective in a similar context in Chapter 4 of this book. The term 'safe space' is often associated with spaces where people who all share the same traits can come together and not feel that they have to justify their positions or views. The more recently developed concept of a 'brave space' (Arao and Kristi, 2013) builds on that, and aims to create an environment in which diverse groups of people can suspend their judgement of one another in order to be brave enough to voice their responses to what people say, sometimes disagreeing or putting forward different perspectives and ideas without fear of judgement. The participants are not trying to persuade their peers to accept pre-existing positions, but rather to create new insights and perspectives, and therefore new knowledge.

Trying to navigate the plethora of views about the type of spaces academics should create in universities can be challenging, and fear of doing or saying the wrong thing can lead to inertia. But it needs to happen – it is not enough to rely on traditional 'investment models' of education (Freire, 2000) and *'the critique-and-imagination of social reality... must occur in contexts and interactions that are not just replications of the unjust social reality'* (Nagda and Roper, 2019, p 117).

So we advocate for the creation of brave spaces – or, indeed, counter-spaces. What critical race theorists originally defined as counter-spaces has been expanded on by Nagda and Roper (2019, p 117) as *'spaces that challenge dynamics, processes, and practices of domination and that foster empowerment for social justice'*. Indeed, counter-spaces *'challenge deficit perspectives, creating interior and external spaces of resistance and, for us, become incubators of critical hope'* (Schwartz, 2014, p 118). In order to avoid the type of 'othering' Sandra experienced, and to incubate the positive interactions with students that she also experienced, perhaps every module taught at any university should commence with time devoted to creating a space appropriate for giving everyone *'the ability to realistically assess one's environment through a lens of equity and justice while also envisioning the possibility of a better future'* (Bishundat et al, 2018, p 91).

The importance of these initiatives

The way Walid describes the importance of Sandra's film and the motivation for extending its reach can be seen as focusing on the 'centrality of experiential knowledge', an essential tenet of critical race theory.

> *Critical race theory recognizes that the experiential knowledge of people of color is legitimate, appropriate, and critical to understanding, analyzing, and teaching about racial subordination.*
> (Solórzano and Yosso, 2002, p 26)

This takes us to our conclusion. Sandra explains that:

> *My experience in Scotland helped me a lot because I learned a lot of things both negative and positive. To begin with, the journey to Scotland was very fruitful because I managed to study at [Queen Margaret University] and I did well in all the modules I studied. And I don't take this for granted because this is what I went for. Another interesting thing is that, when I was coming back from Scotland, I was given some equipment (a camera which is Canon 550D, tripod and other supporting equipment) to produce different videos for the young people in Malawi, more especially children who are not heard, in order to get support from the government and other organisations who can manage to assist them. Another benefit I had in Scotland is that I managed to open*

some doors for opportunity for my siblings at STEKA. This is because I behaved well and people including the university were happy to have more young people from STEKA. If I had behaved badly, I could have prevented these opportunities for them. Today am happy to say that Gift Thomson managed to gain a scholarship at QMU and he achieved a bachelor's degree in sociology. He is now continuing with a master's degree. In addition to that, Abigail also managed to study at [Queen Margaret University] in the same way that I did.

Sandra's experience was an important turning point in motivating her to challenge the single story about people from the Global South being perpetrated in the Global North. Not only has she done this through building her own successful film business in Malawi, but she also went on to co-create the STEKA Critical Dialogue Groups to challenge visiting school pupils from the Global North in their (online) representation of their stay in Malawi, in the Global South (Wood, 2020).

We believe universities should be socially inclusive and that should include creating an opportunity for poverty-experienced people from the Global South to get their voices heard. We do not believe that the problems we have documented here are any individual's 'fault'. We argue that they could be prevented by action being taken at a structural or institutional level. We believe that understanding intersectionality should be a compulsory part of induction for students and staff. Not as a tick box online exercise, but by creating space for face-to-face dialogue leading to an agreement between staff and students on every module about how they will combat inequalities in the way we teach and learn.

Abigail Maseko, another STEKA resident, also took up the opportunity of a six-month placement at Queen Margaret University following Sandra's experience. As a human trafficking survivor, she wanted to commit to getting girls' voices heard about human trafficking. During her stay at Queen Margaret University, she worked with Walid on developing her storytelling techniques and her skills as a filmmaker. She made *Abigail's Film* (edited by Abigail Maseko, 2020), which is available on YouTube. The film was a personal testimony for Abigail, but it has become a powerful tool to challenge everyone's assumptions on survivors, specifically on young women from the Global South. We often use it in our teaching. Likewise, Gift Thompson, another resident of the Malawian STEKA Home, has now spent five years at Queen Margaret University accruing an education that will help him lead and sustain the STEKA Vocational Skills Centre into a strong future. Our positive experiences together by far outweigh any negative ones – but by focusing here on the ways in which we have managed to overcome some negative experiences, we hope that similar future partnerships at other universities can thrive.

Although Sandra is working hard to forge her career as an independent filmmaker in Malawi, unfortunately structural inequalities still stand in her way, as she has to rely on outdated and ageing equipment. To find out more about Sandra, STEKA and STEKAskills go to www.stekaskills.com. To hear more about how Walid Salhab's lived experience has influenced his short films, listen to the Queen Margaret University podcast *From Tripoli to Edinburgh – a Life of Hope and Creativity* (QMU, 2022).

Reflective questions

- Why might academics shy away from overtly addressing inequalities, including race, in the classroom and how can the concepts of brave spaces and counter-spaces help?
- What structural steps can a university take to address 'othering' and achieve social inclusion?
- How can we challenge some students' implicit assumptions about people from the Global South and position lived experience as real expertise that is valued in a university setting?

Recommended reading

- Arao, B and Kristi, C (2013) From Safe Spaces to Brave Spaces: A New Way to Frame Dialogue Around Diversity and Social Justice. In Landreman, L M (ed) *The Art of Effective Facilitation* (pp 135–50). Sterling, VA: Stylus.
- QMU Podcast (2022) *Interview with Filmmaker Walid Salhab: From Tripoli to Edinburgh – A Life of Hope and Creativity*. [online] Available at: www.spreaker.com/user/qmuni/qmu-podcast-walid-salhab-v2 (accessed 12 January 2023).

References

Adichie, C N (2009) *The Danger of a Single Story.* TED Talk. [online] Available at: www.youtube.com/watch?v=D9Ihs241zeg (accessed 20 December 2022).

Arao, B and Kristi, C (2013) From Safe Spaces to Brave Spaces: A New Way to Frame Dialogue Around Diversity and Social Justice. In Landreman, L M (ed) *The Art of Effective Facilitation* (pp 135–50). Sterling, VA: Stylus.

Bishundat, D, Phillip, D V and Gore, W (2018) Cultivating Critical Hope: The Too Often Forgotten Dimension of Critical Leadership Development. *New Directions for Student Leadership*, 159: 91–102.

Flensner, K and Von der Lippe, M (2019) Being Safe from What and Safe for Whom? A Critical Discussion of the Conceptual Metaphor of 'Safe Space'. *Intercultural Education*, 30(3): 275–88.

Freire, P (2000 [1968]) *Pedagogy of the Oppressed.* New York: Continuum.

Grant, J. (2015) Live Aid: Perpetuating the Superiority Myth. *Critical Arts*, 29(3): 310–26.

The Guardian (2017) Ed Sheeran *Comic Relief* Film Branded 'Poverty Porn' by Aid Watchdog. [online] Available at: www.theguardian.com/global-development/2017/dec/04/ed-sheeran-comic-relief-film-poverty-porn-aid-watchdog-tom-hardy-eddie-redmayne (accessed 21 February 2023).

Maseko, A (2020) *Abigail's Film.* [online] Available at: www.youtube.com/watch?v=X_PvSDohPJc (accessed 21 February 2023).

Morrison, T (2019) *Toni Morrison: The Pieces I Am.* Documentary. Dir. Timothy Greenfield-Sanders.

Nagda, B A and Roper, L D (2019) Reimagining Leadership Development for Social Change Through Critical Dialogue Practices. *New Directions for Student Leadership*, 163: 117–36.

QMU (2022) *Interview with Filmmaker Walid Salhab: From Tripoli to Edinburgh – a Life of Hope and Creativity.* Podcast. [online] Available at: www.spreaker.com/user/qmuni/qmu-podcast-walid-salhab-v2 (accessed 12 January 2023).

QMU (2023) International Community: A University Without Borders. [online] Available at: www.qmu.ac.uk/about-the-university/international-community (accessed 12 January 2023).

Schwartz, J (2014) Classrooms of Spatial Justice: Counter-spaces and Young Men of Color in a GED Program. *Adult Education Quarterly*, 64(2): 110–27.

Solórzano, D G and Yosso, T J (2002) Critical Race Methodology: Counter-Storytelling as an Analytical Framework for Education Research. *Qualitative Inquiry*, 8(1): 23–44.

Stengel, B S and Weems, L (2010) Questioning Safe Space: An Introduction. *Studies in Philosophy and Education*, 29: 505–7.

Wood, E (2020) An Alternative to Voluntourism: How Youth Solidarity Groups in Malawi Empower Young Malawians and Scots. *STEKAskills*. [online] Available at: www.stekaskills.com/international-school-workshops (accessed 12 December 2022).

CHAPTER 8

FILM FESTIVALS AND FILM STUDIES: AN ANTI-RACIST APPROACH TO CURATION AND EDUCATION

Stefanie Van de Peer

Introduction

The Africa in Motion (AiM) film festival was founded in Edinburgh in 2006, with the specific goal of addressing a gap in screen space and screen time in the United Kingdom, where at the time, only 1 per cent of content on the big screen was taken up by Black representation. In fact, an extensive research project led by London-based film scholar Dr Clive Nwonka in 2020 revealed that, due to a lack of anti-racist policy in the British film industry, *'racial underrepresentation remains a structural condition within the sector, both on and offscreen'* (Nwonka, 2020, p 17). It is not a problem of the past: it has become worse in terms of what is available on British cinema screens and on university curricula. Most British audiences and young students have an increasingly vocal aversion to so-called foreign language films. Subtitles are a seen as a significant obstacle, and films that would be seen as 'world cinema' are often political in nature – also something with which mainstream audiences are not always keen to engage.

The discourse on diversity in the professional film sector runs parallel with the calls for decolonisation of the university curriculum and the diversification of film studies in higher education. But while growing numbers of voices join the call for the decolonisation of the film industry and of film studies, there is a continued lack of action. This lack of action can be down to availability and accessibility, but it is also due to other obstacles such as self-censorship and the increasing weight given to neoliberal values at universities, where students are seen as customers – and indeed see themselves in the same way. In what follows, I draw parallels between cinema audiences and students, and argue that they have so much in common that as film lecturers we may need to move from planning film content for them to 'curating' it, both with more sensitivity and the expectation of controversy. My own journey towards this understanding was fed by my involvement in the AiM film festival. First, I offer a chronological reflection on the development of my practice as a festival organiser (programmer, curator, adviser, board member) and as a teacher in higher education film studies departments in the United Kingdom. I then look at my interrelated roles as a film festival curator and as a lecturer in film studies – both of which I consider part of the idea of an intersectional 'busting' of the canon. The foundational vision of the AiM festival focused on sharing knowledge of African cinema and offering a new screen experience to Scottish audiences.

Increasingly diverse audiences need more opportunities to see different stories on the screen. I joined the organising team of Africa in Motion in 2007, the year after the festival was founded, and the year I started my PhD research. My research focused (and continues to focus) on the presences and absences of women in North African and Arab film cultures. My approach was informed by the neglect of Northern African films in Arab and African film studies, even though Maghrebi cinema is hugely popular and successful on the global networks of festivals and awards, and Egyptian cinema is a force unto itself, dominating – as it continues to do – the entire Arab film industry since the 1920s. Geographically, North Africa was, at the time that I did my PhD and got involved with AiM, never really seen as a cohesive whole. My work continues to frame this differently by seeing the region north of the Sahara as a crossroads where diverse world cultures meet and blend, a melting pot of influences, and therefore a very lively area of film production. AiM has always had a strong commitment to North African films as an important part of African cinema showcased by the festival, and indeed the festival has learned over the years that North African films (particularly Moroccan and Tunisian films) are often the best-attended and most popular films. As such, AiM's pan-African approach to the on-screen representation of the continent stands out among other festivals that focus on African cinema.

This has directly fed into my teaching in film and media studies, not only at Queen Margaret University but everywhere I have taught over the years at various UK-based institutions. As a postgraduate teaching assistant and early career lecturer, I was always explicitly asked to include Arab and African films on the syllabus for established film genre, film aesthetics, film history and other cinema courses, which translated into my interest in making existing syllabi more inclusive and interesting for an increasingly diverse body of students. As Mistry and Bisschoff (2022) explain, teaching film genre or film history is often accompanied by assumptions on specific canons of film, and they testify that:

> *organising courses with an approach to themes or issues... allows for content to be organised around how film-makers have approached film practices with similar historical and political content but from different perspectives, and often with divergent points of view based on characters and the sociocultural positions they occupy.*
>
> (Mistry and Bisschoff, 2022, p 2)

Indeed, because I see myself as a film historian, rather than copy established approaches to teaching film genre or chronologies of history, my interest was more in the 'broad vision' of film's history: an awareness of the specificities of space and time and a critical reading of socio-political and aesthetic trends. This allows us to *'study similarities and divergences in how certain themes and techniques are represented across a range of films from different perspectives, of resisting the perpetuation of canonisation'* (Mistry and Bisschoff, 2022, p 2).

As my PhD studies and my role in the film festival developed in parallel, I started to understand that my developing specialist knowledge was an asset that established academics wanted to tap into, although it took a very long and circuitous journey for me to become part of the establishment as someone with that specialist knowledge. My positionality, of course, plays a huge part in this process, both its beginning, its change over the course of my learning process and the way it now feeds into my identity as an academic. Even so, the process of decolonising my work has required a difficult journey through the paradoxical forces of speaking up and shutting up. The hunger for global cinema among audiences and students remains focused largely on Western and Eurocentric experiences, where 'different' types of narratives, editing, storytelling techniques and structuring devices are seen as 'low production values', 'slow cinema' or even plain 'boring'. The chapter asks about what we teach in film studies in Britain, the extent to which we see our students as audiences and how we can better curate our syllabi.

What we teach in film studies: programming the canon

Like many PhD candidates, I started teaching in the second year of my PhD as a graduate teaching assistant. I taught on modules coordinated by senior colleagues, and with their guidance about what and how to teach. The seminars I taught were for modules on transnational cinema, post-war European cinema and Francophone cinema, among others. Films included *Fresa y Chocolate* (Gutiérrez Alea, 1993), *Germany, Year Zero* (Rossellini, 1948) and *La Haine* (Kassovitz, 1995). I started to understand that to teach means to learn. Never had I learned so much in such a short timespan as I did when I started teaching. Teaching on other scholars' modules was a treat, and when the time came for me to design my own module, which was a Summer School module on the classics of world cinema, I was excited and enthusiastic as I wanted to inspire the students, which would be an international cohort of mostly American and Asian students. However, the word 'classics' in the title module caused some insecurities. How was I going to decide which 'classic' films to focus on, and what does 'world cinema' really mean? The list of potential films is endless, and considerations around availability (on DVD at that time) were central to the decision-making process. I also wanted to make sure I used my knowledge and growing expertise on African and Arab cinema, so I chose to include films from that geographical location, and I found it important to make sure female filmmakers were 50 per cent of the syllabus too.

My enthusiasm quickly translated into anxiety about what to put on the syllabus, so I started looking at what similarly titled modules at other institutions focused on. Mostly, modules included a majority of (if not only) films by men. If African films were represented (which was not often the case), they would always be by the Senegalese 'father of African cinema' Ousmane Sembène and sometimes by the Egyptian Youssef Chahine: certainly not Senegalese Safi Faye or Algerian Assia Djebar. I started to wonder why these women's works were not represented: do we see the male filmmakers' works as the yardstick, and if so, is that rooted in assumptions about the dominance of the male gender or is it purely a coincidence because they were in fact the first to make films? Likewise, in a module on migrant cinema, I tried to see how I could make the students really understand the migrant experience by presenting it as a journey with a start, a middle and an end. From leaving home in films such as *Tanger, Le Rêve des Brûleurs* (Leila Kilani, 2003), we then looked at films of journeys – for example, *Inch'Allah Dimanche* (Yamina Benguigui, 2001) and the arrival in the new place in *Last Resort* (Pawel Pawlikowski, 2001), alongside the longing for a return home in *The Edge of Heaven* (Fatih Akin, 2007). This structure enabled the students to understand the long, drawn-out process of the narrative and actual journey of the migrant outside of and next to the filmic experience, making sure not to see migrant cinema as a genre but rather as a socio-political state of being, represented in myriad genres.

In addition to the considerations of what to put on the syllabus for specific modules, there is an issue around the availability of the films. Until just a few years ago, we needed to make sure the films we taught were available on DVD, and affordable for the university library to purchase so we could put on screenings of the films for the students. Availability, as well as the cost of the films on DVD, played a significant role in what we were able to include in the syllabus. Students now make the most of the immaterial qualities of film and they find previously unavailable films through their own online networks. Of course, none of Safi Faye's or Assia Djebar's films are available commercially on DVD. However, because I worked for AiM, I had access to these films. My next question was whether I was allowed to screen these films to my students in the context of their education if all the festival had negotiated with the rights-holders was a screening in a cinema for which it had paid a fee? Even when I decided I wanted to try, by contacting the rights-holders and requesting their permission to screen the films in the educational context, I was not (always) allowed to do so. So my determination to include African women's films resulted in a growing awareness of gaps and missing knowledge in the 'canon', and in the world's archives. Where filmmakers or rights-holders did allow me to screen their films to my students, I felt triumphant and as if I had achieved an amazing deal for the students in that I had ensured they had what I saw as a truly unique experience, by enabling them to see films they would not otherwise be able to see anywhere. This was also a 'motto' of the festival: Scottish or UK-wide audiences were provided by AiM with the opportunity to see 'classics' of African cinema because of the educational aspect of the film festival, through which we look back at the past in order to address the present wealth of African cinema. The initial vision for AiM was exactly that: to ensure that Scottish and British audiences were able to engage with African cinema on the big screen – both historical cinema and contemporary works.

This is where the distinction between programming films and curating a film festival needs to be made clearer. The two terms are often conflated, assumed to mean the same or at least similar things: putting films into a programme for people to see. In this understanding, festival organisers programme films for audiences and film educators programme films for their students. However, the meanings of the terms 'programming' and 'curating' are subtly different, and this starts to create clarity in approaches to the relationship between the person or team showcasing films and those to whom they showcase these works. In Bosma's (2015) conceptualisation of programming, the audience is central in terms of quantity: putting films on a programme that will attract the largest possible audience. Curation, by contrast, is rooted in research, putting together a programme that emphasises cohesion, expands a sense of understanding and invites critical engagement – perhaps even inspiring transformative action. For Bosma, a curator designates *'a more sophisticated level of cinematic knowledge than simply "programming" specific screenings'*. The curator is a *'custodian of cinema culture'* or *'cultural intermediary'*, which means presenting *'a diverse selection of the most recent releases... [while] simultaneously keeping the varied and complex past of cinema alive through screenings of all sorts of film heritage'* (Bosma, 2015, p 1). So curation is about quality: the quality of the work(s), the context in which they are presented and the way they are cohesively offered to the audience – which is presumed to be an audience willing to be informed or instructed towards a new insight or new knowledge.

What the students want

Students are not audiences, though, and my module was not a commercial opportunity for me to 'programme' a series of films the way I was used to from working at AiM. I was using my curatorial skills in my approach to teaching, but I had not borne in mind that students are young people with their own ideas about what the title of a module might mean. So, when I dealt with a student cohort consisting mainly of American students, I quickly learned that there was a resistance to what I presented to them. Their expectations about 'classics' or 'world cinema' were very different from mine: they wanted the types of films that featured at the top of end-of-year lists voted for by experts, such as the films of Orson Welles, Alfred Hitchcock and John Wayne. Not *Caramel* (Nadine Labaki, 2007), *Paris is Burning* (Livingston, 1990) or *Battle of Algiers* (Pontecorvo, 1966). In fact, one male student said *Caramel* was a woman's film, about which he had nothing to say. He thought it was *'silly'* because it is set in a beauty salon. The privilege that emanates from such a statement was repeated by another male student, who claimed he did not have anything in common with the queer subjects of *Paris is Burning*, effectively trying to shut down any opportunity for him to engage with the film at all.

The fact that such students expect a connection with the films' subjects through their own lived experiences is interesting in itself, but also highly problematic, and it shows the individualisation of neoliberal educational structures, where students are encouraged to see themselves as customers. Another male student told me that he had seen *Battle of Algiers* in the context of his military training, which resulted in a class discussion about terrorism, Islamism and the conflation of the two, and what it means for Americans. While it was a necessary discussion that I sensed made some of them at least reflect more critically on how they saw the Arab world, this was not a discussion about the film and the impact it had on Algerian cinema, neorealism and the representation of Arab women on global screens. In the years that followed, I kept *Battle of Algiers* on the syllabus but took *Caramel* off and replaced it with *West Beirut* (Doueiri, 1998), which was slightly more to the taste of the students. From sub-Sahara Africa, I found that *Moolaade* (Sembène, 2004) was more acceptable to students than *Xala* (1975), by the same filmmaker. I suspect that this may have to do with what they expect to see from sub-Sahara Africa: a confirmation of their monolithic view of oppressed women instead of a complex satirical film about neocolonial mismanagement.

This begs the question of whether we need to heed feedback from students that is concerned with taste. If they do not like a film, and discussions in class veer off course due to the cultural and emotional sensibilities, aesthetic expectations and personal or professional experiences of the students, what can a tutor do? Find a balance between the confidence they are finding in their knowledge of and expertise in their field of research on the one hand and the wish to ensure the relevance of the work discussed in class for the experience of the student cohort on the other? Because of this and other experiences over the years, I have come to acutely understand the subjective/personal nature of any list of experts, any sensibility of what is important and what is not, and any choice on any syllabus in all the universities in the world. Even at a Russell Group university where I later taught and was given free reign with 'diversifying' an existing first-year module on film histories, feedback from students and the more experienced lecturers showed that the choices I made about which films to put on the syllabi did not align with student expectations. I have learned to embrace this, and to assure my students that they can, in fact, very easily see *Citizen Kane* on any platform they like and read 100 scholarly articles about the film, but that the films I discuss in class are meant to contribute to an expanding worldview that intensively destabilises their thinking about and expectations of the terms 'classics' and 'world cinema'. Bringing films from the film festival into the classroom has emancipated my responses to feedback about film choices. The lack of accessibility of works by women that have impacted film history without being acknowledged for it likewise feels important, and indeed I increasingly receive positive feedback where my defiance of popular taste and availability are praised. The key is openly explaining to students at the start of the module what 'classics' are and how the canon is a construct they must learn to critique through the works of 'world cinema' that I present to them.

Learning is achieved when students are exposed to difference and diversity, when *'the world does not meet parts of the learner's expectations'* and *'a student's pre-existing knowledge is challenged, thus stimulating "change" – ie learning'* (Pirnay-Dummer et al, 2012, p 68). Making sure they get content that is different from what they may expect challenges them as well as me, and creates an atmosphere of curiosity – not only about the content of the module, but also about one another as people involved in the exchange of teaching and learning. This in turn has led to more confidently diverse and research-based teaching, where students (especially those in levels 3 and 4) are requested to contribute to the decision-making process regarding what they learn. At least one slot on the syllabus is left open, and students are asked what they expect to see on the syllabus that is not there, or what they want to learn more about. This process of co-creation emancipates students' learning. bell hooks (1994) shows that by co-creating content, learning can be revolutionary, nurturing and enabling. A two-way interactive way of learning enhances one's capacity to be free. Indeed, particularly at institutions that advocate for social justice, *'education is a potential site for personal transformation and prefigurative politics*', but one has to acknowledge that education institutions, especially higher education institutions, are also '*colonial tools of control*' (Chetty et al, 2022, p 1). Government intervention and the core neoliberal values of institutions challenge us as transformational teachers to be brave about our positionalities and acknowledge these as part of our identities as people standing in front of students and encouraging critical thinking. The importance of recognising our performativity as teachers is central to being anti-racist. The self-reflexive mode enables humility and acceptance of our limitations and the constant challenge to these limitations, both self-imposed and those imposed by the institutions that sustain our livelihoods. Humility is difficult, but it is necessary as part of a commitment to transforming people's lives through education.

Reflection upon the world is likewise essential – it is at the very heart of what it means to be human says Paolo Freire (2000), but he also emphasises that thinking cannot and must not be separated from doing, as real reflection must lead to action if we want the world to transform (Balani, 2022, p 11). As Azumah Dennis (2015) shows, teaching should emphasise dialogue, respect and commitment to co-building a future. Finding out what students expect teaches me about their sensibilities and how to deviate from them during the module, and as these expectations are discussed in class; it also shows individual students how the rest of their cohort responds and where they fit into the group. It enables them to see how diverse large groups can be, and how to accommodate others' voices. These discussions inform future content of modules. In the rapidly changing world of film and media, this is crucial.

Teaching film and media requires us to engage critically with the neoliberalist worldviews of popular media, and to encourage the difficult process of self-reflexive criticality in how media students engage with the media in their own lives outside of the classroom. Demanding such critical thinking inside and outside of the classroom is sometimes a lot to ask, and defensive attitudes surface easily. As Balani (2022, p 16) says In her article on pedagogical defiance, educators may start to '*fear the consequences of expressing*' political leanings in the classroom due to the immediacy of student feedback and the centrality of student feedback to the image of the neoliberal university. In writing, academics are more able to do so as it may be seen as an example of free speech. But the discussion in class is more important: anti-colonialism and anti-racism '*create spaces in which new types of knowledge are produced*' and '*a pedagogy of defiance produces the knowledge to liberate the self from false limits*' (Balani, 2022, p 17). Honest dialogue between tutor and students enables a reflexive process in the planning stages, and co-creation of module content has inspired a '*curatorial aspect*' to the design of modules (Bovill, 2019, p 1023). Freire (2000) tells us that '*there is no such thing as neutral education. Education functions as an instrument to bring about conformity or freedom*' (cited in Garson, 2022, p 6), and brave dialogic education can cultivate '*alternative ways of thinking and of being*' (Balani, 2022, p 18). Indeed, being '*braver in sharing our concerns about the limits of institutional reform with our students*' in an open and honest conversation with them (either at the start of a semester in co-creating and co-curating what the module will cover or at the end of the semester when discussing their feedback) is a crucial developmental tool in changing the students' self-identification as customers. But it is also important in our identity as educators wishing to critically think about how we may change the institutionalised discourse on 'decolonisation' to develop into a more active anti-colonial and anti-racist dialogue. '*Decolonising the curriculum or decolonising education [is] a desire to recognise the humanity in all of us*' (Dennis, 2022, p 35), while it is also '*an epistemological project where we delink ourselves from the structure of knowledge imposed by the West, and then to reconstitute our ways of thinking, speaking and living*' (Cusworth, 2022, p 48). In selecting films to screen to my students and discuss in class, I therefore attempt to move beyond 'programming' films for my students as audiences, and instead curate – and indeed co-curate – the content of modules with them, which results in more dialogic processes of learning – my own learning included.

Curating an anti-colonial film syllabus

With experience, and an increased security in my position at the institution where I currently work, I have been able to reflect critically on my own anti-racist journey and the meaning of the decolonisation of higher education. My research in film feminisms, film histories and African and Arab film cultures has fed into this directly, and my experience as an organiser of the AiM film festival consolidated my access to and broad view of the importance of film as a tool to educate. In many ways, the decolonisation discourse has been disappointing and frustrating, mostly because I felt that it has been and remains precisely that: a discourse, especially at the institutional level. It is a buzzword, as Kathy Davis (2008) explored in her work, and one that the neoliberal university has embraced cynically in its marketing strategies. But at the same time there is also a sense of urgency and vindication in the collaborative nature of the work we can do as people in relative power positions. With our privilege as lecturers comes a responsibility that we can develop through the ground swell of teacher-activism, as we are located at precisely the institutions that allow us to think critically about concepts, words and their meaning for younger generations. Even in the face of some students not being ready or willing to broaden their worldview by watching African films, there is the space of the classroom where we can coax them into thinking differently, in a new way, about what challenges their comfortable positions. The same is true for audiences: if we move away from the assumption that we just programme films to get people into the cinemas or in front of their screens for new experiences, and instead transparently curate showcases of films that challenge familiar notions of diversity and representation, we can also start to respect students and audiences as active agents for change.

With this creative curatorial approach to the anti-colonial and anti-racist syllabus, where our positions are destabilised and challenged, but we allow that challenge to encourage us to think harder and deeper about the power of our work to renew and refresh critical thinking inside the classroom, teachers can learn as much as their students do. This is possible only through engaged and sincere dialogue with students (and audiences) around their expectations about which films to see and how to discuss them. In the design of my modules, I attempt to be transparent about how we develop our thinking from one week's theme or topic to the next. Being explicit and open about this process is crucial. Through such discussions, students and audiences feel emancipated in all meanings of the word: that their voices and opinions are heard, that the classroom is a space where we necessarily move beyond words and opinions, towards critical thinking and an increased awareness of students' voicefulness. This sense of classroom emancipation includes an awareness that the classroom is part of an institution but can also act as a 'brave space' where opinions are turned into critical engagement with visual culture, and engender '*a full and equitable participation of people from all social identity groups in a society that is mutually shaped to meet their needs*' (Adams et al, 2016). An understanding that independent thought and critical thinking are not the same thing as opinions emancipates the students' self-awareness and liberates them from an individualistic way of thinking towards a thinking that enables criticality rooted in self-criticality. As such, including 'difficult' films as challenges to comfortable worldviews and emphasising the classroom as a defiant space for discussion can result in students' intellectual transformation, emancipation and freedom, where those with lived experience of being racially othered may feel seen, heard and empowered, as well as encouraged to testify and challenge mainstream White worldviews.

Reflective questions

- What is the significance of a canon, and who, historically, has decided on what is included and excluded?
- How can we be more open about which films we (can) include on our syllabi and why? How often do we revise the films?
- Should we listen to student feedback when it comes to 'tastes' in film? What can we do with 'taste' in the classroom, and how can we critically engage students with the limitations of 'taste'?

Recommended reading

- Akande, L (2020) Film Education Pedagogy in Nigeria: A Nation-Specific Approach to a Non-Western University Curriculum. *Film Education Journal*, 3(1): 1–12.
- Dovey, L, Mangalanayagam, N and Mistry, J (2022) Perspectives: A Round-Table Discussion on Decolonial Pedagogies. *Film Education Journal*, 5(1): 24–33.
- Mistry, J (2021) Decolonizing Processes in Film Education. *Film Education Journal*, 4(1): 1–13.
- Shamash, S (2022) A Decolonising Approach to Genre Cinema Studies. *Film Education Journal*, 5(1): 41–54.

References

Adams, M, Bell, L A, Goodman, D J and Joshi, K Y (2016) *Teaching for Diversity and Social Justice*. London: Routledge.

Azumah Dennis, C (2015) Blogging as Public Pedagogy: Creating Alternative Educational Futures. *International Journal of Lifelong Education*, 34(3): 284–99.

Balani, S (2022) Pedagogies of Defiance. *Wasafiri*, 37(4-111): 4–18.

Bosma, P (2015) *Film Programming: Curating for Cinemas, Festivals, Archives.* London: Wallflower Press.

Bovill, C (2019) Co-creation in Learning and Teaching: The Case for a Whole-class Approach in Higher Education. *Higher Education*, 79: 1023–37.

Chetty, D, Golding, A and Rollock, N (2022) Editorial: Reimagining Education – Where Do We Go from Here? *Wasafiri*, 37(4-111): 1–3.

Cusworth, H (2022) Diversifying or Decolonising: How Do We Teach Black History? *Wasafiri*, 37(4-112): 42–51.

Davis, K (2008) Intersectionality as Buzzword: A Sociology of Science Perspective on What Makes a Feminist Theory Successful. *Feminist Theory*, 9(1): 67–85.

Dennis, N (2022) Educational Grief. *Wasafiri*, 37(4-112): 33–41.

Freire, P (2000 [1968]) *Pedagogy of the Oppressed.* New York: Continuum.

Garson, K (2022) Weaving Critical Education Perspectives in Teaching for Social and Ecological Justice. In Farrell, A J, Skyhar, C and Lam, M (eds) *Teaching in the Anthropocene: Education in the Face of Environmental Crisis* (pp 4–15). Toronto: Canadian Scholars.

hooks, b (1994) *Teaching to Transgress: Education as the Practice of Freedom.* London: Routledge.

Mistry, L and Bisschoff, L (2022) Editorial: Decolonising Film Education. *Film Education Journal*, 5(1): 1–9.

Nwonka, C J (2020) *Race and Ethnicity in the UK Film Industry: An Analysis of the BFI Diversity Standards.* London: London School of Economics and Political Science.

Pirnay-Dummer, P, Ifenthaler, D and Seel, N M (2012) Designing Model-based Learning Environments to Support Mental Models for Learning. In Jonassen, D and Land, S (eds) *Theoretical Foundations of Learning Environments* (pp 77–115). London: Routledge.

CHAPTER 9

CREATIVE STRATEGIES FOR UNKNOWING: TAKING RISKS TO ENCOURAGE EQUITABLE RELATIONSHIPS IN THE CLASSROOM

Anthony Schrag

A relationship of equivalents

Before I began teaching in higher education, I was a professional artist working in community settings. In brief, in my artistic practice I did not aim to make singular aesthetic objects to be exhibited in the hallowed spaces of museums and galleries. Instead, the work focused on how community groups or individuals may be positioned as collaborators and co-authors within a participatory context, in creative and challenging ways. It is beyond the scope of this chapter to go into depth about this practice, or indeed to examine the nuances of socially engaged art, although I do touch on some of their key problematics below. However, it is perhaps sufficient to say that working with people in such a manner is complicated because, in order to function effectively, the process needs to be cognisant of power dynamics, navigate dominant hegemonies and negotiate complex intersocial exchanges. I will discuss some of this work in what follows, but I raise this practice in this introduction because my experience with such engagements has helped me to develop, incorporate and enact some de-colonial and anti-racist strategies in my teaching. I aim to present some of these strategies below. I do this to make an equivalence of practice between myself as artist and as educator. In both conditions, my role as an educator-artist is premised in relation to public audiences/learners and arts organisations/educational institutions, as explored in Figure 9.1.

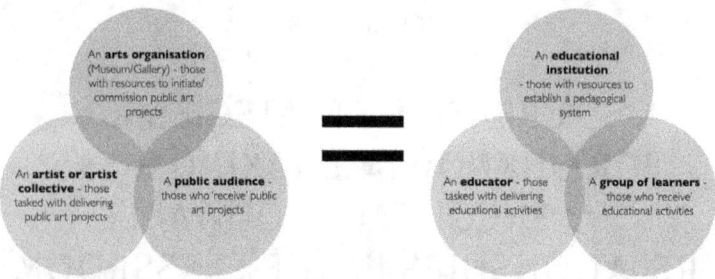

Figure 9.1: A Venn diagram of equivalences between the domains of socially engaged art and education (Schrag, 2022)

My art practice is premised on developing and prioritising egalitarian exchanges between and within groups of people (Kester, 2004; Schrag, 2016) and in an artistic context this manifests as dialogue with a diversity of forms, including curated discussions, talks, workshops, events, activities and debates. As such, dialogue is central within my creative work, and as with all forms of speech, it is infused with power: who has the resources to speak? Or, thinking of it in another way: who has the choice to not speak? Why are some bodies required to speak and what are the (emotional) labour demands of that act? Within any social domain, this can be difficult to negotiate, but these boundaries are sharper still in higher education: in a system wherein there is a paid lecturer and paying students, can a student's voice ever be equal? What might an egalitarian education system look like?

For transparency's sake, it is important to note that I am a child of colonisers, and I can trace my White African lineage back to the 1700s. I therefore come from a long line of racists, and I also come from extensive privilege. I thus do not claim to have solutions, nor do I wish to speak unduly when voices other than mine can offer far more insightful critique and direction, and are indeed more important to hear than that of another middle-aged White man. Instead, I hope to present some creative strategies that have been useful for me in subverting the traditional educational structures of my sector in ways that – I hope – provide alternative potentialities for learning. I should also be clear that what follows is not specifically focused on race; instead, I hope that the present work is helpful to think about infrastructural power of any kind, and ways in which dialogue has been helpful to challenge such infrastructures.

In what follows I start with a description of my artistic practice, which will help to frame some of my thinking (and theoretically aligns this work to collaborative anthropology), and then go on to discuss two short case studies of my teaching practice, where I have drawn from this creative practice to help decolonise the classroom. While there is extensive literature on dialogue in the field of education (eg Bloom, 1956; Freire, 2000; Vella, 1994), my own pedagogical understanding of this concept came through Tazos Kazepides' (2010) education as dialogue, where I noticed the similarity of this approach to approaches of socially engaged art, specifically the aim of creating the conditions for equitable exchange (Kester, 2004). Importantly, this equitable exchange within education – like art – must contain *'cognitive conflict and puzzlement'* (Pirnay-Dummer et al, 2012, p 66). Pirnay-Dummer et al (2012, p 68) suggest that these dialogic exchanges are most effective when students are exposed to difference and diversity, when *'the world does not meet parts of the learner's journey, and a student's pre-existing knowledge is challenged'*, thus stimulating *'change'* – that is, learning. It is through dialogue that a learner can have *'explicit opportunities to confront the old beliefs and to construct new aspects into them'* (Pirnay-Dummer et al, 2012, p 72). If the anti-racist project within education is to work, this confrontation is central for everyone involved.

Kill Your Darlings: socially engaged art and collaborative anthropology

I will now discuss a recent artistic project, Kill Your Darlings, which will function as an example of this confrontation and provide the concept of collaborative anthropology as a theoretical framework through which to ground this work.

In 2019, I was invited to develop a participatory artwork for the Perth Museum and Art Gallery (PMAG) in Scotland, pertaining specifically to its Museum Collection. This collection is of national significance and comprises over half a million individual items, including exceptional fine art, socially important heritage objects, rare archaeological findings, extensive spoils of colonisation and a substantial natural sciences collection. While the collection ultimately belongs to the citizens of the area, it is managed by Culture Perth and Kinross

(CPK), which cares for – and develops – the collection on behalf of this public, including its safe storage, display, preservation and general management. The majority of the collection is kept locked away in the museum store, with only 1 per cent on display at any one time. A small group of collection managers select which items are to be on public display.

Considering this, I was interested to explore how this collection could truly be considered public if it was both invisible/inaccessible to the general public and curated by a small group of gatekeepers. While I recognise the practical and managerial requirements of such processes, I also recognise that museum collections have considerable gaps where important stories should be (Museum Association, nd). Where are the women's stories? Where are the stories of people of colour? Public collections such as those in Perth and Kinross can only really be said to represent *some* of the citizens of Perth. What about the other public(s)?

Levinas (1989) suggests that humans, as social creatures, can only ever understand ourselves through the Other. In other words, we understand ourselves in opposition, in the same way that light can only be understood through darkness, or joy through sadness. In witnessing difference, we see contrasts that define our own edges more clearly. Levinas goes on to say that this engagement with something other can be very difficult because it exposes us to the essentially socially plural nature of human culture: it shows that the world is made up of multiple, different – sometimes opposing – systems of value and otherness. In regard to this collection, I became interested in how I could explore and expose some of those multiple, different publics, both as a way to value the hidden stories and in order to challenge the hierarchies of power embedded in traditional museum management.

I therefore devised a project that publicly presented objects from the collection and invited the public of Perth and Kinross to (collectively) select a single item that was the 'most' valuable. The definition of valuable was intentionally left open to interpretation. This item would be selected by democratic public vote, with each visitor receiving one vote. I also included the provocation that the item receiving the lowest number of votes would be symbolically destroyed at the end of the exhibition as the least valuable object within the collection.

The project was called Kill Your Darlings, after the William Faulkner quote that challenges authors to pay attention to the characters a writer may adore, but that are not helpful to the storytelling, and – if necessary – to kill those darlings. Similarly, the project was trying to draw attention to the different types of value(s) at play, and to discuss (through the voting) the values (as represented by the objects) that are worth forgetting.

Alongside this gallery exhibition, I engaged multiple constituents of the community in conversations about how represented they felt they were by the collection, using the elements of the collection itself to speak to their interests and values – local history, identity, sports, agriculture, ownership, historical problematics, gender, class and so on. These activities also fed into the public vote, and a growing tally within the gallery highlighted which items were being valued (or not), while also indicating which item was slated for destruction (Figures 9.2, 9.3 and 9.4).

Figures 9.2, 9.3 and 9.4: Installation of the objects of value, including voting tokens. The weekly tally is visible in the posters above each item (Schrag, 2022)

Figure 9.2

(Continued)

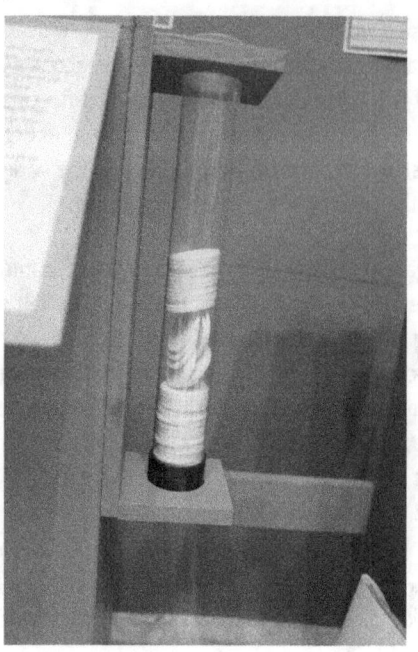

Figure 9.3

Figure 9.4

The weekly tally therefore functioned as a mechanism to illustrate the plurality of values in the public realm. The project resulted in over 7000 public votes, a publication, anecdotal evidence of extended engagement, a variety of well-received events and significant positive feedback from audiences, press and industry bodies. Rather than focus on the outcomes, however, here I would like to consider the way in which the project provided multiple publics with an opportunity to assert their own voice and tell different (and multiple) stories about their collection, rather than the traditional monolithic museum deciding which stories are most important.

This egalitarian approach to representation is a central tenet of collaborative anthropology, which emerged in the late 1990s from ethical concerns that sought to both redress the mechanisms that sustained colonial practices, and to develop collaborative and egalitarian relationships with other people. Jacques Rancière's (1991) argument about politics is employed by collaborative anthropologists to reconfigure the notion of politics away from specific party politics (Tory, Liberal, Green, etc.) and instead uses it do draw attention to what happens when bodies shift *'from their assigned place, of making visible what was once not allowed to be seen, and making heard what was once only noise'* (Hopkins, 2003). Anthropologist Kiven Strohm (2012, p 107) draws from this argument and suggests that collaborative anthropology is concerned with equity, and that this can only occur when politics is supported as *'a disruption of the police order, a disidentification with its spatial and temporal ordering of bodies'*. As he writes, *'politics is dissensus'* (Strohm, 2012, p 108). Collaborative anthropology thus aims to shift *'control of the research process out of the hands of the anthropologist and into the collective sphere of the anthropologist on an equal basis with community researchers'* (Rappaport, 2008, p 108). This could mean co-authoring films, collaborating on papers or even developing site-responsive and context-specific research with a community that renegotiates the final resting place of the knowledge formed during the project as appropriate to – and truly representative of – the constituent participants' values. Likewise, socially engaged artists aim to provide a critical space to explore, critique and reimagine new potentialities of how the world can be organised. As Chantal Mouffe (2007) suggests, *'According to the agonistic approach, critical art is art that forms a dissensus – that makes visible what the dominant consensus tends to obscure and obliterate, aiming to give voice within the existing hegemony.'* It is in this space that multiple voices that may have

Figures 9.5, 9.6 and 9.7: Some comments illustrating difference of values and insights (Schrag, 2022)

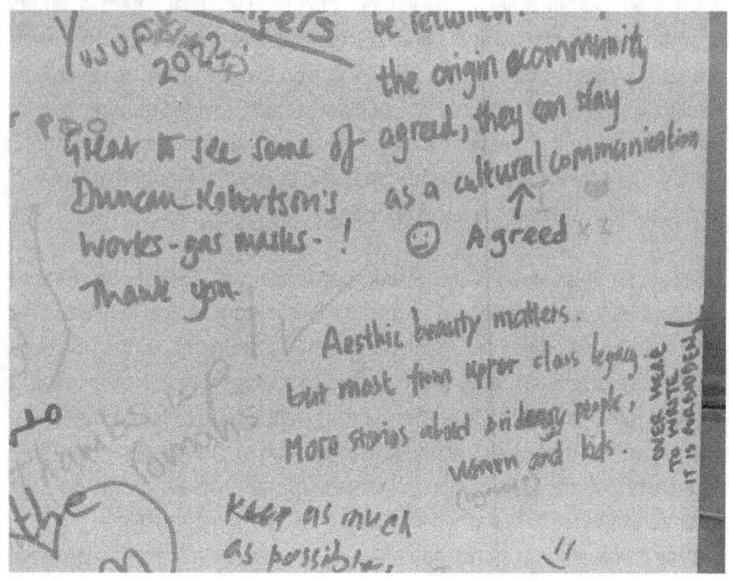

Figure 9.5

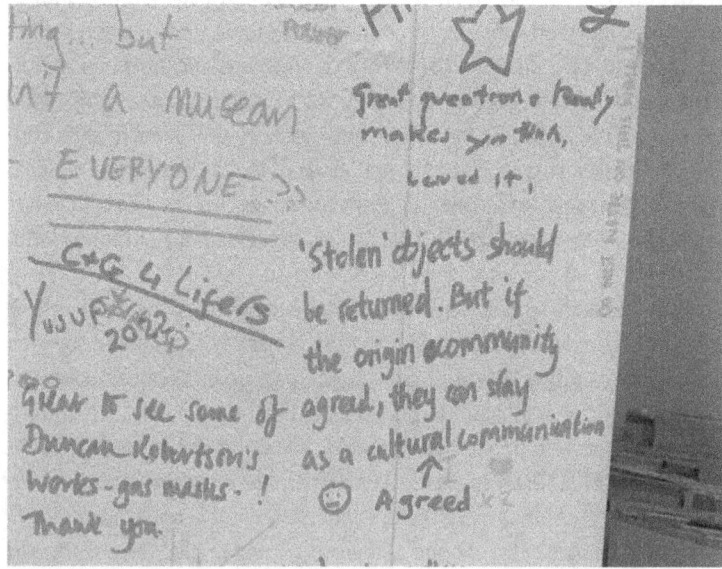

Figure 9.6

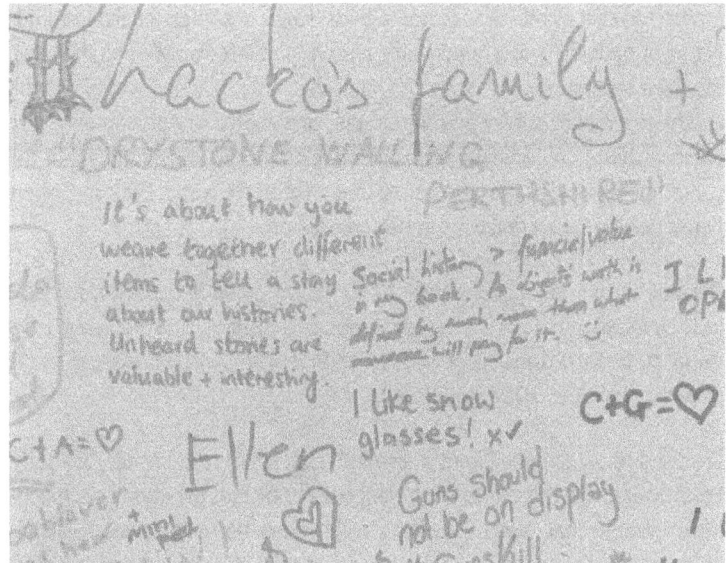

Figure 9.7

been obscured or obliterated can come together in a productive dissensus in a way that challenges dominant hegemonies. That is the principle that underpins all my artwork. I include my own disruption and discomfort in this process, and have realised that such an approach can also be useful in a radical reconsideration of educational processes within higher education, as explored below.

Learning to be uncomforted

In 2015, I was invited to develop and teach a module called Contemporary Issues of Art and Design Education for the MA in Art and Design Education, at the Piet Zwart Institute in Rotterdam in The Netherlands. As I had been lecturing in higher education institutions (HEIs) for eight years by that point, I promptly and perfunctorily sketched the learning outcomes, decided topics and themes, developed a few PowerPoint lectures, proposed assignments and closed the laptop, escaping to a glass of wine and a TV boxset binge. Easy. But when I returned to the plan the next day it felt wrong: something did not fit, and I was not sure what it was. Using the critical friend approach (Costa and Kallick, 1993), I reflected and realised that the student body did not have a homogenous profile. It included a wide range of professionals, from directors of national programmes to recent BA graduates working on their own localised community art projects. Thus, what I had planned would only be a very generalised survey and unsuitable for the diversity of learners. I also realised that it could only inform the students of my understanding of the contemporary issues, not the issues they might face within their respective fields, nor the issues that were important to them.

Reading further in Jacques Rancière's (1991) *The Ignorant Schoolmaster* project reminded me that it is a false assumption that *'in order to teach, a teacher needs to be in possession of knowledge that s/he can then explain to the students'* (Pelletier, 2008, p 201).

I realised that if I applied Rancière's (1991) concept of relationships of equity, I could adapt the module to be student led and disrupt the traditional monolithic narrative that often exists within higher education institutions. To do this practically, I adjusted my module and tasked each student to develop a short text on an issue they faced within their own field.

In the following session, after a short lecture about my personal insights and further presentations from the students about their perspectives, the texts that had been developed were passed along to other students to adapt and add to from their particular context; and in the following session, after another discussion and presentation, these texts were passed on again to different students to explore from yet another context. Over the course of the module, this was repeated eight times, resulting in each student contributing to the conceptual strands initiated by their colleagues. In other words, rather than a traditional structure of master/student, I was keen to allow collaborative creativity to provide different knowledge potentialities where information was shared between students and their own particular interests guided the content. The students were therefore taking ownership of their own knowledge, and their research informed my insights too. The Piet Zwart Institute felt the approach to be so successful in covering the breadth of contemporary issues and its appropriateness for the diversity of the students and the master's level that it was replicated the following year.

One student wrote to me the following year to indicate that the project was successful because I was a part of their educational process, and able to make decisions if needed.

> *You led the way for a collaborative assignment, but there was space for us students to question your decisions, or to act in a different way. Relinquishing the process to us made you feel uncomfortable, I think, but being open about this made the interaction valuable and your commitment to teaching made me feel important as a student.*
>
> (email from student, 2016)

While I recognise there are curriculum requirements within any formal education structure that will necessitate specific learning, the salient reflection I have regarding this experience was that in destabilising my role as module leader, there was an equity of sharing and learning that presented a different structure of knowledge – one that was responsive, equitable and ethical. Like the museum in Kill Your Darlings, the authority (in this case, me as lecturer) had to relinquish some control to allow space and time for significant dialogue and innovation. In an educational context, this led the students to not only to take ownership of their learning, but also to establish a more nuanced, equitable power structure that valued multiple perspectives.

The School of kNOw

In 2014, I was invited be artist-in-residence at Drama for Life, a drama therapy Masters programme at the University of the Witwatersrand (Johannesburg) in South Africa. Part of the residency involved supporting students with the design and execution of their final projects in the socio-economically deprived communities in which they worked. On arrival, I found it problematic that I – a White male from the colonial Global North – was tasked with educating middle-class students from the unique context of the Global South, who were working with poor, Black communities.

The embedded power dynamics within education settings are obviously a concern (Pelletier, 2008) and, despite my good intentions, I was worried that I would inadvertently replicate unethical power systems, and that the students might similarly replicate such problematic dynamics within their own projects. I therefore attempted to establish a para-educational institution (Harris, 2005) called the School of kNOw, which would offer points of negation to any embedded, unethical power dynamic.

This parasitic school within the Masters programme aimed to provide the students with an opportunity for un-knowing that would bring into question the types of knowledge we each held, and the power embedded within those knowledges. Practically, this consisted of weekly exchanges around a desk shaped like a question mark. The very shape of this desk changed the dynamic of teacher–student relationship, as we were all required to constantly negotiate how/where to sit in relation to each other. Simply put, it altered the infrastructures of the classroom, and this in turn altered the ways we engaged with each other: we were forced to think differently about power structures.

Around this difficult table, we began to discuss their projects in a call-and-response process in a variety of formats, including group critiques, anonymous written provocations, group/individual exchanges and other non-traditional formats such as walks, meals and activities that reconfigured the traditional hierarchy and allowed us, as a collective whole, to challenge assumptions of operating in the context of the Global South, question my role as a privileged outsider and critically engage with their individual projects. This process not only challenged the content of the sessions, but also explored how the classical format of teaching – such as organised desks or time structures – can replicate habits that might not be conducive to developing egalitarian exchanges.

Some students did not like the experience; they had not expected an international academic such as me to be so informal. Nor did I particularly enjoy being challenged on my own assumptions and inherent prejudices at each step of the way. But in the art world, I have always believed the artist should be as uncomfortable as the people they are challenging. Through this project, I realised this can and must be the same in educational contexts too; to learn about pedagogy, assumptions of not only what we teach, but also how we teach, must be challenged. This was – like the Piet Zwart Institute module described above – an uncomfortable place for me to sit. But in such restructuring of the hierarchies, new possibilities emerged.

Despite the discomfort I felt, the process was vitally illuminating as it proved the insight that the mechanisms of teaching are just as important as the content, and the project's success was illustrated by the students' reconsideration of the ethical relationships between artist and community that I was hoping

Figure 9.8: The School of kNOw desk (Schrag, 2022)

to explore. For example, a student had initially planned to develop a performance that would tell the stories of a community of taxi drivers, but because of the School of kNOw she shifted the context so that the taxi drivers could tell their own story in a way that was important to them.

Conclusion: unlearning

In the three projects I have presented in this chapter, there has been a process of unlearning and unknowing – not just about information and facts, but also assumptions and infrastructures. And in this unknowing, new opportunities emerged. In the classroom context, these have not been significantly difficult to enact, but they have resulted in a significant restructuring of power; nurtured a more nuanced, equitable relationship; and presented new insights in new and innovative ways. Both have been significantly risky, I admit, but new knowledge is always risky and if we want work in anti-racist ways, risks must be taken.

Reflective questions

- In what ways can a lecturer or education system be uncomforted? Or, put differently, what opportunities do you take to unlearn?
- What are the physical or conceptual infrastructures of your daily teaching that can be altered? What makes it difficult to change them?
- How can we nurture creative, risky thinking in the classroom?

Recommended reading

- Hyde, L (1998) *Trickster Makes This World: How Disruptive Imagination Creates Culture.* Edinburgh: Canongate.
- Kester, G (2004) *Conversation Pieces: Community and Communication in Modern Art.* Berkeley, CA: University of California Press.

References

Bloom, B (1984 [1956]) *Taxonomy of Educational Objectives.* Boston, MA: Allyn and Bacon.

Costa, A and Kallick, B (1993) Through the Lens of a Critical Friend. *Educational Leadership*, 51(2): 49–51.

Freire, P (2000 [1968]) *Pedagogy of the Oppressed.* New York: Continuum.

Harris, J (2005) *Art, Money, Parties: New Institutions in the Political Economy of Contemporary Art.* Liverpool: Liverpool University Press.

Hopkins, B (2003) The Artist as Ethnographer – Annotations. University of Chicago. [online] Available at: http://csmt.uchicago.edu/annotations/fosterartist.htm (accessed 4 August 2022).

Kazepides, T (2010) Education as Dialogue: Its Prerequisites and its Enemies. Montreal: McGill-Queen's University Press.

Kester, G (2004) *Conversation Pieces: Community and Communication in Modern Art.* Berkeley, CA: University of California Press.

Levinas, E (1989) Substitution. In Hand, S (ed) *The Levinas Reader* (pp 88–126). Oxford: Blackwell.

Mouffe, C (2007) *Agonistic Politics and Artistic Practices* (Lecture), Glasgow School of Art, Glasgow, 2 March.

Museum Association (nd) Our Statement on Decolonisation. *The Museum Association.* [online] Available at: www.museumsassociation.org/campaigns/decolonising-museums (accessed 12 August 2022).

Pelletier, C (2008) Emancipation, Equality and Education: Rancière's Critique of Bourdieu and the Question of Performativity. *Discourse: Studies in the Cultural Politics of Education,* 30(2): 137–50.

Pirnay-Dummer, P, Ifenthaler, D and Seel, N M (2012) Designing Model-based Learning Environments to Support Mental Models for Learning. In Jonassen, D and Land, S (eds) *Theoretical Foundations of Learning Environments* (pp 77–115). London: Routledge.

Rancière, J (1991) *The Ignorant Schoolmaster: Five Lessons in Intellectual Emancipation.* Stanford, CA: Stanford University Press.

Rappaport, J (2008) Beyond Participant Observation: Collaborative Ethnography as Theoretical Innovation. *Collaborative Anthropologies,* 1: 1–31. Project MUSE. [online] Available at: https://muse.jhu.edu/view_citations?type=article&id=367015 (accessed 22 February 2023).

Schrag, A (2016) *Agonistic Tendencies: The Role of Conflict within Institutionally Supported Participatory Art Projects.* PhD thesis, Newcastle University, Newcastle.

Strohm, K (2012) When Anthropology Meets Contemporary Art: Notes for a Politics of Collaboration. *Collaborative Anthropologies*, 5: 98–124.

Vella, J (1994) *Learning to Listen, Learning to Teach: The Power of Dialogue in Educating Adults*. San Francisco: Jossey-Bass.

CHAPTER 10

WHITE IS THE COLOUR OF MY NAME: ANTI-RACISM IN THEATRE AND PERFORMANCE PRAXIS

Bianca Mastrominico

Preamble

In the West, what is the degree of Whiteness that spares an individual from becoming Other? As an Italian in the United Kingdom, I am aware that it is not widely understood that my name, Bianca – which I inherited from my paternal grandmother – in English translates as a woman who is, literally, White. Some say it comes from the German *blank*, which means 'of bright and luminous skin' and others from the Latin *blancus*, which again means the colour White. According to Catholicism, my name is traditionally associated with the fourth century CE Italian Madonna della Neve (Our Lady of the Snows), referring to both her purity and her White skin, as madonnas are usually depicted in Western artworks. In exalting the White skin tone as a beauty norm, my name encapsulates both patriarchy and White supremacism. So, when speaking about anti-racism, I will need to remember that I carry an intrinsically racialised name, which I did not choose for myself.

As a European citizen living in the United Kingdom since 2002, I have spent considerable time and energy integrating, but how do I confront the legacy of British colonialism and what does decolonisation mean for me in a cultural context that inevitably highlights my own diversity? As a self-proclaimed anti-racist, my effort goes into defamiliarising myself from my host culture in order to reflect on my position in it. To this purpose, in this chapter I follow the serendipity of inspiring encounters, events and people who have empowered me in my personal and professional life to discover the true colour of my name.

The racialised body

As an Italian-born, White, cisgender woman, performance-maker and lecturer in British higher education institutions since 2007, I understand anti-racism as a pact of alliances, a tool for exercising human wisdom, for consciously preserving my cultural identity and actively counteracting processes of othering and inequality. I learn from scholars who speak out about race issues, as well as their lived and/or learnt experiences of racism. As a performer and an educator who shares knowledge through practice, I believe the most effective (and affective) way to understand those experiences is by channelling them into an embodied pedagogy. I value learning through the body as a transcultural somatic process of apprenticeship, and my professional background is rooted in a deep appreciation and first-hand practice of non-Western forms of theatre, dance and performance. As a tutor, I work through a personal need to break cultural barriers and foster critical discussion in the classroom, and this orientates my teaching towards the recognition of behaviours and historical processes from which racial inequalities and divisiveness arise.

Evaluating how colonialism is embedded in institutional systems and entangles with higher education institution curricula for me requires a conscious choice of vocabulary, and an act of questioning *'which words are really necessary to talk about difficult legacies of White dominance and the power struggle embedded in our system'* (Finkel and Mastrominico, 2021). I believe that central to this articulation is the language of the racialised body, shaped by the disturbing presence of historical perpetrators, even in the form of statues, flowing into rivers of intra-generational transmission of traumas, inherited from silenced ancestors. I see our bodies as the loci of decolonising narratives, and if these do not take into account the physical experience of racism within the colonised institutional body, the risk is partaking in superficial chit-chat about what Tom Conford (2019) defines as *'the breadth of diversity... diluting awareness of justice'*, which reinforces – instead of eroding – the White systemic gaze resulting in stigmas of otherness. Creating safe spaces within institutions, where the oppressed body can express legitimate anger and its resilience can be witnessed and validated, is not only an act of human compassion and solidarity, but also a necessary step towards the intellectual rigour needed to recognise racial oppression in all its chameleonic forms – for me, a vital skill to master as an anti-racist.

Decolonising/diversifying the curriculum

While the Black Lives Matter movement is shifting the course of history, educators are joining together and forming alliances to question whether changes to the status quo can be achieved solely through reviewing institutional curricula, or whether more grassroots activity is needed to target policies and mindsets. Within British theatre, dance and performance studies, scholars from the global majority have been proactive in generating discussions among students and colleagues about what decolonising might mean, and how it could really work in higher education contexts. A prime example is the 2019–20 Education Incubator project Decolonising the Curriculum/Diversifying the University, organised by Professor Jerri Daboo at the University of Exeter, which used *'creativity to explore and give space and voice to students' experiences'* (Daboo, 2020, p 6). The project culminated in *The Rest of Us – Stories*, an e-magazine collating the written contributions of the students who took part in performances and writing workshops, and it is defined by Daboo as *'a small step along the path of change and action'*. It is not only an invaluable resource created by students, but also a template for how to start a dialogue about anti-racism among students and staff within academic institutions. As Daboo (2020, p 6) states, the collection of stories validates that *'universities have a major part to play in shaping the way we think, what we know, who is given voice, and how we make the future'*.

In 2018, Daboo also initiated and convened a focused group of academics working on anti-racism in Exeter, which generated further meetings in London instigated by Professor Royona Mitra (Brunel University), as well as collegiate responses on equality and diversity within the discipline. According to Conford (2019), these highlighted that, *'rather than focusing on the historical legacies of racist ideology… we should interrogate and seek to repair the historical processes that have produced oppression and inequality'*. This is a standpoint for my approach to the decolonising agenda in my higher education institution, where I take action joining in monthly readings and discussions with colleagues of the Decolonising our Research group, and inviting performing arts students to engage with anti-racism through performance practice. In promoting anti-racism through participation and in my pedagogy,

I am renewing my commitment to address systemic racism and work intentionally towards structural changes.

I find this an essential challenge, as Ibram X Kendi (2019, p 9) so aptly indicates, unlike what he calls *'not racist neutrality'* – which is *'a mask for racism'* and blocks you from dismantling it; as an anti-racist, you locate *'the roots of the problems in power and politics'*. Therefore, activating collective strategies (including this book chapter) of reporting, documenting and reflecting on personal and social experiences from an anti-racist perspective empowers me to identify and respond to instances of racism in my scholarly role. As a White person, I might not like what I will discover about myself from embarking on a process of self-scrutiny – from personal prejudices and implicit biases, and of course the assumptions derived by my White privilege. However, I am aware that it is from this uncomfortable position of questioning that I can take emotional and intellectual responsibility in denouncing and counteracting White supremacist behaviours in a place of learning and teaching. It is of course always my personal choice whether I stand for my own limitations, or I take agency to seek social justice and nurture my own sense of humanity in a transformative way.

Anti-racism as a creative and critical compass

Acknowledging my racial prejudices is an essential step towards maturing and nurturing a conscious anti-racist behaviour. In so doing I validate that the discussion around decolonising the curriculum in university contexts should be based on individual accountability, and should serve to *'question whose viewpoint the information is coming from'* and *'identifying that we are learning a story'* (BBC Bitesize, 2020), not the victor's story. On the other hand, I am aware that the victor's story is not just one story among others, but a specific and individual narrative that carries the ghosts of the perpetrators and their privileges, reinforcing them within the generational trauma of racism. However, these narratives are losing meaning as, looking at how young White people are struggling with their identity since the Black Lives Matter protests, human development expert Anthony Ataekong (2022) notes:

> *The global racial awakening is upending and shaking up 'Whiteness', forcing its beneficiaries to seek alternative sources of meaning, self-esteem and self-confidence rather than the false, spurious, and pernicious theory that being White automatically conferred these values.*

For a White, Southern Italian woman working with mostly White students in a predominantly White UK university, Ataekong's analysis has a consequence, as it implicitly asks me, the scholar and the educator, how I can operate and take action to dismantle the pernicious theory of White supremacy and White privilege from my own mindset. The pedagogical pathways of theatre and performance practice have offered me the possibility to facilitate a learning environment that looks at race and identity as social and political constructs imposed upon the body. Through the embodiment of these constructs, I am interested in finding out what I can learn about the dynamics of racially motivated oppression of the body in different cultures, as this also shapes me as a person, as well as my attitude of behaving according to internalised racial views and cultural conditionings. Furthermore, I am keen to reflect on how the false sense of privilege that comes with Whiteness can be released through embodied practice, when I truly and honestly embrace anti-racism as a creative and critical compass in my teaching and performance work, and in establishing and nurturing relationships and networks, both in academia and in professional contexts.

The anti-racist collective

One of the most public achievements of an anti-racist action within the British theatre, dance and performance studies community has been the political statements from scholars and researchers united in Revolution or Nothing. This was set up as an informal network of 'Black and Global Majority Scholars in UK Theatre, Dance, and Performance Studies' (Revolution or Nothing, 2020), a definition that, as the members say, *'while not perfect, attempts at signalling a political, collective and positive identification, so that we are not categorised in relation to Whiteness'*. Through open letters, the network has been denouncing systemic racism, racial inequalities and racialised power politics within the discipline and in higher education institutions in general.

In the letter titled 'WHITE COLLEAGUE LISTEN!*', the authors call for *'a fundamental re-examination of the racist values that shape our fields'* (Revolution or Nothing, 2020), expressing frustration and disempowerment through personal and anonymously shared stories that expose deeply ingrained inequalities in their workplaces. The letter brings examples of career aspirations suffocated by petty colonial-style bureaucracy and the dim tale of scholars and researchers sidelined, mistrusted and silenced. Searching for a dialogue within their scholarly community, the network directs the collective writing to *'individual colleagues, friends, and peers'* rather than to the institutions, asking them *'to recognise and undo your roles in upholding racist structures and systems of oppression'*.

This public mobilisation fluctuated between the condemnation of the systemic and racially motivated abuse of power to the more nuanced potential for change, resting in individual action within a collective and underlining that *'when responsibility is passed on to an "institution", it absolves the responsibility, culpability, and complicity of individuals in perpetuating racist power structures'*. The authors of the letter also appear to protest against the lack of access to work and academic recognition, and it could be observed that to obtain it from the very institutions oppressing growth and career prospects problematises the aims and objectives of the message in relation to the power struggle it seeks to denounce. However, there is no easy way of provoking change in the thick racialised fabric of an institution, if you cannot move an inch from your position and you are actively discouraged – if not pushed back at every attempt – to develop and achieve.

In reporting their experience of systemic oppression in higher education institutions, the Revolution or Nothing network made a conscious decision to individually embody anti-racist solidarity. Members joined forces to speak with one strong voice, bringing their questioning of structural racism and processes of othering to the forefront of the social and political concerns within the discipline, which echoes those discussed within the creative and professional sector. While the network's protest was geared towards imagining and invoking a whole new system, where anti-racist consciousness and practice is operating at a structural level regardless of our disciplines, these anti-racist socio-political tensions are a useful reminder of the necessity to decolonise our minds before addressing institutional racism.

The roots of othering

Since the 1990s, my practice-based learning of non-Western performance has led me to problematise the supposed centrality of Western theatre, dance and performance-making. Through physical and dance training with Asian and Afro-Brazilian artists and teachers, I was pushed to interrogate the roots of othering within myself. Between 1997 and 1999, on two different journeys to

India, I became an apprentice of Milòn Méla, an ensemble of traditional Indian artists teaching at Theatre House – Khele Danga (Village of the Red Earth), a work centre for intercultural performance research created by Calcutta-born theatre director Abani Biswas and based near Shantiniketan in Bengal, India. In the 1970s, Biswas had collaborated with the revolutionary Polish director Jerzi Grotowski on the Theatre of Sources project, aimed at finding the transcultural sources of human behaviour through artistic practice. Since the group started in 1986, Milòn Méla has continued working in this direction, inviting participants – mainly White Europeans – to work at the centre. The daily routines were structured around the workshops with Kalaripayattu martial artists from Kerala, Chhau and Gotipua dancers, Patua storytellers, Muslim Fakir musicians and Hindu Baul singers, the Bengali minstrels devoted to Krishna, whose singing and music is rooted in a spiritual quest for the divine and the interconnection between all human beings. During my stay at Theatre House, I was asked to respect silence when engaging in the activities and at meals. These conditions heightened the observation of how my body reacted to the environment and to others in a mutual state of responsiveness, overcoming language as the crucial human ability to facilitate social interactions.

Sustaining silence provoked not only deconditioning and mindfulness, but most importantly helped shift the focus from vocal communication to body language, and from the outer to the inner gaze. Every silent interaction engenders a form of (re)connection through the body, while the perception of otherness becomes less and less impellent. Through letting go of unnecessary verbal cues, I was able to recognise the biases and prejudices in my thinking, which I was dragging around, preventing me from fully trusting and releasing into human encounters. Re-learning to trust the intelligence of the body through training and practising in silence is what I often bring into my classroom, inviting my students to keep words at bay and to observe the tendency to speak as a social habit in order to clarify their thoughts and switch off the rational mind. When this is achieved even minimally, it is possible to appreciate the uniqueness and energetic quality that each of us holds, beyond our diverse cultural backgrounds.

Intercultural performance pedagogies

In seeking opportunities to work and learn from artists who did not align with my pre-existing knowledge of predominantly White performance-makers and teachers, I was privileged to experience how their craft, formed with years of technical learning and discipline, carried deep embodied knowledge of their own culture. These powerful performers provoked a real earthquake in my practice and values, through their creativity, work ethic, humour and luminous stage presence. To celebrate these encounters, between 2007 and 2008, with my intercultural performance laboratory Organic Theatre – which I founded in 2002 with British-born actor and director John Dean – I co-organised the International Training and Performance Residencies in the southwest of England, in collaboration with Asian Arts Agency and the Tobacco Factory Theatre in Bristol. Invited artists were the late Afro-Brazilian performer, dancer and choreographer Augusto Omolú, Indian Kathakali dancer Kottakkal Sasidharan Nair and the Milòn Méla ensemble I visited in India. The project offered internship opportunities to UK-based university students, who could become involved in different capacities, as translators, facilitators and stewards in parades, as well as taking part in the pedagogical activities, meeting the artists and attending performances.

The intention behind the residencies, mostly centred in the Bristol area, was to give voice and space to the mastery, pedagogy and performance work of international artists from India and Brazil, some of them coming to the United Kingdom for the first time. The collaboration with Asian Arts Agency, a dynamic arts development agency promoting South Asian music and arts in Bristol, aimed to involve the city's POC communities in the activities open to the public. As a company, a great part of our effort went into questioning at every step who this project was for, what the social repercussions were for the communities we aimed to involve, and what the benefits were for the artists and the university students involved.

Scottish-born Jonathan Webster, who lives and works as Head of Primary Arts in Hong Kong, was a student at Queen Margaret University when 14 years ago he joined Organic Theatre for the Milòn Méla residency. I asked Webster to recall his emotional and sensorial memory of that encounter, and his first reminiscence is linked to food, and the action of buying very specific ingredients for the visiting performers and cooking with them.

The communal process of cooking and eating together was very important to the group visiting and helped us to be together, even though verbal communication was occasionally challenging. This was not food that I would usually cook and eat, so the 'Otherness' was contrasted with the communal way of eating... the experience of cooking together was important.

(Webster, 2022)

Webster also recalls the intensity of the working day with the Indian artists-teachers, not only in terms of the long periods of physical work, but the way in which *'my brain had to engage when communication was all non-verbal'*. He also remembers wondering *'whether the performers of Milòn Méla had been trained or learned specifically about communication between cultures'*. In making connections between the experience of participating in the residency and his current life in Hong Kong, Webster reflects that:

Living openly and receptively enables me not to be closed off to learning opportunities and different ways of thinking, but also to connect with other people on a human level — finding what unites us rather than what separates us... perhaps rather pertinent for our post-Covid world.

(Webster, 2022)

Freedom is love

In a perspective on the International Training and Performance Residencies written for *Total Theatre Magazine*, I note dancer and choreographer Augusto Omolú saying during a work session that *'the key to achieving things is freedom, and to achieve freedom you need respect, will and love'* (Mastrominico, 2008). Then I comment that this was *'almost a revolutionary slogan in the working space of the Tobacco Factory Theatre, at the heart of a vibrant western city still coming to terms with its obscure past as a major British port for the African slave trade'*. Alongside the tacit embodiment to overcome language barriers, being together through the work and in daily and (apparently) mundane tasks, the residencies in Bristol became a shared experience of intercultural embodiment and learning through doing. Most importantly, the presence of the artists in a British city battling with the harmful legacies of its colonial past became an anti-racist statement, vindicating and problematising notions of heritage and historical contexts linked to racial oppression.

Towards anti-racist performance practice

As a migrant, I have experienced how important body language is when addressing or being addressed by someone you do not understand. Being exposed to a culture for long enough that it becomes sufficiently familiar that one stops paying attention to the difference, and more to the commonality of humankind, is a journey that in itself embraces the logic of anti-racism. Moreover, when you invite silence into a learning space and let bodies speak, it opens pathways to a much deeper listening and compassionate understanding. How does this sit in an educational context, where discourse and words are the primary medium to convey knowledge? What do I hope to know if I neglect what I learn through my body? How can I be an anti-racist if I do not understand in my body the dynamics of pain caused by racist behaviour?

In Autumn 2021, returning to teach on campus face to face for the first time since the Covid-19 pandemic – and following the tsunami of social and political unrest around the globe – I decided to invite my third-year drama and performance students to consider anti-racism as a subject for creating devised performance work. I proposed that they would embark on a journey of embodied research, to gain a better understanding of racialisation, which Adam Hochman (2019) explains as *'the process through which racialised – rather than racial – groups are formed'* and through which racist behaviours emerge. Actively embracing the spirit and practice of anti-racism in a creative process; two groups of students worked on texts and original performance material towards a final 20-minute ensemble performance. Over a three-month period, the students committed to understand, discuss and transform their thinking about anti-racism, and how it could translate and resonate through performance making for their academic assessment. In my feedback to one of the groups, I wrote:

> *The implications brought by anti-racism to your devising process was that openness in form was bound to honesty and fairness towards the argument and the implicit biases you were all navigating in the making of the performance. The resulting meaning was achieved... visualising the struggle to speak about, understand and act as an anti-racist.*
>
> (Mastrominico, 2021)

Creatively embodying their own struggle in understanding and applying anti-racist practice to their creative work and thinking patterns, students who identify as White started to become aware of how the privileges of Whiteness shape their life experience. They also started to appreciate the need of constantly discussing their positioning with humility and the acknowledgement of the discrimination and suffering inflicted by racial inequality.

[There is never a] conclusion on living as an anti-racist

Every year on 5 August, my name day is celebrated in a district of Naples, my birthplace in Italy, and the eighteenth-century statue of our Lady of the Snows swings around the streets on top of a 17 metre-tall wooden chariot. She is carried on the shoulders of 100 believers, who are all local men moving slowly in contorted spasms of pain because of the massive weight on their backs. I carry my first name with the same weight. My skin colour is not fair, and I am not as White as snow. I have brown hair and eyes ostensibly not of a Nordic type. In Italy, I am from the South; in Europe, I am a Mediterranean. The colour of my name does not help me to disappear in a crowd of Northern people, nor does it protect me from xeno-racist aggressions from those to whom I 'look' different. In the United Kingdom, I am often asked where I am from and I am frequently stared at as if I stand out as an anomaly. Despite this, my very name contains the weight of patriarchy, and the racial taxonomy with which I struggle, and that I rebel against as an anti-racist. In post-Brexit Britain, I can feel oppressed because I am a European citizen, and in Italy because I am from the South of the country. As a cosmopolitan who has broken the boundaries of nationalities and political borders, wherever I find myself to be I consider myself at risk of experiencing social rejection because either I do not conform or I do not renounce displaying my roots, or I provocatively and ironically accentuate my exoticism. Most of the time, an insidious degree of oppression comes from trying to relax my nervous system, to feel at home and safe, when I am relentlessly reminded that I do not belong.

White is the colour of my name, but then I saw a rainbow and jumped in.

Reflective questions

- How can performance be a tool for investigating internalised racism?
- How can individual stories of racial oppressions be shared through creative means?
- How can creative practice and embodiment challenge the racial discourse?

Recommended reading

- Daboo, J (2018) Women and British South Asian Theatre. *Theatre.Conflict. Change*, 14 August. [online] Available at: https://theatreconflictchange.com/professor-jerri-daboo (accessed 18 October 2022).

- McCluney, C L, King, D D, Bryant, C M and Ali, A A (2021) From 'Calling in Black' to 'Calling for Antiracism Resources': The Need for Systemic Resources to Address Systemic Racism. *Equality, Diversity and Inclusion*, 40(1): 49–59.

- Narang, A (2021) Expanding Notions of Pedagogy to Empower Change. *AdvanceHE*, 4 February. [online] Available at: www.advance-he.ac.uk/news-and-views/expanding-notions-pedagogy-empower-change (accessed 18 October 2022).

References

Ataekong, A (2022) The Negative Impact of Whiteness on the Mental Health of Adolescents in the UK. LinkedIn, 14 August. [online] Available at: www.linkedin.com/pulse/negative-impact-Whiteness-mental-health-adolescents-uk-ataekong (accessed 11 October 2022).

BBC Bitesize (2020) Decolonising the Curriculum. [online] Available at: www.bbc.co.uk/bitesize/articles/z7g66v4 (accessed 11 October 2022).

Conford, T (2019) Anti-Racism in Theatre & Performance Studies. *Theatre Matters: Research@Central*, 24 July. [online] Available at: https://rcssdtheatrematters.wordpress.com/2019/07/24/anti-racism-in-theatre-performance-studies (accessed 10 October 2022).

Daboo, J (2020) Introduction. In *The Rest of Us – Stories* (30 November). [online] Available at: https://issuu.com/therestofus/docs/tbgdc_uoe_the_rest_of_us_stories_issuu_pages (accessed 10 October 2022).

Finkel, R and Mastrominico, B (2021) Cooking Up a Storm: Discussions about Decolonisation. Queen Margaret University, 24 March. [online] Available at: www.qmu.ac.uk/campus-life/blogs/staff-dr-rebecca-finkel-bianca-mastrominico/cooking-up-a-storm-discussions-about-decolonisation (accessed 10 October 2022).

Hochman, A (2019) Racialization: A Defense of the Concept. *Ethnic and Racial Studies*, 42(8): 1245–62. https://doi.org/10.1080/01419870.2018.1527937

Kendi, X I (2019) *How to Be an Anti-Racist*. New York: One World.

Mastrominico, B (2008) Come Together: Connecting Worlds Apart. *Total Theatre Magazine*, 19(4). [online] Available at: http://totaltheatre.org.uk/archive/features/come-together-connecting-worlds-apart (accessed 18 October 2022).

Mastrominico, B (2021) Assessment Feedback [Blackboard Hub]. T3219 Devising Practices. Queen Margaret University, 15 December.

Revolution or Nothing (2020) WHITE COLLEAGUE LISTEN!* An open letter to UK Theatre, Dance and Performance Studies. [online] Available at: https://medium.com/@revolutionornothing/White-colleague-listen-2d098d6a4a5d (accessed 18 October 2022).

Webster, J (2022) WhatsApp Message to Bianca Mastrominico, 21 August.

CHAPTER 11

MAD STUDIES AND ANTI-RACISM

Anne O'Donnell

Introduction

In the field of mad studies, the words 'mad' and 'madness' are reclaimed terms. As derogatory words, they have been reappropriated. They are non-medical terms, reclaimed in the Mad Pride movement and in mad studies. While they are difficult terms for many, who feel they are too negative or divisive (Beresford et al, 2016), they have actually become terms that imply a radical, political critique of psychiatry. In this chapter and in my work, I use them as a political position rather than a personal identity. The terms we use to describe ourselves collectively are likewise contested. I use the terms 'service user' and 'survivor', often together. Sometimes I will use the term 'with lived experience of mental health issues' as is the currently preferred term in Scotland. In this chapter, I will first explain what mad studies is and why it is important to decentre Whiteness in this emerging field. The second part of the chapter is about my role as an educator.

What is mad studies?

Mad studies is *'an umbrella term that is used to embrace the body of knowledge developed by [mad] people'* (LeFrançois et al, 2013, p 337). Mad studies has also been described as *'an area of education, scholarship, and analysis about the experiences, history, culture, political organising, narratives, writings* and, most importantly, the people who identify as [mad]' (Costa, 2014). Mad studies emerged first in Canada, with its roots in survivor activism going back to the 1970s and to survivor/user-led research in the late 1980s (Sweeney, 2016). It has since spread internationally, as demonstrated by the *Routledge International Handbook of Mad Studies* (Beresford and Russo, 2022). Mad studies is an emerging field, and Queen Margaret University is one of the pioneers in teaching and researching it in a more coherent form (Armstrong and LeFrançois, 2021, p 323). We are a small team of four lecturers, three of whom are part time.

Mad studies at Queen Margaret University has its roots in a partnership with a local user-led organisation, CAPS Independent Advocacy, which is funded by NHS Lothian. From the Oor Mad History community history project at CAPS, we developed a widening participation module called Mad People's History and Identity in 2013 (O'Donnell and Maclean, 2019). It welcomes people with lived experience of mental health issues, regardless of previous academic experience, and offers space to explore those experiences through a mad studies perspective. The first course was delivered in 2014, and since then we have delivered it five times with the next delivery in April 2023. In 2021, we offered the only postgraduate mad studies degree in the world. I have been involved in developing and delivering these courses, first as a visiting lecturer and since January 2022 as a university employee.

How I came to mad studies

I have been involved in survivor/service user activism since the mid-1990s and had become very disillusioned by how little we had achieved (Sapouna and O'Donnell, 2017). We felt our initial energy and passion had been diluted by the constant demand from the mental health system to be involved (O'Donnell and Maclean, 2019) and this led us to set up a project called Oor Mad History, a community history project that records and celebrates service user activism in Lothian. We were inspired and supported by David Reville and Kathryn Church from what is now called the Toronto Metropolitan University. They worked in the School of Disability Studies, offering courses in the history of madness and mad people's history (Church 2013, 2015; Reville 2012, 2022). Through Oor Mad History, we connected with Elaine Ballantyne at Queen Margaret University and began to develop the idea of the Mad People's History and Identity course.

Developing this work connected us to mad studies. We were inspired by Lucy Costa (2014), who challenged us by asking, *'Maybe it's time we stop answering [user involvement] questions and have Mad Studies develop our own questions and research agendas.'* I was also interested in going beyond focusing on mental health services and oppression. In the words of Helen Spandler and Dina Poursanidou, mad studies:

> *can ask wider questions about society and culture. For example, it can explore mad people's histories, cultures, politics, and communities, including before the invention of psychiatry; and use mad-centred knowledge to critique existing cultures and practices.*
> (Spandler and Poursanidou, 2019, p 9)

The undoings of mad studies

In 2015, Brenda LeFrançois delivered a powerful keynote speech at the Making Sense of Mad Studies conference. In her presentation, she called on us to consider the *'undoings of mad studies'*. One of the main undoings is the potential disconnection between mad studies in the academy and mad activism and knowledge production outside the academy. Beresford (2020) reminds us that intellectual activity – user-led research and the like – happens outside universities.

I think mad studies can and should be in the university. But it has to be in the community too. It happens in our activist spaces and in our community building spaces. But we do not often call the knowledge produced in those places 'mad studies'. Armstrong and LeFrançois (2021) claim that without a connection to the community and to activism, mad studies in the university is really critical mental health studies. In other words, mad studies could become a totally academic critique of mental health services and discourse, detached from the experiences and intellectual work by mad people. It would lose its emancipatory purpose. Mad studies is still very new, and it is fragile. It generally exists as individual lectures and modules on a range of degree programmes. Mad scholars and mad people generally are *'granted inferior credibility and discriminated against in the distribution of power, legitimacy and resources'* (Beresford, 2020, p 1341). So those of us in the academy need our comrades in the community.

We have to recognise that it was activists who created the space for us to do research in the first place and that mad studies has roots in user-led research (Sweeney, 2016). Only a small number of mad people will study mad studies at university level. There is a danger that we create an elite mad studies cohort that splits the movement. This may be a bit rich coming from a university lecturer and a PhD candidate, but I come from an activist background: my teaching and research are deeply connected with my experiences of mental distress, use of services and activism. My intellectual and professional home is in community education, inspired by Paolo Freire (2000) and bell hooks (2003, 2014), among others. I see education as a practice of freedom. The Mad People's History and Identity course at Queen Margaret University is a good example of how we connect the academic and the activist and the personal (Ballantyne et al, 2019). It is proof of the richness of keeping that connection. I am inspired by David Reville's (2022, p 327) call for us to *'take madness back out into the community'*. Yet there is more that we can do.

The second undoing, according to LeFrançois (2015), is that mad studies is in danger of being White mad studies unless those of us involved in its development continuously aim to decentre Whiteness. LeFrançois argues that unless mad studies attends to both of these concerns, it will be 'undone'. Beresford (2020) agrees, and calls for mad studies to engage with scholars and activists in the Global South and Indigenous people on their terms. Mad studies is taught mostly in English-speaking countries in the Global North. Most writers and activists I know of are White and live in the Global North. However, it is racialised people and Indigenous people who experience the worst of the mental health system in these countries. For example, in the United Kingdom, Black people experience higher rates of detention, diagnoses of serious mental health issues and forced treatment (Gilroy, 2019). Activists and scholars such as Raza Griffiths (2018), Jayasree Kalathil (2013) and Colin King (2022) have pointed out the problems of survivor activism that centres White activism. Gorman et al (2013) wrote their *Mad People of Colour: A Manifesto* because the *'racism, sexism and oppression circulating in the system are also circulating in the mad movement'* (Gorman et al, 2013, p 1). Despite a growing awareness of the need for anti-racist action within mad people's activism and mad studies, Whiteness is still dominant. And the activism of Mad People of Colour has been sidelined and forgotten (Kalathil, 2013). Indeed:

> Knowledge producers who are not BME service users must better recognise the value of the knowledge that BME service users produce. They should also develop greater self-reflexivity around their own knowledge production in terms of White privilege, Eurocentrism, sanism and other biases that disempower BME service users and strive to work with BME service users to correct these blind spots.
>
> (Griffiths, 2018, p 7)

Mad studies needs to work against societal and systemic racism, and within mental health services as well as within survivor activism. We also need to look beyond the Global North.

Mad studies: possibilities for anti-racist teaching

While Queen Margaret University is a small university in Scotland, the MSc is an international course offered both on campus and online to an increasingly wide geographic spread. We currently have students from all over the United Kingdom, as well as from Canada and Australia. In comparison, the students on the Mad People's History and Identity course are all local because of the funding coming from the local NHS board, NHS Lothian. As reflected in our student body, a lot of the writing on decentring Whiteness in mad studies is also written by people in Canada, Australia and Aotearoa New Zealand. We have to bear in mind that the context in Scotland is different, and we must explore what this means in terms of anti-racist education.

I write this from my perspective as a White Irish woman who came to Scotland in the early 1990s. I wanted to believe that both Ireland and Scotland were better than England and the United States when it came to racism. I wanted to believe that we were both victims of empire and of prejudice and so could not be perpetrators of racism and colonialism. However, I was constantly being challenged in these beliefs. For example, when I read *Don't Touch My Hair* by Emma Dabiri (2019), a Black Irish writer, I got upset at her description of racism growing up in Ireland. This was a very visceral reaction, which shocked me in its intensity. She challenged my fantasy, of which I was only vaguely aware, that somehow my own country was better than England or America. Since then, I have sought out material that challenges and complicates this assumption.

Teaching in Scotland means I must pay attention to how racism operates here in our society as a whole, and how that affects me and my complicity in it as a person, as a mad activist and as an educator. The idea that racism is 'not a problem here' is increasingly being challenged in Scotland. I want to be part of that challenge, and to do that I find myself listening and reading to the perspectives from a variety of places and spaces. Supporting the students in their developing understanding of to how address racism is core to mad studies. We assign some readings that address this, such as those by Bhargavi Davar (2016), Gorman et al (2013), Raza Griffiths (2018), Jayasree Kalathil (2013) and Colin King (2022).

As we begin to attract students from beyond the United Kingdom, we look forward to having our knowledge and awareness expanded. We also seek out mad studies scholarship that 'de-provincialises' our European-based epistemology (Mbembe, 2015). Achille Mbembe criticises Western epistemic traditions for *'claim[ing] detachment of the known from the knower'*, which aligns with mad studies. We too claim that this 'objectivity' is bogus. We challenge the Western split between reason and nature. Mad studies enacts situated knowledge (Haraway, 1998) and standpoint theory (Harding, 2004) and places the insider within knowledge (Hill Collins, 1986). We have a lot to gain from looking beyond where we are situated within the Western framework of knowledge.

Colin King (2022, p 353) has a vision of mad studies that could *'contribute to the decolonisation of the hegemonic power of Whiteness'*. There can be pushback, so we are clear that this is not about 'shaming people for being White', but an honest acknowledgement of what has happened to the meaning of Whiteness and how it continues to impact on us all. Being open to these ideas and to new scholarship, even if I do not use it directly in my teaching, keeps me fresh and engaged.

All the students I have met through MPHI and the MSc are mature students, with a wealth of life experiences and previous activism and intellectual work. However, the vast majority have been White and have grown up in the United Kingdom. There can be a range of previous knowledge and thinking about race, which can lead to tensions; I need to work with these. I am focused on how I can make sure everyone can learn. How can I support someone to develop their awareness and knowledge of how insidious racism is in society and challenge their own racism? How can I do that without shaming that person? And how can I do it without making the classroom unsafe for students of colour? I have no easy answers to this. My experience so far is with people who are ignorant but willing, at least to some degree, to be challenged and to change their minds.

So far, I have not had to deal with a student who is so immersed in racism that I would need to ask them to leave the room or take disciplinary action. On the whole, students are very keen to engage with these perspectives. They see the relevance and importance of talking about race. Indeed, some students are more informed and knowledgeable than I am – for example, on abolitionism – and this enriches our shared educational experience. My responsibility as an educator is to manage any tension that may arise in classroom discussions, and to support all my students while also learning from my own and their mistakes.

In my teaching, I make the connection between colonialism and psychiatry (Eromosele, 2022) about the whole concept of the way in which rationality marginalised not just mad people but also non-mad marginalised people – based on a concept of a White, upper-class, able-bodied male accepted as standard. And some attempts at redressing the balance – for example, through women's suffrage – inconsiderably threw people of colour and mad people under the bus. Bruce (2017, p 304) notes that *'any critical investigation of madness and modernity must confront the matters of Blackness and antiBlackness in the foundation of modern Reason'*. Indeed, he observes that: *'The fact is that far more modern violence has been perpetrated under the aegis of Reason than committed by rogue madmen and madwomen'* (Bruce, 2017, p 307). Students generally respond well to this argument; however, one problem I have come across – and not just in the mad studies classroom but in mad activism generally – is the idea that there is an equivalence of oppression between mad people and Black people. I find this really difficult to challenge in a useful way. By useful, I mean to be able to support a student to question this simplistic idea and not shut them down. Eromosele (2022) criticises many mad studies writers who conflate psychiatric oppression and colonisation. He describes it as:

> *a rhetorical move that gathers all psychiatrically oppressed individuals into a transnational, transcultural and transethnic (post) colonial*

> community. What this does is that it effectively erases the ways that both madness and psychiatric oppression are experienced differently
>
> (Eromosele, 2022, p 328)

I think one reason why this happens is because of a lack of understanding of what colonisation actually means – that is, it is not a simple metaphor for oppression. By applying colonisation to the oppression experienced by mad people, we are homogenising mad people and mad experiences. Another reason is that we focus on the familiar and assume that what 'we', as mostly White mad people in the Global North, experience as the norm as well as our forms of activism can apply in every context. They do not.

Another problematic trope is that in 'other cultures' people with experiences we consider mad are treated much better or much worse than they are in 'the West'. Many of us pick out poorly understood ideas – for example, that mad people are respected as shamans – as evidence against psychiatry's narrow conceptualisation of these experiences as individual, medical problems. This feeds into an exoticism that I challenge, both in the material I assign and in the classroom discussions. For this reason, I assign Bhargavi Davar's (2016) powerful chapter 'Alternatives or a Way of Life?', which complicates our simplistic views of how mental health is understood and responded to in India and asks what happens when Indian 'ways of life' are appropriated as alternative healing.

Of course, there is much more that I and the mad studies team could be doing. We are an all-White team, and the majority of our students are White. We need to hire more visiting lecturers of colour and encourage them to apply for future posts. We need to attract a wider range of students of colour as well. We must be particularly sensitive to issues that affect people of colour such as visa restrictions through the Prevent strategy. We also need to expand our readings to include more scholarship by mad people of colour – and their critiques of mad studies. We already make the connections between material conditions and madness.

However, I want to reach beyond narrow disciplinary boundaries – it helps that mad studies is so interdisciplinary at its roots. We look to the increasing scholarship coming from queer studies, critical race theory, geography and social work, which connects with the concerns of mad studies. As a scholar,

I try to engage with ideas and writing that do not seem directly relevant to my teaching – such as pre-colonial African history. Sometimes I will be surprised to find something that does connect very strongly to mad studies. But that is not the main reason why I seek this out. I want to broaden my intellectual development – continuing to learn is central to how I teach. Sometimes it can seem like a burden, like I am adding extra work – but I have found it deepens my work, both in my research and in the classroom. My reading adds new understandings, raises new questions and allows me to better appreciate the experiences of my students. Connecting with others doing similar work is vital. Not long after I joined Queen Margaret University as a member of staff, I went to a meeting called Decolonising Research, where I met people from other disciplines, some of whom have contributed to this book. Having this space has been very helpful in looking beyond my immediate workload and my field, to see what else is happening. The solidarity of being together is powerful. We are all focused on what we can do in this university at this time to challenge the White-centric nature of our own thinking, disciplines and practices as well as the university itself. We held a teach-out in the summer of 2022, coming together to raise the awareness of racism in education.

Conclusion

In this chapter, I have outlined what mad studies is and why it needs to be anti-racist. I have also explained how I try to teach it in ways that challenge racism and decentre Whiteness. I acknowledge that this is difficult, but it is essential work. From my position as a White person in a small Scottish university, my efforts are limited and incomplete. However, I continue to grow and develop in community with other educators at Queen Margaret University, and with mad studies scholars across the world. This work is ongoing and unceasing.

Reflective questions

- What is the importance of a working as a collective rather than doing this individually? Who around you is doing similar work? What is going on more widely in your workplace and beyond?

- What are the key issues in your field? Where does race fit – is it invisible?
- Who are you citing? What topics and concerns are you including? Whose knowledge matters?
- Where are the spaces in the current curriculum to include the perspectives and experiences of racialised people?
- Do you feel burdened by 'having to' do this work? Why? What can you do to lessen that sense of being burdened and to be better able to engage in the work?

Recommended reading

- Abdul, A (2020) Racism – the Threat to Our Mental Health. [online] Available at: www.theantiracisteducator.com/post/racism-the-threat-to-our-mental-health (accessed 20 January 2023).

  This blog post is necessary reading for understanding racism and mental health in a Scottish context.

- Davidson, N and Verdee, S (2017) Introduction. In Davidson, N, Liinpää, P, McBride, M and Virdee, S (2017). *No Problem Here: Racism in Scotland*. Edinburgh: Luath Press, pp 9–12.

  This short reading really challenges the idea that Scotland is not racist.

References

Armstrong, V and LeFrançois, B A (2021) Interrogating Mad Studies in the Academy. In Russo, J and Beresford, P (eds) The *Routledge International Handbook of Mad Studies* (pp 315–26). London: Routledge.

Ballantyne, E, Maclean, Collie, S, Deeming, L and Fraser, E (2019) Mad People's History and Identity. In Scandrett, E (ed) *Public Sociology as Educational Practice* (pp 25–36). Bristol: Policy Press.

Beresford, P (2020) 'Mad': Mad Studies and Advancing Inclusive Resistance. *Disability & Society*, 35(8): 1337–42

Beresford, P, Nettle, P and Wallcraft, J (2016) *From Mental Illness to a Social Model of Madness and Distress?: Exploring What Service Users Say*. London: Shaping and Lives and National Survivor User Network (NSUN)

Beresford, P and Russo, J (2022) *The Routledge International Handbook of Mad Studies*. London: Routledge.

Bruce, L (2017) *How to Go Mad Without Losing Your Mind: Madness and Black Radical Creativity*. Durham, NC: Duke University Press.

Church, K (2013) Making Madness Matter in Academic Practice. In LeFrancois B A, Menzies, R and Reaume, G (eds) *Mad Matters: A Critical Reader in Canadian Mad Studies* (pp 181–90). Toronto: Canadian Scholars Press.

Church, K (2015) 'It's Complicated': Blending Disability and Mad Studies in the Corporatising University. In Spandler, H, Anderson, J and Sapey, B (eds) *Madness, Distress and the Politics of Disablement* (pp 261–70). Bristol: Policy Press.

Costa, L (2014) *Mad Studies – What It Is and Why You Should Care*. London: Mad Studies Network. [online] Available at: https://madstudies2014.wordpress.com/2014/10/15/mad-studies-what-it-is-and-why-you-should-care-2 (accessed 20 January 2023).

Dabiri, E (2019) *Don't Touch My Hair*. Harmondsworth: Penguin.

Davar, B V (2016) Alternatives or a Way of Life? In Russo, J and Sweeney, A (eds) *Searching for a Rose Garden: Challenging Psychiatry, Fostering Mad Studies* (pp 14–19). Monmouth: PCCS Books.

Davidson, N, Liinpää, P, McBride, M and Virdee, S (2017) *No Problem Here: Racism in Scotland*. Edinburgh: Luath Press.

Eromosele, F (2022) Madness, Decolonisation and Mental Health Activism in Africa. In Beresford, P and Russo, J (eds) *The Routledge International Handbook of Mad Studies* (pp 327–39). London: Routledge.

Freire, P (2000 [1968]) *Pedagogy of the Oppressed*. New York: Continuum.

Gilroy, R (2019) Mental Health Detention Rate Over Four Times Higher for Black People. *Nursing Times*, 30 October. [online] Available at: www.nursingtimes.net/news/mental-health/mental-health-detention-rate-over-four-times-higher-for-Black-people-30-10-2019 (accessed 20 January 2023).

Gorman, R, saini, a, Tam, L, Udegbe, O and Usar, O (2013) Mad People of Color: A Manifesto. *Asylum*, 20(4): 27.

Griffiths, R (2018) *A Call for Social Justice: Creating Fairer Policy and Practice for Mental Health Service Users from Black and Minority Ethnic Communities.* London: Kindred Minds.

Haraway, D (1988) Situated Knowledges: The Science Question in Feminism and the Privilege of Partial Perspective. *Feminist Studies*, 14(3): 575–99.

Harding, S G (2004) Introduction: Standpoint Theory as a Site of Political, Philosophic and Scientific Debate. In Harding, S G (ed) *The Feminist Standpoint Theory Reader: Intellectual and Political Controversies* (pp 1–16). London: Routledge.

Hill Collins, P (1986) Learning from the Outsider Within: The Sociological Significance of Black Feminist Thought. *Social Problems,* 33(6): s14–32.

hooks, b (2003) *Teaching Community: A Pedagogy of Hope.* London: Routledge.

hooks, b (2014) *Teaching to Transgress*. London: Routledge.

Kalathil, J (2013) *Dancing to Our Own Tunes: Reassessing Black and Minority Ethnic Mental Health Service User Involvement.* London: National Survivor User Network and Catch-a-Fiya.

King, C (2022) Madness as a Term of Division, or Rejection. In Beresford, P and Russo, J (eds) *The Routledge International Handbook of Mad Studies* (pp 351–62). London: Routledge.

LeFrançois, B A (2015) Acknowledging the Past and Challenging the Present, in Contemplation of the Future: Some (Un)Doings of Mad Studies. *Making Sense of Mad Studies.* Durham University. [online] Available at: https://youtu.be/5An8Bf8CY6I (accessed 20 January 2023).

LeFrançois, B A, Menzies, R and Reaume, G (2013) *Mad Matters: A Critical Reader in Canadian Mad Studies.* Toronto: Canadian Scholars Press.

Mbembe, A (2015) Decolonizing Knowledge and the Question of the Archive. [online] Available at: https://wiser.wits.ac.za/system/files/Achille%20Mbembe%20-%20Decolonizing%20Knowledge%20and%20the%20Question%20of%20the%20Archive.pdf (accessed 20 January 2023).

O'Donnell, A and Maclean, K (2019) Reclaiming Agency Through Oor Mad History. In Gijbels, H, Sapouna, L and Sidley, G (eds) *Inside Out and Outside In: Alternatives to Mainstream Mental Health Services* (pp 245–60). Monmouth: PCCS Books.

Reville, D (2013) Is Mad Studies Emerging as a New Field of Inquiry? In LeFrancois, B A, Menzies, R and Reaume, G (eds) *Mad Matters: A Critical Reader in Canadian Mad Studies* (pp 170–80). Toronto: Canadian Scholars Press.

Reville, D (2022) Taking Mad Studies Back Out into the Community. In Beresford, P and Russo, J (eds) *The Routledge International Handbook of Mad Studies* (pp 307–14). London: Routledge.

Sapouna, L and O'Donnell, A (2017) 'Madness' and Activism in Ireland and Scotland: A Dialogue. *Community Development Journal*, 52(3): 524–34.

Spandler, H and, Poursanidou, D (2019) Who is Included in the Mad Studies Project? *The Journal of Ethics in Mental Health*, 10. [online] Available at: http://clok.uclan.ac.uk/23384 (accessed 23 February 2023).

Sweeney, A (2016) Why Mad Studies Needs Survivor Research and Survivor Research Needs Mad Studies. *Intersectionalities*, 5(3): 36–61.

CHAPTER 12

IMAGINING DEFRAGMENTED UNIVERSITY SPACES

Arek Dakessian, Anthony Ataekong, Joy Owojuyigbe, Olutayo Burrows, Misbah Haqani, MD Rezaur Rahman and Georgina Pearson

Introduction

This chapter was co-authored with members of the student cohort of 2021–22. It is worth reflecting, even briefly, on the importance of writing with students: as academics, whether we like to admit it or not, we have already – to varying extents – been socialised into the everyday exclusions and discriminations of the UK university system. The everyday policing of international students, for instance, has already unfortunately been normalised to some extent in our everyday lives. So precisely because, as academics, we have worked our way to successful (even if somewhat precarious) employment at UK universities, our structurally privileged positions mean we are perhaps no longer as sensitised to some of the extant power dynamics and subjectivations of UK university spaces. Our student co-authors, by contrast, have not been. For reasons too numerous and complex to fully consider within the confines of this chapter, including the incisive clarity that their positions as students afford them on such matters, their co-authorship is fundamental to any reflection on anti-racist education. Upon receiving the co-editors' generous and caring agreement, then, we invited our student cohort to co-author this chapter. We set up a shared iCloud folder in which we minuted our wide and varied discussions over the next six months and shared writing with each other, as well as a WhatsApp group where we coordinated meeting times, and in this way arrived at this chapter.

We have organised the chapter along the same lines as our discussions played out. We began by asking questions to which we wanted to find answers: What are we trying to achieve through anti-racism? Who are the beneficiaries of such a project? What can be achieved through anti-racism? How do we deal with anti-racism's necessary extension beyond university spaces into the national and global? How do we navigate anti-racism's close association with identities (eg minorities) when we conceive it as having *something to teach the one race to which we all belong* (Appiah, 1992, p 27)? We wanted our chapter to identify specific problems and propose specific practical solutions. But we were also mindful that even as we stood on the shoulders of giants, inspired by those fellow humans past and present who have dedicated their lives to anti-racist projects, our contribution would at best amount to a humble raindrop in the ocean. Below, we show the cycle of our reflections and conversations: reckoning with the world in which anti-racism is embedded, grappling with the provocations of science and finding silver linings in defragmentations.

Positionality

It is important to begin by noting how we came together, as a group of faculty and students through a UK-based master's level teaching programme in Global Health. We have been grappling with questions on legacies of colonialism and imperialism, on hierarchies of power, representation, voice and activism within this largely ill-defined field of global health. These legacies are not just a passive infrastructure that we inherit, but rather a part of our present, reproduced through institutions and discourse and rhetoric. Reflecting on our own positionality, we could consider our individual (geographical, epistemological, professional) backgrounds and identities in a way that mirrors the categories defining the status of groups and individuals that we are forced to interrogate in our quest to understand our own positionality: 'student', 'staff', 'home', 'international'. We are staff and students, teachers and learners, researchers and researched, North and South, practitioner and activist – for many, both at the same time.

In teaching the history of global health, we often talk of the trajectory from tropical medicine to international health to global health, and the changing influences of various institutions that govern to a greater or lesser extent. Global health represents an evolution, a change in direction shaped by processes of globalisation, post-globalisation, and shifting economic and political orders. But it also presents a moral gloss – a more neutral term that recognises a shift from structures of thinking around unilateral flows of aid, knowledge and discourse from higher-income to lower-income settings to a consideration of multiple bilateral flows, and nationally led agendas and initiatives. But while the nomenclature and phraseology change, the hierarchies of power remain (Abimbola et al, 2021). Being in an institution in the Global North raises questions on the multiple disconnects between where institutions of global health are situated, where the focus of study is, and where students of global health are coming from. As raised in one of our discussions, when students travel across continents to study global health, and receive an education steeped in its own colonial roots, it begs the question of where one can study an 'anti-colonial global health'.

Reckonings

The first step in reflecting on the possibilities of anti-racist education in UK universities is to locate the project within the standpoint and situated experience of a student, including international students – some of whose nationalities were not too long ago considered 'high risk' by the institutions governing the terms of their studentships. UK revenue from higher education-related 'exports' grew by 26 per cent from 2010 to 2016, contributing an estimated £19.9 billion (Department for Education, 2019). In this period, fee income from EU students rose by 133 per cent (a £4.6 billion increase) and that from non-EU students by 68 per cent (a staggering £18 billion increase) (Department for Education, 2019, p 5). According to the National Audit Office (2017), a three-year university education leaves the UK home student (something only one in four 18-year-olds from the most disadvantaged backgrounds can call themselves) with an average debt of £50,000. And with 87 out of the 90 'top' institutions charging the maximum permissible tuition fee of £9000 per year in 2016/17, only 32 per cent of undergraduate students from England considered their courses to offer value for money in 2017, a sharp decrease from the 50 per cent of 2012. It is also worth noting that international students have outnumbered home students in the United Kingdom since 2016/17 (HESA, 2022). There is added complexity post-Brexit. In Scotland, between 2007/08 and 2020/21, EU undergraduate students on eligible courses were entitled to a tuition fee waiver (supported through Students Award Agency Scotland). Since Brexit, this has been withdrawn and EU students are no longer eligible for home fees or Scottish Government funding; they are classed as international students, which carries implications for both fees and visas (see Scottish Government, 2022).

While ostensibly not directly relevant to a discussion on the possibilities of anti-racist education in UK universities, these figures nonetheless give a sense of the systemically extractive structuring backdrop against which staff–student relationships – those same relationships that *do* anti-racism – play out in everyday life. These systemic racisms are worth laying out here as they are infrastructural to any anti-racist relationship: since the mid-2010s, staff at UK universities have been required by the British government to register attendance in classrooms not for pedagogic purposes but simply to police international student visa compliance. This leads to a two-tiered attendance system where for some non-attendance could lead to a withdrawal of their student visa, while for others it has no implications. International students today are required to 'tap in' to campus with their smartcards, in the most recent expansion of the human and-non-human assemblages that uphold the everyday racisms of UK university studentship. That the key distinguishing feature in these requirements is nothing but the different pieces of paper that legislate the presence of human beings in classrooms is an inherently racist practice of everyday bordering (Yuval-Davis et al, 2018) that gives those doing the work of bordering no choice but to comply (lest the educators themselves be found in breach).

The point of departure for any reflection on the possibilities of anti-racist education in UK universities, then, is a reckoning with the systemic racisms that preclude, predicate and thus already compromise any possible anti-racist relationship. Put differently, with the intention of (1) displacing all reduction (in the words of Martiniquan poet and philosopher Edouard Glissant (1997, p 190), the likes of whose marginalisation from curricula we engage with below) and (2) distancing our discussions from the metaphorisations of decolonisation that Tuck and Yang (2012) warn us against: the point of departure for any reflection on the possibilities of anti-racist education in the United Kingdom must necessarily be a reckoning with the inherently racist nation-state systems or prerogatives in which higher education is embedded.

'Sciences'

The core problem with statistics such as that regarding value-for-money degrees – apart from the prevalence of the much-criticised marketised clientelist language that such figures draw upon (eg Molesworth et al, 2011) – is the slippage between the education premium-paying students expect to receive and the education they do receive. During the meetings in which we developed this chapter, our discussions always to some extent problematised knowledge production's discursive upholding and perpetuation of racisms and other exclusions throughout history. This is the kind of orientation sometimes called 'anti-social science' because of its incisive challenges to what constitutes scientific knowledge. Jacques Rancière's oeuvre forms part of this tradition, not least through his insightful questioning of the seminal correlation Bourdieu found between people's tastes and their place in the social order in *The Philosopher and His Poor* (Rancière, 2004), where he argues that such social scientific accounts serve to maintain the status quo much more than they actually explain the social world. Willem Schinkel's (2013, 2017, 2018, 2019; Boersma and Schinkel, 2018) extensive and substantive critique of integration also forms part of this tradition. Among the multitude of provocative illustrations that Schinkel contributes to integration research, we pick here his problematisation of the distinction in integration between first-, second- and third-generation migrants for its relevance to what we teach at our institutions. Schinkel (2013, p 1156) argues: '*This ... is something of a paradox, as second-generation immigrants have not immigrated.*' Here he is taking issue with racisms and exclusions that pass as 'science'. There is a slight irony that such an orientation is often referred to as anti-social science when its project is to root social scientific knowledge production more rigorously in science.

With this commitment to rigour in what presents as scientific, anti-racist education becomes not only a form of activism but an academic pursuit of correction. In our own classrooms, this has led to a consistent questioning of the global health programme we offer, not least its upholding of such problematic categories as 'Global South', 'low and middle income', 'fragile' and 'hard to reach.' These don't just evacuate history and metaphorise the 'global' in global health; considered in the light of the possibilities for anti-racist education, they also erode trust in the educational relationship. How can students trust that the education for which they pay a premium, for which they subject their bodies to constant surveillance, and that impels them to engage critically and rigorously and scientifically, has itself engaged critically and rigorously with its own colonial and imperial underpinnings?

The question is not about cancelling or cancel culture as is often reported, but rather about a broad and uncomfortable – though necessary – reckoning as a precondition for trust that can and should be localised across disciplinary boundaries. In sociology, we might ask what is at stake, and for whom, when the very same Max Weber (2011) who warned of *'African and Asiatic savages'* in 1917 is considered a founding father of the discipline in classrooms full of 'African and Asiatic' international students (Allen, 2004, p 6)? This is neither a call to 'cancel' Weber nor a desire to question his status as a founding father of sociology; rather, it is a wish to take issue with the pervasive and convenient sweeping aside of such racist articulations in contexts where a commitment to rigour should ostensibly outweigh convenience. Students are asked to justify, explain, elaborate and critically engage with their research choices and decisions, but the courtesy of justifying, elaborating and critically engaging with the disenfranchising discriminations of disciplinary foundations is not always reciprocated. A common retort to challenges such as these is that such language 'was not uncommon at the time'. Yet, to us at least, this retort is reminiscent of an Arabic axiom, 'an excuse that's worse than the crime itself', because it looks at then willingly sees past the problem at hand. To be clear: that White supremacist views pervaded the history of the West is not the problem here; the metaphorisation of the project of reckoning with its continued pervasiveness in the academy today is.

(De)fragmentations

Who, then, decides what the premium-paying, surveillance-accepting, debt-laden student is expected to learn? On whose shoulders rests the impossible responsibility of upholding in the educational space the violence and one-directionality of the civilising process? It is from these questions (which begged themselves in light of our discussions described above) that we arrived at the final reflective frontier. Citing John Thompson's critique of Bourdieu, Kwame Anthony Appiah (1992, p 179) argues:

> It may be a mistake to think that social reproduction – the processes by which societies maintain themselves over time – presupposes 'some sort of consensus with regard to dominant values or norms'. Rather, the stability of today's industrialized society may require 'a pervasive fragmentation of the social order and a proliferation of divisions between its members'. For it is precisely this fragmentation that prevents oppositional attitudes from generating 'a coherent alternative view which would provide a basis for political action'.

The argument is foundational to any critical orientation, including that of anti-racism. The rigidity of boundaries between educator and educated that upholds in education the one-directionality of the civilising process inheres to the somewhat normalised impositions of the status quo, undermining possibilities for anti-racist education. Indeed, at the level of embodied, situated experience there is no fragmentation. As students and staff, we both grapple with the racisms, discriminations and alterities of the world we inhabit and the world as it is bordered, however geographically near or far they may be; we both find inspiration in each other's navigations, the moral commitments that drive them and the knowledges that they produce – no matter how marginal these may be. We do not teach and learn on a binary; we teach each other across the differential affordances of the structural positions we occupy.

And here we must confront the uncomfortable truth that, as staff occupying structural positions of power, we simply must do better. Rampant student solidarity with staff in industrial disputes compares somewhat uncomfortably with the paucity of staff responses to the everyday borderings and racialisations of student bodies, for instance. We might well be outraged at the requirement to police student presence on campuses and in classrooms, but our outrage has been somewhat muted. Without taking a paternalistic stance on our responsibilities here, the fact remains that the educational experience is the responsibility of academic staff, not students. Taking this responsibility seriously requires a critical engagement with institutional silences and the picking of political battles because the moral commitment to the equality of all human beings espoused by anti-racist orientations in education is not a political contingency but an ontological torsion that we must right.

The relationships between staff and students are rendered increasingly precarious by the racisms of the world, including those of the academy. These prosper through the pervasive fragmentations that they are predicated on, such that everyone is assigned a hierarchical position within the status quo – a contingent equality. Against these constraints, our attempt in this chapter – and indeed in our discussions – has been to illuminate possibilities for a defragmented world, *'generous, tolerant, benevolent and reassuring'* (Caduff, 2019, p 788). These possibilities only come into view if premised on the acknowledgement of the axiomatic equality of everybody to everybody.

This equality is palpable in those unplanned, random moments when we grapple with the racisms of the world together, revealing them as the collective problems of all people, and that must be tackled by all. They are further manifest in the unrelenting collective attempts to escape disciplinary and identitarian silos irrespective of social location within systems of power. The moral clarity/commitment that has informed and forged solidarities demands uncomfortable reflections (Pillow, 2003; see also Johnson, 2020), profoundly placed at the heart of all our work here and forming the driving force of any and all anti-racist undertakings. With this acknowledgement of equality and moral commitment towards restoring it, we envision an education that paves the way to annihilate the many divisions and alterities of our world. That, in all its enormous simplicity, is the project.

Reflective questions

- In light of structural barriers undermining the possibilities for anti-racist education, how can anti-racist educational practice undermine structural barriers in return?
- What does an anti-racist curriculum look like? In global health and other disciplines?
- How might we move university spaces from bordering subjects to nurturing learning?

Recommended reading

- Johnson, A (2019) Throwing Our Bodies Against the White Background of Academic. *Area*, 52(1): 89–96.
- Lorde, A (1997) The Uses of Anger. *Women's Studies Quarterly*, 25(1/2): 278–85.
- Pelletier, C (2009) Rancière and the Poetics of the Social Sciences. *International Journal of Research & Method in Education*, 32(3): 267–84.

References

Abimbola, S, Asthana, S, Montenegro, C, Guinto, R R, Jumbam, D T, Louskieter, L, Kabubei, K M, Munshi, S, Muraya, K, Okumu, F, Saha, S, Saluja, D and Pai, M (2021) Addressing Power Asymmetries in Global Health: Imperatives in the Wake of the COVID-19 Pandemic. *PLoS Medicine*, 18(4): e1003604.

Allen, K (2004) *Max Weber: A Critical Introduction*. London: Pluto Press.

Appiah, K A (1992) In My Father's House. *Africa in the Philosophy of Culture*. Oxford: Oxford University Press.

Boersma, S and Schinkel, W (2018) Imaginaries of Postponed Arrival: On Seeing 'Society' and its 'Immigrants'. *Cultural Studies*, 32(2): 308–25.

Caduff, C (2019) Hot Chocolate. *Critical Inquiry*, 45(3): 787–803.

Department for Education (2019) UK Revenue from Education Related Exports and Transnational Education Activity in 2016. [online] Available at: https://assets.publishing.service.gov.uk/government/uploads/system/uploads/attachment_data/file/773167/SFR_Education_Exports_2016.pdf (accessed 23 February 2023).

Glissant, É (1997) *Poetics of Relation*. Ann Arbor, MI: University of Michigan Press

Higher Education Statistics Agency (HESA) (2022) Where Do HE Students Come From? [online] Available at: www.hesa.ac.uk/data-and-analysis/students/where-from (accessed 23 February 2023).

Johnson, A (2020) Throwing Our Bodies Against the White Background of Academia. *Area*, 52(1): 89–96.

Molesworth, M, Scullion, R and Nixon, E (2011) *The Marketisation of Higher Education and the Student as Consumer*. New York: Routledge.

National Audit Office (2017) *The Higher Education Market*. [online] Available at: www.nao.org.uk/wp-content/uploads/2017/12/The-higher-education-market.pdf (accessed 23 February 2023).

Pillow, W (2003) Confession, Catharsis, or Cure? Rethinking the Uses of Reflexivity as Methodological Power in Qualitative Research. *International Journal of Qualitative Studies in Education*, 16(2): 175–96.

Rancière, J (2004) *The Philosopher and His Poor*. Durham, NC: Duke University Press.

Schinkel, W (2013) The Imagination of 'Society' in Measurements of Immigrant Integration. *Ethnic and Racial Studies*, 36(7): 1142–61.

Schinkel, W (2017) *Imagined Societies: A Critique of Immigrant Integration in Western Europe*. New York: Cambridge University Press.

Schinkel, W (2018) Against 'Immigrant Integration': For an End to Neocolonial Knowledge Production. *Comparative Migration Studies*, 6(31). [online] Available at: https://comparativemigrationstudies.springeropen.com/articles/10.1186/s40878-018-0095-1 (accessed 23 February 2023).

Schinkel, W (2019) Migration Studies: An Imposition. *Comparative Migration Studies*, 7(32). [online] Available at: https://comparativemigrationstudies.springeropen.com/articles/10.1186/s40878-019-0136-4 (accessed 23 February 2023).

Scottish Government (2022) Total Costs of Educating EU Students in Scotland: FOI Release. [online] Available at: www.gov.scot/publications/foi-202200282430 (accessed 23 February 2023).

Tuck, E and Yang, K W (2012) Decolonization is Not a Metaphor. *Decolonization: Indigeneity, Education & Society*, 1(1): 1–40.

Weber, M (2011 [1917]) *The Methodology of the Social Sciences*. London: Routledge.

Yuval-Davis, N, Wemyss, G and Cassidy, K (2018) Everyday Bordering, Belonging and the Reorientation of British Immigration Legislation. *Sociology*, 52(2): 228–44.

CHAPTER 13

CRITICAL CONVERSATIONS ON DECOLONISING THE PHYSIOTHERAPY CURRICULUM

Kavi C Jagadamma, Judith Lane and Jane Culpan

Introduction

This chapter discusses the journeys of three academics in physiotherapy from different backgrounds in their campaign of anti-racist action. We describe our shared struggle to identify and subjugate the impact of coloniality on the physiotherapy curriculum. As a transformative campaign, decolonising the physiotherapy profession and curriculum is still in its early stages. We all had different reasons to engage in this campaign, different starting points and different challenges. In this chapter, we explore our growing understanding of coloniality in physiotherapy by reflecting on our own motivation and learning. Drawing from our experience, we also provide our readers with suggestions for personal action they could take to understand and challenge coloniality.

Where we started

We each entered this campaign with different motivations. We brought together our disorienting dilemmas (Mezirow, 1991) for the first time when each of us decided to do a lightning talk on decolonising curriculum at our university (Lane et al, 2022). As explained by Mezirow (1975, p 7), a disorienting dilemma is a *'developmental challenge'* or *'life crisis'* that challenges one's *'embedded beliefs'*. Judith's disorienting dilemma arose from her doubt about her own credibility to facilitate anti-discriminatory and anti-racist discussions – what right did she have as a Scottish, White, middle-class woman to speak of such issues? When speaking to a class of mainly White, middle-class young people, how could they connect with the healthcare experiences of people from Black and minority ethnic communities? Kavi's disorienting dilemma arose through a realisation that he had perceived himself as 'moving up the ladder' when moving from India to become an academic in the United Kingdom. Over time, conversations and reflections uncovered deeply rooted biases and beliefs influenced by the coloniality that permeated his cultural and educational upbringing. Jane's dilemmas resonated with Kavi's, as she realised her choice of physiotherapy as a career direction in Aotearoa New Zealand had been influenced by its status within the hierarchy of Western health professions. Her discomfort was reinforced by growing difficulties in reconciling practices within the physiotherapy profession and the needs of people from diverse backgrounds.

A common factor linking our disorienting dilemmas is our increasing awareness of the othering of knowledge and experience within the physiotherapy profession, while at the same time recognising international drivers for person-centred practice (House of Commons, 2014; World Health Organization, 2016). There are many views on what person-centred care means, and how person-centred practice is enacted. McCormack et al (2021) identify person-centred practice as a movement that focuses on humanising health services and establishes the patient/client at the centre of care. With much more focus on all persons involved in the care and organisational culture that enables person-centred practice, we align ourselves with the following definition.

> *An approach to practice established through the formation and fostering of healthful relationships between all care providers, service users and others significant to them in their lives. It is underpinned by values of respect for persons, individual right to self-determination, mutual respect and understanding. It is enabled by cultures of empowerment that foster continuous approaches to practice development.*
>
> (McCormack et al, 2013, p 193)

Person-centred practice is rooted in humanistic principles (McCormack et al, 2021). Humanising healthcare through person-centred approaches relies on holistic care and respect for persons. Coming from a decolonising perspective, we believe that it is not possible to enact person-centredness in physiotherapy when professional education and practice in the United Kingdom are underpinned solely by Eurocentric knowledge, principles and values. As academics, we are faced with the question of how it is possible to humanise healthcare (and physiotherapy in particular) without accepting the plurality of knowledge?

Being and becoming a physiotherapist

The UK Standards of Proficiency state that physiotherapists must not engage in discriminatory behaviours (Health and Care Professions Council, 2022) and as physiotherapy lecturers we have a responsibility to promote anti-racist and anti-discriminatory practice. In 2021, the UK professional body for physiotherapy, the Chartered Society of Physiotherapy (CSP), launched its Equality, Diversity and Belonging Strategy, which acknowledges the power imbalances in society and outlines its aim to *'create a profession that reflects the diversity in society'* (Chartered Society of Physiotherapy, 2021, p 6). The CSP also acknowledged the need for education of members to make sure that diversity is valued within the profession.

In our higher education institution, the physiotherapy student body is predominantly White and female, reflecting research showing that physiotherapy is perceived to be a 'White' profession (Naidoo et al, 2021; Yeowell, 2013). When students from Black and minority ethnic backgrounds do enter physiotherapy education, many report that they must work harder to demonstrate those characteristics that they feel are part of the physiotherapy persona (Hammond et al, 2019). Vazir et al (2019) have described how students felt the need to 'act' White to be assimilated into the physiotherapy profession. It seems that decolonising physiotherapy requires us to go beyond ensuring that the profession reflects the diversity in society (Naidoo et al, 2021). Consequently, physiotherapy needs to question what factors influence the 'becoming' of a physiotherapist and what it means to 'be' a physiotherapist.

Unlike some other healthcare professions, physiotherapy traditionally has paid little attention to concepts of being and becoming from either personal or professional perspectives. An internet search for *'being and becoming AND physiotherapy'* revealed many websites explaining the academic skills needed to be a physiotherapist, but none talking about what it means to be a physiotherapist. Understanding what is meant by the culture in physiotherapy seems to be implicit. Students in the studies by Hammond et al (2019) and Vazir et al (2019) reinforced this when they talked about the difficulties in assimilating into a profession that seemed to value specific personal characteristics that potentially were at odds with their cultural background. At our institution, we no longer interview prospective students for our programmes because of the inherent bias present in the interview process, which tends to disadvantage underrepresented groups and particularly Black and minority ethnic groups. All three of us have, at some point in our professional career, had discussions with physiotherapy clinicians who have felt that interviewing is essential to get the 'right' students and to reject those who do not possess the desired personal characteristics. Furthermore, we have all had conversations with students about how to 'act' as a physiotherapist (Vazir et al, 2019) to satisfy expectations of certain practice educators. Chambers (2012) describes this as *'learning to play the game by adjusting my performances... to get in, fit in and get through'*. This idea of the 'model physiotherapist' presents yet another challenge in our struggle to understand how we can develop anti-racist actions in physiotherapy education.

Reflecting on how these 'norms' of the 'model physiotherapist' are developed leads us to consider what students learn and assimilate rather than what is planned into the curriculum. As Gilborn (2005, p 485) puts it, *'although race inequity may not be a planned and deliberate goal of education policy, neither is it accidental'*. This resonates with the approach taken to the physiotherapy curriculum in the West. While the profession and formal curriculum have inclusivity as an intention, the latter is not intentionally considered with an anti-racism lens, and the impacts of the informal and hidden curriculum are neglected. Concepts of the informal and hidden curriculum contrast with the intended learning with what students learn in other ways during their studies. This includes implicit aspects of the profession such as *'organizational systems, workplace cultures, power dynamics and professional behaviours'* (Barradell, 2017, p 443). In the context of medical education, Hafferty (1998) maintains that in fact most student learning is gained from the hidden curriculum.

We have therefore come to an understanding that decolonising physiotherapy requires a deeper review of its history as well as analysis of the canons of knowledge that underpin the profession. This may cast light on the implicit facets of the physiotherapy discipline which are perpetuated unintentionally.

A brief history of physiotherapy and canons of knowledge

One definition of 'canon' in this context is *'a body of principles, rules, standards, or norms'* (Meriam-Webster, 2022). We are on a journey of exploring canons of knowledge and ideologies within physiotherapy. While it is not possible within the scope of this chapter to explore the breadth of canons and ideologies, here we want to illustrate some examples to show our growing understanding of the area.

It is argued that the canons of knowledge or ideologies informing physiotherapy practice were codified for the first time with the formation of the Society of Trained Masseuses (STM), which later became the Chartered Society of Physiotherapy. In 1894, the formation of the STM was achieved *'by nurses wanting to protect their profession after stories in the press warn young nurses and the public of unscrupulous people offering massage as a euphemism for other services'* (Chartered Society of Physiotherapy, 2020). After the four founders, Misses (Mary) Rosalind Paget, Lucy Robinson, Elizabeth Anne Manley and Mrs Margaret Palmer, formally established the STM, they developed a curriculum and professional code of conduct. In an analysis of the conditions and influences prevalent at the time, Nicholls and Cheek (2006) suggest that some of the core ideologies for the 'new' STM profession continue to resonate and inform physiotherapy practice today. A biomechanical view of the body was seen as necessary for the establishment of the STM, to both remove any intimation of sensuality or sexual response to treatment and to gain the approval of the medical association for professional recognition. This continues to be a core construct of the curriculum (Nicholls, 2018). As fundamental as it remains, the idea of the body-as-machine also contributes to dehumanising physiotherapy practice, preventing practitioners from seeing people holistically, or being able to *'hand over the power of decision making to our patients and communities'* (Nicholls, 2018, p 139).

Modern physiotherapy curricula are changing and there are educators and academics addressing the dehumanising dominance of the biomedical view of the body-as-machine (Barradell, 2017; Hammond, 2013; Nicholls and Larmer, 2005; Nicholls et al, 2009; Nicholls, 2018). Despite this, there remains a lack of widespread support in addressing alternative epistemologies within physiotherapy practice (Mescouto et al, 2022; Shaw and

DeForge, 2012). This is exacerbated by an ongoing dominance of biomedical views perpetuated through informal and hidden curricula. This is not dissimilar to the challenges in the medical curriculum, heavily influenced by supporters of biomedicine who reject other views as lacking an evidence base. In their attempt to decolonise medical education, Wong et al (2021, p 1) identified the epistemic dominance of biomedicine and advocate for '*epistemic pluralism*'. Shaw and Deforge (2012) argue that physiotherapy is ontologically complex, and practice requires multiple ways of knowing (epistemic pluralism). This deeper, more explicit exploration of epistemologies underpinning the physiotherapy practice is, however, lacking in the literature (Edwards and Richardson, 2008).

We advocate for an in-depth analysis of epistemologies underpinning physiotherapy and canons of knowledge. This will involve sustained work over time. One example comes from our personal journey, and a realisation that our physiotherapy education conditioned us to see particular bodies as the ideal normal. Key textbooks such as that by Kendall et al (2005) provide detailed drawings and photographs of healthy, athletic, White men and women. These images do not represent the range of body shapes of people that we see in practice, but they tell us what normal, good or perfect postural alignment should look like. We did not understand the 'standing-at-attention' military influences conveyed by these representations. We understand now that this posture was an idealised form. This was rooted in medical science and the social and cultural concerns of the late nineteenth and early twentieth centuries, when posture became the '*litmus test for the healthy modern body of the perfect citizen*' (Gilman, 2014, p 57; Kripa and Kaur, 2021; Slater et al, 2019; Smythe and Jivanjee, 2021). With increasing awareness of these Eurocentric biases and cynicism about the biomechanical model (Lederman, 2011), we find ourselves questioning some of the traditional physiotherapy practices they underpin (Mintken et al, 2018).

Some may argue that these are examples of unintended discrimination rather than intentional racism, that these practices are simply a product of their time and practice will evolve, in line with professional values and the developing evidence base. This view suggests that this is not a problem and explicit action is not required. Nicholls (2018, p 8) argues, however, that physiotherapists '*do not possess the necessary historical, philosophical, political, and socio-cultural vocabulary*' to describe ourselves. Without this, it is not possible to see the unintended impacts of our wider understanding of health on our tendency to focus on physical function. This means that a conscious effort is needed to decolonise the physiotherapy curriculum by identifying and dismantling racist practices and building a humanistic knowledge base to inform practice. To build our physiotherapy vocabulary and broaden our understandings of health, physiotherapy educators must do more than add a sociology or philosophy module to an already crowded curriculum. As advocated by our peers in South Africa, we suggest a careful consideration of what is needed to go '*beyond add-on or elective courses in the humanities and social sciences*' (Pentecost et al, 2018, p 222) and consider how these ideas might be integrated into our local curricula (Nicholls, 2018).

Planning a course of action

Following a disorienting dilemma and the resulting critical reflection, the sixth step in Mezirow's (1975) '10 phases of transformative learning' highlights the need for an action plan in order to effect change. Here we propose actions to further our campaign of anti-racist action in physiotherapy.

Reflecting on self and profession

Our 'disorienting dilemmas' highlight that the process of personal change is inherently destabilising. Judith's anxieties around 'credibility' to facilitate discussions on racism and discrimination within healthcare illustrate this point. We have all found value in the process of reflecting on our role in promoting an anti-racist curriculum and a key learning point for each of us has been acceptance of ourselves as neophytes. Our process of deep reflection has raised our awareness of how the profession privileges biomedical approaches, basing the development of professional knowledge on the rigorous application of the Socratic method of knowledge generation (Greenfield et al, 2015). Along with this have come binary narratives that fail to recognise other knowledge systems. All three of us received this classical 'scientific' education and have been professionally raised to believe in the power of positivist thinking. In contrast, person-centred approaches to practice demand a more humanistic view of knowledge generation. To resolve this dissonance, physiotherapy must explore the epistemic oppression that has shaped its knowledge base.

In doing so, physiotherapists must question all that has been taken for granted as significant and important in our practice. As Popova (2016, p 184) shows, you also need to ask yourself, *'What hidden lessons do I perpetuate as I teach and as I research?'*

Addressing the informal and hidden curriculum

In accordance with the UK Health and Care Professions Council (HCPC) Standards of Proficiency (HCPC, 2022), the majority of clinical and academic physiotherapists believe that their practice is non-discriminatory. However, this 'intention to include' does not necessarily result in a 'sense of belonging'. We have suggested that the informal and hidden curriculum fosters exclusive practices. It is therefore critical that the content of the informal and hidden curriculum is made more explicit if its impact is to be better understood. Webb et al (2022) evaluated the experiences of hidden curriculum on Black and minority ethnic students in health and social care programmes. Through focus groups, authors identified key themes around visibility of ethnicity, problematisation of lived experiences of Black and minority ethnic students, internalising of systemic problems affecting self-confidence and segregation between ethnic groups. While the focus of the study was to look at lived experiences of hidden curriculum on Black and minority ethnic students, the study also identified problematic representation of people of colour within the formal curriculum, where the Black and minority ethnic population was represented as *'poor and unhealthy'* (Webb et al, 2022, p 316). This is an example of an exploration of hidden curriculum and the experiences of people of colour. The scope of this research needs to be further developed to foster better understanding of how the messages perpetuated by educators unintentionally impact the formative views of all students towards diversity in terms of people, knowledge and ideologies.

Communicative action

We have argued that 'being and becoming' a physiotherapist is an inherently biased process, which tends to advantage the White, Western female and disadvantage minority groups. This arises not only through skewed representations of different groups within the profession, but also through the tacit public relations that underpin physiotherapy practice. Habermas's theory of communicative action offers a lens through which this can be achieved

(Trede, 2012). Habermas (1970) distinguishes 'knowledge-interest' into three areas: technical, practical and emancipatory. Links, Wilkinson and Campbell (2019, p 93) note that practical questions are *'communicative questions of human relationship, comparison, culture, and society'* which require interpretation. Emancipatory questions explore individual perspectives, involve the questioning of assumptions and are intended to bring about change or improvement. We posit that the application of communicative action theory could provide a useful process by which we can reflect on our professional practice and engage in meaningful anti-racist activism. Part of this process involves a commitment to learning the vocabulary necessary to engage in anti-racist discourse.

Accountable spaces

> *To move forward, we don't need to promise safety or expect bravery. We need to embrace accountability.*
>
> (Ahenkorah, 2020)

Our journey in understanding decolonising the curriculum and taking anti-racist action has led us to the brave spaces developed for social justice classrooms in the United States (Ali, 2017; Arao and Clemens, 2013). This is a concept that builds out of the divergent views of safe spaces being either places of refuge offering comfort for excluded or marginalised students, or places to hide from challenging or disagreeable views and perspectives (Ellison, 2016, cited in Grieve, 2016). However, language matters, and the use of the term 'brave spaces' acknowledges that one can never promise a safe space because any authentic dialogue required for learning involves risk and controversy. To promise otherwise is to avoid your responsibility as an educator. Learning environments, including classrooms and clinical placements, are challenging and students are expected to contribute. An educator's role is to facilitate that contribution and acknowledge the differing risks and challenges these spaces offer students, depending on their group membership and identity (Arao and Clemens, 2013).

In physiotherapy education, it is vital to have conversations that make explicit the hidden and informal curriculum, and that expose the exclusionary and racist spaces found within the profession and health service. Critical debates are necessary for our students to explore and develop more nuanced understandings of their identity (Hammond et al, 2019; Nightingale et al, 2022). We think these challenging conversations are better served by educators who can facilitate brave spaces – environments that acknowledge the challenges when attempting to have discussion around difficult topics such as race, power and privilege, where respect, trust, compassion, humility and forgiveness are essential (Arao and Clemens, 2013).

Our anti-racist journey continues with the serendipitous finding of the blog post titled 'Safe and Brave Spaces Don't Work (and What You Can Do Instead)'. In it, Ahenkorah (2020) tells us that from her experience designing spaces for social justice, anti-racism and equity, brave spaces negate the everyday bravery required by members of marginalised and oppressed communities to negotiate their lives in a demonstrably unequal and discriminatory world. Brave spaces ask more of these people than more privileged groups – not just to be brave, but to be brave and educate others (Verduzco-Baker, 2018). Her step beyond these brave spaces therefore is to offer us guidelines for accountable spaces that facilitate more inclusive discourse. As physiotherapy educators, we have collectively identified that one of our challenges is to build inclusive discourse into our practice, *'creating accountable spaces that place an equal amount of onus for all to behave equitably and inclusively, to foster a deeper understanding of diverse lived experiences in real-time'* (Ahenkorah, 2020).

Conclusion

The decolonisation of contemporary health and social care practice, and physiotherapy in particular, faces challenges in reconciling a more humanistic approach with existing ideas of what knowledge is considered valid and important. Despite intentions and strategies to improve equality and diversity within healthcare, the enduring current informal and hidden curriculum is inherently excluding, as evidenced by the experiences of students from Black and minority ethnic backgrounds who feel they have to act in certain ways to be seen to 'get in' and 'fit in'. A critical disruption of the underpinning epistemologies and canons of knowledge in physiotherapy is necessary if we are to embrace other ways of knowing and being. While we relate our journey as physiotherapy educators, there are parallels in other professions and we hope our insights are of value to others who are embarking on similar campaigns to challenge exclusionary practices. We have found this reflective process useful. This chapter may offer you a starting point in your anti-racist journey as an educator, or you may have found other routes to action and be further along in your journey.

Reflective questions

- What messages did you learn about 'being and becoming' during your own education, and how has this shaped your professional development?
- How does the informal and hidden curriculum influence practice in your profession?
- Where are you in your journey of anti-racist action and what are you doing in your classroom to challenge discriminatory practices?

Recommended reading

- Ali, D (2017) *Safe Spaces and Brave Spaces: Historical Context and Recommendations for Student Affairs Professionals.* London: NASPA. [online] Available at: www.naspa.org/images/uploads/main/Policy_and_Practice_No_2_Safe_Brave_Spaces.pdf (accessed 30 August 2022).
- Hammond, J A, Williams, A, Walker, S and Norris, M (2019) Working Hard to Belong: A Qualitative Study Exploring Students from Black, Asian and Minority Ethnic Backgrounds' Experiences of Pre-registration Physiotherapy Education. *BMC Medical Education*, 19: 372–83.
- Nicholls, D A (2018) *The End of Physiotherapy.* London: Routledge.
- Wong, S H M, Gishen, F and Lokugamage, A U (2021) Decolonising the Medical Curriculum: Humanising Medicine Through Epistemic Pluralism, Cultural Safety and Critical Consciousness. *London Review of Education*, 19: 1–22.

References

Ahenkorah, E (2020) Safe and Brave Spaces Don't Work (and What You Can Do Instead). [online] Available at: www.medium.com/@elise.k.ahen/safe-and-brave-spaces-dont-work-and-what-you-can-do-instead-f265aa339aff (accessed 30 August 2022).

Ali, D (2017) *Safe Spaces and Brave Spaces: Historical Context and Recommendations for Student Affairs Professionals*. London: NASPA. [online] Available at: www.naspa.org/images/uploads/main/Policy_and_Practice_No_2_Safe_Brave_Spaces.pdf (accessed 30 August 2022).

Arao, B and Clemens, K (2013) From Safe Spaces to Brave Spaces: A New Way to Frame Dialogue Around Diversity and Social Justice. In Landreman, L M (ed) *The Art of Effective Facilitation: Reflection from Social Justice Educators* (pp 135–50). Sterling: Stylus.

Barradell, S (2017) Moving Forth: Imagining Physiotherapy Education Differently. *Physiotherapy Theory and Practice*, 33 : 439–47.

Chambers, A (2012) Student Physiotherapists' Narratives and the Construction of Professional Identities. PhD thesis, University of Manchester.

Chartered Society of Physiotherapy (2020) CSP History. [online] Available at: www.csp.org.uk/about-csp/who-we-are/csp-history (accessed 30 August 2022).

Chartered Society of Physiotherapy (2021) Equality, Diversity and Belonging Strategy. [online] Available at: www.csp.org.uk/about-csp/equity-diversity-belonging/strategy (accessed 30 August 2022).

Edwards, I and Richardson, B (2008) Clinical Reasoning and Population Health: Decision Making for an Emerging Paradigm of Health Care. *Physiotherapy Theory and Practice*, 24: 183–93.

Gillborn, D (2005) Education Policy as an Act of White Supremacy: Whiteness, Critical Race Theory and Education Reform. *Journal of Education Policy*, 20: 485–505.

Gilman, S L (2014) Stand Up Straight: Notes Toward a History of Posture. *Journal of Medical Humanities*, 35: 57–83.

Greenfield, B H, Jensen, G M, Delany, C M, Mostrom, E, Knab, M and Jampel, A (2015) Power and Promise of Narrative for Advancing Physical Therapist Education and Practice. *Physical Therapy*, 95: 924–33.

Grieve, P (2016) University to Freshmen: Don't Expect Safe Spaces or Trigger Warnings. *The Chicago Maroon*. [online] Available at: chicagomaroon.com/22405/news/university-to-freshmen-dont-expect-safe-spaces-or-trigger-warnings/#:~:text=News-,University%20to%20Freshmen%3A%20Don't%20Expect%20Safe%20Spaces%20or%20Trigger,creation%20of%20intellectual%20'safe%20spaces (accessed 30 August 2022).

Habermas, J (1970) Knowledge and Interest. In Emmet, D and MacIntyre, A (eds) *Sociological Theory and Philosophical Analysis* (pp 36–54). London: Palgrave Macmillan.

Hafferty, F W (1998) Beyond Curriculum Reform: Confronting Medicine's Hidden Curriculum. *Academic Medicine*, 73: 403–7.

Hammond, J (2013) Doing Gender in Physiotherapy Education. PhD thesis, Kingston University.

Hammond, J A, Williams, A, Walker, S and Norris, M (2019) Working Hard to Belong: A Qualitative Study Exploring Students from Black, Asian and Minority Ethnic Backgrounds' Experiences of Pre-registration Physiotherapy Education. *BMC Medical Education*, 19: 372–83.

Health and Care Professions Council (2022) *Standards of Proficiency for Physiotherapists*. [online] Available at: www.hcpc-uk.org/standards/standards-of-proficiency/physiotherapists/ (Accessed 30 August 2022).

House of Commons Health Committee (2014) *Managing the Care of People with Long-term Conditions, Vol. 1*. London: The Stationery Office.

Kendall, F P, McCreary, E K and Provance, P G (2005) *Muscles: Testing and Function with Posture and Pain* (5th ed). Baltimore, MD: Lippincott Williams and Wilkins.

Kripa, S and Kaur, H (2021) Identifying Relations Between Posture and Pain in Lower Back Pain Patients: A Narrative Review. *Bulletin of Faculty of Physical Therapy*, 26: 1–4.

Lane, J, Jagadamma, K C, Culpan, J and Bulley, C (2022) Exploring Decolonising the Curriculum in Physiotherapy: Our Learning Stories as Dedicated Novices. *International Practice Development Journal*, 12: Art 10. [online] Available at: https://doi.org/10.19043/ipdj.122.010 (accessed 9 December 2022).

Lederman, E (2011) The Fall of the Postural-structural-biomechanical Model in Manual and Physical Therapies: Exemplified by Lower Back Pain. *Journal of Bodywork and Movement Therapies*, 15: 131–8.

Links, M J, Wilkinson, T and Campbell, C (2019) Discourses of Professionalism: Metaphors, Theory and Practice. *Medical Teacher*, 41: 91–8.

McCormack, B, McCance, T, Bulley, C, Brown, D, Martin, S and McMillan, A (eds) (2021) *Fundamentals of Person-centred Healthcare Practice*. Oxford: Wiley-Blackwell.

McCormack, B, McCance, T and Maben, J (2013) Outcome Evaluation in the Development of Person Centred Practice. In McCormack, B, Manley, K and Titchen, A (eds) *Practice Development in Nursing* (2nd ed.) (pp 189–214). Oxford: Wiley-Blackwell.

Merriam-Webster Dictionary (2022) *Canon*. [online] Available at: www.merriam-webster.com/dictionary/canon (accessed 2 September 2022).

Mescouto, K, Olson, R E, Hodges, P W and Setchell, J (2022) A Critical Review of the Biopsychosocial Model of Low Back Pain Care: Time for a New Approach? *Disability and Rehabilitation*, 44: 3270–84.

Mezirow, J (1975) *Education for Perspective Transformation: Women's Reentry Programs in Community Colleges*. New York: Columbia University Press.

Mezirow, J (1991) *Transformative Dimensions of Adult Learning*. San Francisco: Jossey-Bass.

Mintken, P E, Rodeghero, J and Cleland, J A (2018) Manual Therapists: Have You Lost that Loving Feeling?! *Journal of Manual and Manipulative Therapy*, 26: 53–4.

Naidoo, K, Yuhaniak, H, Borkoski, C, Levangie, P and Abel, Y (2021) Networked Mentoring to Promote Social Belonging Among Minority Physical Therapist Students and Develop Faculty Cross-cultural Psychological Capital. *Mentoring and Tutoring: Partnership in Learning*, 29: 586–606.

Nicholls, D A (2018) *The End of Physiotherapy*. London: Routledge.

Nicholls, D A and Cheek, J (2006) Physiotherapy and the Shadow of Prostitution: The Society of Trained Masseuses and the Massage Scandals of 1894. *Social Science and Medicine*, 62: 2336–48.

Nicholls, D A and Larmer, P (2005) Possible Futures for Physiotherapy: An Exploration of the New Zealand Context. *New Zealand Journal of Physiotherapy*, 33: 55–60.

Nicholls, D A, Reid, D A and Larmer, P J (2009) Crisis, What Crisis? Revisiting 'Possible Futures for Physiotherapy'. *New Zealand Journal of Physiotherapy*, 37: 105–14.

Nightingale, J, Parkin, J, Nelson, P, Masterson-Ng, S, Brewster, J, Labinjo, T, Amoakoh, D, Lomas, D, Salih, I and Harrop, D (2022) Multiple Stakeholder Perspectives of Factors Influencing Differential Outcomes for Ethnic Minority Students on Health and Social Care Placements: A Qualitative Exploration. *BMC Medical Education*, 22: 17.

Pentecost, M, Gerber, B, Wainwright, M and Cousins, T (2018) Critical Orientations for Humanising Health Sciences Education in South Africa. *Medical Humanities*, 44: 221–9.

Popova, D (2016) Decolonization of the Self. In Tilley-Lubbs, G A and Calva, S B (eds) *Re-telling Our Stories: Imagination and Praxis*. Rotterdam: Sense.

Shaw, J A and DeForge, R T (2012) Physiotherapy as Bricolage: Theorizing Expert Practice. *Physiotherapy Theory and Practice*, 28: 420–7.

Slater, D, Korakakis, V, O'Sullivan, P, Nolan, D and O'Sullivan, K (2019) 'Sit Up Straight': Time to Re-evaluate. *Journal of Orthopaedic and Sports Physical Therapy*, 49: 562–4.

Smythe, A and Jivanjee, M (2021) The Straight and Narrow of Posture: Current Clinical Concepts. *Australian Journal of General Practice*, 50: 807–10.

Trede, F (2012) Emancipatory Physiotherapy Practice. *Physiotherapy Theory and Practice*, 28: 466–73.

Vazir, S, Newman, K, Kispal, L, Morin, AE, Mu, YY, Smith, M and Nixon, S (2019) Perspectives of Racialized Physiotherapists in Canada on Their Experiences with Racism in the Physiotherapy Profession. *Physiotherapy Canada*, 71: 335–45.

Verduzco-Baker, L (2018) Modified Brave Spaces: Calling in Brave Instructors. *Sociology of Race and Ethnicity*, 4: 585–92.

Webb, J, Arthur, R, McFarlane-Edmond, P, Burns, T and Warren, D (2022) An Evaluation of the Experiences of the Hidden Curriculum of Black and Minority Ethnic Undergraduate Health and Social Care Students at a London University. *Journal of Further and Higher Education*, 46: 312–26.

Wong, S H M, Gishen, F and Lokugamage, A U (2021) Decolonising the Medical Curriculum: Humanising Medicine Through Epistemic Pluralism, Cultural Safety and Critical Consciousness. *London Review of Education*, 19: 1–22.

World Health Organization (2016) *Global Framework on Integrated, People-centred Health Services*. [online] Available at: tinyurl.com/WHO-integrated-framework (accessed 30 August 2022).

Yeowell, G (2013) 'Isn't It All Whites?' Ethnic Diversity and the Physiotherapy Profession. *Physiotherapy*, 99: 341–6.

CHAPTER 14

WALKING THE TALK: CHANGING AND CHALLENGING THE CONVERSATIONS IN OCCUPATIONAL THERAPY EDUCATION

Michelle L Elliot and Zaynab Akhtar

Introduction: the narrative journey

In this chapter, the two authors reflect upon some of the personal and professional experiences, challenges and insights that have informed their current understandings about microaggressions, racism and anti-racism. Using the framings offered by Thambinathan and Kinsella (2022), the experiences in this chapter are conceptualised as anti-racism praxis. The authors are aware that this work is lifelong. In the collaborative discussions and writing, Michelle and Zaynab shared uncomfortable learnings, knowledge gaps and the importance of staying present within difficult conversations.

In addition to representing a narrative journey within and between these two authors, the chapter also offers critical perspectives on the professional and educational discourses in occupational therapy. 'Journey' and 'narrative' are intentional word choices that invoke a sense of discovery and dislocation. *'The value of dislocation is in the way it moves us beyond illusion so we can see "in the round" – since what we are able to see depends entirely on where we stand'* (hooks, 2003, p 21). Narratives, as with journeys, have endings, beginnings and points of departure and intersection. The headings throughout this chapter offer waymarkers through perspectives on racism and anti-racism that are contributing to the construction of different narratives within the occupational therapy profession, practice and education. The chapter sections offer places to pause, reflect and locate your positionality as you enter the narrative journeys of Michelle and Zaynab.

The authors are conscious of the power of words and discourse to marginalise, acknowledge the echoes of silence when words are not spoken and humanity not recognised, and engender personal and collective responsibility to speak up and stand up. *'There is an educational imperative to take care of language, taking responsibility for our words and their meaning, and to take care with language, acknowledging that we cannot fully know what our words will mean to others'* (Pirrie et al, 2021, p 45). There is a growing body of anti-racist scholarship within and beyond occupational therapy that takes care of and with language, and some of this literature will be referred to throughout this chapter. It is not possible to acknowledge all the authors, activists, practitioners, educators, learners and anti-racist allies whose views are agentic and challenging. You are encouraged to seek out that work, join those networks and mobilise your own words (and theirs) into action.

Entering conversation from different perspectives

Michelle and Zaynab worked together over four years during Zaynab's studies in occupational therapy at Queen Margaret University. During that period, Michelle was a lecturer who coordinated several later-year modules taken by Zaynab. They learned from and with each other in the university's personal academic tutor (PAT) system and now connect through their professional identities as qualified occupational therapists. The stories they live are different and presented separately. The desire to cultivate and contribute to systems of change is shared and integrated in later sections.

Call me by my name

Name

In September 1997, my mum made the decision to name me Rebecca. Though biblical, this was not a commonly used name among our community of South Asian Muslims. Travelling on religious missionary work, my dad was not present when I was legally named. Upon his return, he was adamant that my name be changed. Growing up with some bitterness, I imagined how different (easier) introductions and conversations might have been had my name been Rebecca rather than Zaynab. Zee is my nickname among friends, yet I have perpetuated this into adulthood within employment and university contexts so that it was easier for White people. Every time I introduced myself, I would say my name (with the wrong pronunciation for ease), quickly followed by *'but you can just call me Zee!'* with the intention of saving the person any hassle of trying to pronounce my name. I believed, and at times still do, that correctly pronouncing my name results in conversations about how accents differ depending on ethnic background. For example, my family and I pronounce my name as 'Ze-nub', which is common within our Pakistani community. However, the originating pronunciation of my name is from the Middle East and phonetically is pronounced 'Zu-ee-nub'.

The Black Lives Matter movement ignited a long reflection of my own experiences regarding my race, religion and ethnic background. I am now using my full name in emails and correspondence, as well as pronouncing it correctly in conversation. It feels uncomfortable to think that I would purposely mispronounce my own name to fit more easily into the mouths of my Western counterparts.

Identity

As a person of colour residing in the UK, there are numerous ways in which I and my family have been and continue to be racialised and racially profiled. The following examples are presented as evidence that our identities and the stories constructed about them exist in the realities of everyday life.

I identify as a British-Pakistani Muslim. As someone who has grown up in a predominately White geographic area, racist, derogatory and stereotypical remarks regarding my brown skin and religion are familiar to me. I stopped wearing the hijab at the age of 18 after years of experiencing contradictory treatment from peers and friends. When I wore the hijab, for example, I felt excluded from my friend group and was mocked by boys in my school. The days I would not wear the hijab I received compliments on my appearance and felt included in conversation. I still struggle to understand what the hijab symbolised to create such a barrier to social inclusion. The impact became cyclical; while wearing the hijab, I was more reserved and perhaps this was what caused my peers to react as they did. Yet my shyness was a result of the stares and bullying I often received. For me, these school experiences destroyed the beauty and purpose of the hijab to the point that I did not – and at times today, sometimes still do not – want to visibly identify as a Muslim.

When out with family, travelling abroad, taking short day trips or out for a meal, I am always conscious of how we appear to others. If there are social inconveniences, such as my family holding up the airport check-in queue due to overweight luggage, I wonder if the stares would be the same if we were White. There were times I did not want my parents to laugh out loud because I did not want people to stare. My dad wears a hat (topi), South Asian clothing and has a long beard. With guilt and regret, I recall a time when he and I went to a sandwich shop after he picked me up from school. Arriving at the shop, I noticed there were classmates inside. Instead of sitting inside to eat, I begged him to let us take the food home. I did not want to be seen with him, a man who wore his Muslim identity so visibly. I feared the 'banter' that would follow if we were seen together. Was my dad aware that his daughter felt uncomfortable about their shared culture and religious identity?

Positionality and privilege

As an educator, occupational therapist, occupational scientist and narrative researcher, I sit with Zaynab's narratives with the realisation that many of the theoretical perspectives I have drawn from to date have been inconsistently enacted in my various personal and professional roles. I reflect on my journey to this current place of awareness and position my own narrative alongside Zaynab's. I also reflect on my first meeting with her. *'Call me Zee'*, she said.

I grew up in northern British Columbia, Canada and acknowledge that my childhood existed across the unceded territory of the Lheidli T'enneh Nation. I hold awareness today that I held very limited awareness then of the complexity of health inequities, generational traumas, sociocultural and historical oppression, and institutional, interpersonal and epistemic racism (Greenwood et al, 2018). Decades on, these realities remain, though they are more present in everyday conversation and the school curricula in Canada and abroad. I have not lived nor worked in Canada for many years. Yet feelings of connection and dislocation from 'home' and 'identification with' Canada have followed me around the world, and they are increasingly present in my teaching, learning and scholarship.

Challenging complicity

I am aware that the privileges I hold as a White woman, educated and socialised in Western systems and structures, have contributed to what is primarily an intellectual understanding of racism. I have arguably benefitted from these privileges, and in the early years of my professional career, I shied away from conversations that elicited conflict, criticality and challenge. With a propensity to think with alliteration, I recognise that the c's just mentioned have now extended to include curiosity and considerations of complicity. An additional c, complexity, is also increasingly present in not only my work but that of my colleagues (Pentland et al, 2018).

The following story is offered as an example of how the option to challenge or comply can occur at unexpected times and requires conscious awareness to reveal the choices at hand. As I settled into my seat at the back of the plane returning me to the United Kingdom after presenting at the 2018 World Federation of Occupational Therapy (WFOT) Congress in Cape Town, South Africa (Nicholls and Elliot, 2019, 2021), the White person in the seat beside me asked where I was from. In response to my reply, *'Canada'*, they said *'That's a beautiful country, and you don't have any of the racial issues like we do here (South Africa).'* Realising that my seatmate and I would be together for over nine hours, I had some choices to make in that moment. Did I simply nod and pull out my book? The easier choice, perhaps. Did I engage with an abridged history lesson that challenged the friendly and welcoming stereotype of Canadians and breached the social norms of small talk among strangers? I chose the latter and offered this fellow passenger some insight into Canada's legacy of racism and oppression. To be quiet in that moment was to be complicit in the historical and ongoing silencing of many individuals experiencing marginalisation. For the remainder of this long flight, we separately and collectively experienced a different form of silence.

The danger of a single story (Adiche, 2009) is an important reminder. Dominant narratives persist for many reasons and in many forms, in part because they often reflect desired or expected narratives (Beagan, 2021)? If language of race is masked with alternate words such as 'culture', consciousness-raising and responsibility-taking are compromised (Adiche, 2013; Nicholls and Elliot, 2019). The cohorts of pre-registration occupational therapy students with whom I have worked have been predominately White. Engaging in critically grounded conversations about racism, anti-racism, oppression and anti-oppressive practices within a university community that may not see or experience such realities is part of my reflective journey. That talk must also be walked.

My formative anti-racism work and reflections and questions for provoking dialogue and debate are described in the next sections, along with Zaynab's reminder that for many people this is familiar and not formative work.

Challenges and contexts

As was mentioned at the start of this chapter, words and talk matter. Different ways in which racism and racialised interactions occur can be understood through different concepts, two of which are introduced here.

> 'Casual racism' refers to the use of adverse stereotypes of individuals based on their race, ethnicity, or religious beliefs.
> (Australian Human Rights Commission, 2011)

Most of the time this is not intended to cause harm or offence; rather it is indicative of racism that exists collectively in society and is a result of ignorance and lack of education surrounding race. The word casual implies that these instances are common; they are often not taken seriously by the perpetrators or those unaffected by them. Thus, these instances can be brushed aside as imaginary or insignificant by individuals who are subjected to racism. The second concept of oppression are microaggressions, notable for the *'non-conscious intention of the offender or perception of the target, these are deniable acts of racism (or other oppressive acts) that reinforce pathological stereotypes and inequitable social norms'* (Williams, 2020, p 4).

If there are non-conscious and non-intentional dynamics, what are the practical and tangible ways whereby anti-racism theories and approaches can become part of the classroom and practice-based learning and working contexts (Osbourne et al, 2022; Sterman et al, 2021)? Casual racism and microaggressions exist in everyday experiences. How, then, is consciousness raised in such a way that these are named and identified for what they are? In their critical interpretive synthesis of occupational therapy and occupational science literature, Pooley and Beagan (2021) conclude that the axes of oppression, including racism, are addressed but not readily classified with the language of oppression. As they and others in the field are doing, Michelle and Zaynab invite you to consider the question: what's in a name?

Within a critical gaze

Occupational therapy within the United Kingdom, according to the Royal College of Occupational Therapists (RCOT), is a profession that has historical foundations with and aspirations to uphold values of equity, diversity and belonging (RCOT, 2022). Individual actions aligned with collective efforts are necessary to mobilise challenges to the power and privileges of institutions and systems that have reproduced racist, colonial and/or oppressive practices (Bheero et al, 2021; Kendi, 2019; Moore and Simango, 2021). There are movements on the ground and in the social media sphere – BAMEOT Network (2022) in the United Kingdom, for example – that challenge perspectives, bodies of knowledge and practices that have long existed within the dominant narratives of 'the way things are'.

For learners within occupational therapy programmes, introducing a critical gaze and welcoming debate can feel disorienting. Anti-racism work requires a challenge to 'the system' and an acknowledgement that 'it' may be flawed or at fault. But systems do not exist 'out there'; they are comprised of and are constructed by individuals. Of us. The national and international membership of this professional community professes a desire to advocate for change on behalf of others, and this must include within our own local communities and contexts. For us. Marginalisation and oppression are happening within our professional communities, not just 'out there' (Grenier, 2020). By us. This inquiry is growing in education and practice, with frameworks, tools and ongoing learnings shared for everyone involved in the disruptions and deconstructions of curriculum, conversations and communities (Ahmed-Landeryou et al, 2022; Atwal et al, 2021). With us.

Questions to think with

Tools, frameworks and strategies may offer some directional assistance into and with anti-racism work. In different contexts, provocations for individual and collective reflection may also be useful. The following are questions that could be explored with personal (you) and collective reflections.

- Where and how do you learn to speak up when you do not see or feel or experience learning and practice environments as reflective of your own or your profession's values?
- When issues arise that do not have direct personal impact on you due to your positionality and privilege, what reminds you that such impact may be experienced by others?

The challenges faced by Zaynab as an occupational therapy student would not have been resolved with a single class discussion or learning activity addressing this question. There has been personal, programmatic and institutional learning as an outcome of these experiences. However, learning and awareness are insufficient within anti-racism praxis, as Zaynab's narrative in the next section reveals.

'You have to be careful'

I experienced casual racism while on my lunch break during one of my practice-based learning experiences. The discussion with my practice educator and a ward clerk centred around airport security measures and protocols. I shared experiences that my family and I had encountered as Pakistani Muslims. One specific example involved a story of my dad, who travelled to the United States shortly after the 9/11 events. Upon arrival, he was interrogated for 13 hours and placed in an overnight airport cell. With his beard, hat, clothing, skin colour and Arabic name, he was identifiably an Asian Muslim man attempting to enter the United States after terrorist attacks orchestrated by Muslim men. In telling this story, my intention was to describe the struggles ethnic minorities and Muslim people may face when travelling. However, this conversation then took a turn when one of the people at lunch said:

When I see a man with the beard and the bag at the airport, I do look twice – I do.

You have got to be careful you know, you just don't know.

Having grown up witnessing and hearing comments such as these, my interpretation was that this person had perhaps been socialised to fear 'visibly' Muslim men. In response to statements of 'caution' when seeing men who looked like my father, I too have been socialised. To stay quiet. Moments before, I had shared that my dad matched that same description, yet I said nothing. With the permission implied through my silence, this person steered the conversation towards talk of further terrorist incidents. Feeling increasingly uncomfortable, I defaulted to my habit of inserting humour into the situation. Dismissive of my intended (or attempted) deflection and distraction, the racist perspectives continued.

Taking action

I had been unsure whether to take the matter further and raise a formal complaint as I did not believe the onus was on me, a person of colour, to educate anyone on racism. There is a legacy of such responsibility, unfortunately (Eddo-Lodge, 2017). What pushed me to act was the realisation that I had let casual racism, ignorance and microaggressions slide my whole life; now I wanted to stand up for myself. I was motivated by the Black Lives Matter movement. Furthermore, this situation occurred in a workplace, which is an environment that is expected to reflect and uphold professional standards.

Once I gathered the courage to make a formal complaint, there was some confusion regarding the process. My university programme advised me to make the complaint through the placement site. My practice educator claimed that a formal complaint needed to be made through the university. The confusion resulted in back and forth between institutions and at one point I considered abandoning the matter. This lack of clarity regarding a complaints process felt indicative of how ill-equipped institutions can be to receive and respond to complaints (Ahmed, 2021). In the end, the event occurred on placement and the workplace agreements for that site informed the complaints procedure that was to be followed.

After the complaint was escalated to senior management, swift action was taken. A total of 160 staff members across the local health board were to complete an equality and diversity training module. When hospital management apologised to me on behalf of the ward clerk, they admitted that many staff members had not ever or recently completed diversity training. At the time, I was content with this response; however, I remain sceptical about the meaningfulness of required training to prevent future racist actions and comments.

Learning

As Zaynab's personal academic tutor, I (Michelle) was supportive of her desire to formalise her complaint and ignorant about the mechanisms of doing so. Practice-based learning is facilitated primarily within health and social care or third-sector services in partnership with the university. Different situations may require different plans of action; it was the Dignity at Work policy that was used to formalise Zaynab's complaint. Greater reflective awareness of and active engagement in praxis that challenges the casual racism and microaggressions that are experienced by members of the professional community (Sterman et al, 2022) is a significant learning need for myself and colleagues who are involved with health professionals education.

Engaging with anti-racism and anti-oppressive practices and perspectives, and bringing these into my teaching and learning, has required me to acknowledge – to myself and to the learners with whom I work – that I will make mistakes. I will and do not know. I will 'get it wrong'. I will misinterpret and misdirect. I will read and speak from my position of privilege. I want to learn, share and champion actions and discourses of accountability that are facilitative rather than defensive.

Questioning

'Aspiring towards an anti-racist praxis involves unlearning and disrupting' (Thambinathan and Kinsella, 2022, p 1). What follows are a selection of ideas and examples of anti-racism approaches that I am 'actioning' in my teaching and learning. Zaynab's stories and experiences importantly remind myself and my team that there is much more to be done.

You are invited to reflect on your own facilitation processes or learning experiences, and to generate further examples and perspectives that are relevant to your contexts.

- If case studies are used as part of teaching and learning materials, is race or ethnicity mentioned?
  - If it is not, how do you engage students in exploring racialised experiences of health and illness?
  - What narratives are privileged and perpetuated with such default assumptions?
- If activities of daily living are discussed or assessed, assumptions are associated with the values and practices of them?
  - Is independence universally valued, expected and understood?
  - Do assessments and interventions reflect different clothing, cooking, self-care or spiritual practices?
- What aspects of equity, diversity and inclusion are represented in the videos, films and non-academic literature brought into learning environments and discussions?
- Where and when are academic and profession-specific literature from scholars and practitioners in the Global South introduced?
  - How are critical conversations of contextual 'relevance' introduced?
- Theories, conceptual models and therapeutic practices related to occupation are globally exported from the Global North. How is this incorporated and critiqued within curriculum?

The journey forward

At the start of the chapter, Michelle and Zaynab acknowledged that their stories are different and evolving. The decision to close this chapter with a 'where to from here' section risks simplifying the complexity of the issues and narratives presented or distilling them down into a selection of 'take-home messages'. The authors aspire to take care with language here and reflect upon the past in order to contribute to the transformation of current and future narratives and actions. For Michelle, the small steps taken thus far are part of a much longer journey that must be navigated with curiosity and criticality. Her alliteration stylings are not a play on words; they are a resonant reminder for her of the power, privilege and responsibility held within them.

For Zaynab, there remains an expectation that she will be racialised throughout her life. She retains hope that the voices, experiences and challenges of people of colour are heard, recognised, valued and supported. Zaynab wants her generation to catalyse real change. Her parents shrugged off racism with a view that they should just 'get on with life' and not make a big deal of it. But it *is* a big deal. For both authors, there is a shared desire and commitment to show up, speak up and stand up. And then walk that talk, being conscious to call things by their names.

It is not enough to say you are 'not racist' (Deggans, 2020). To align the talk and the walk of anti-racism requires a further intention to generate evidence of these actions (Miller, 2021). What are or might be your 'receipts'?

Reflective questions

- What helps you to stay present, contribute openly and listen for understanding in conversations that may be difficult?
- Where and with whom do you practise asking questions that disrupt 'how things are'? How do you receive such questions when they are addressed to you?
- What are the support and reporting infrastructures in your institution for anyone experiencing racism and/or oppression?

Recommended reading

- *The Colour of Fear* (1994) Directed by Lee-Mun Wah [Documentary film]. Stirfry Seminars and Consulting.
- Freire, P (2000 [1968]) *Pedagogy of the Oppressed.* New York: Continuum.
- Mannix, K (2021) *Listen: How to Find the Words for Tender Conversations.* London: William Collins.

References

Adiche, C N (2009) *The Danger of a Single Story*. [online] Available at: youtu.be/D9Ihs241zeg (accessed 14 December 2022).

Adiche, C N (2013) *Americanah*. New York: Alfred A Knopf.

Ahmed, S (2021) *Complaint!* Durham, NC: Duke University Press.

Ahmed-Landeryou, M J, Emery-Whittington, I, Ivlev, S R and Elder, R (2022) Pause, Reflect, Reframe: Deep Discussions on Co-creating a Decolonial Approach for an Antiracist Framework in Occupational Therapy. *Occupational Therapy Now*, 25(2): 14–16.

Atwal, A, Sriram, V, McKay, E A and BAMEOT Network (2021) Making a Difference: Belonging, Diversity and Inclusion in Occupational Therapy. *British Journal of Occupational Therapy*, 84(11): 671–2.

Australian Human Rights Commission (2011) *National Anti-Racism Strategy Consultation*. [online] Available at: https://humanrights.gov.au/sites/default/files/casual-racism-faqs.pdf (accessed 14 December 2022).

Beagan, B L (2021) Commentary on Racism in Occupational Science. *Journal of Occupational Science*, 28(3): 410–13.

Bheero, L, Mafethe, P and Billing, L (2021) *Racism, Power and Truth: Experiences of People of Colour in Development*. London: Bond.

Black, Asian and Minoritised Ethnicities Occupational Therapy (BAMEOT) Network (2022) About Us. [online] Available at: www.bameot.uk (accessed 11 December 2022).

Deggans, E (2020) 'Not Racist' is Not Enough: Putting in the Work to be Anti-Racist. [Podcast]. 25 August 2020. [online] Available at: www.npr.org/2020/08/24/905515398/not-racist-is-not-enough-putting-in-the-work-to-be-anti-racist (accessed 12 September 2022).

Eddo-Lodge, R (2017) *Why I'm No Longer Talking to White People About Race*. London: Bloomsbury.

Greenwood, M, de Leeux, S and Lindsay, N (eds) (2018) *Determinants of Indigenous Peoples' Health in Canada: Beyond the Social* (2nd ed). Toronto: Canadian Scholars' Press.

Grenier, M-L (2020) Cultural Competency and the Reproduction of White Supremacy in Occupational Therapy Education. *Health Education Journal*, 79(6): 633–44.

hooks, b (2003) *Teaching Community: A Pedagogy of Hope*. New York: Routledge.

Kendi, I X (2019) *How to Be an Antiracist*. London: Bodley Head.

Miller, P (2021) 'System Conditions', System Failure, Structural Racism and Anti-Racism in the United Kingdom: Evidence from Education and Beyond. *Societies*, 11(2): 42–56.

Moore, T and Simango, G (eds) (2021) *The Anti-Racist Social Worker: Stories of Activism by Social Care and Allied Health Professionals*. St Albans: Critical Publishing.

Nicholls, L and Elliot, M L (2019) In the Shadow of Occupation: Racism, Shame and Grief. *Journal of Occupational Science*, 26(3): 354–65.

Nicholls, L and Elliot, M L (2021) Authors in Dialogue: Why Race Matters – Then, Now and For the Future. *Journal of Occupational Science*, 28(3): 419–22.

Osbourne, L, Barnett, J and Blackwood, L (2022) Black Students' Experiences of 'Acceptable' Racism at a UK University. *Journal of Community Applied Social Psychology*, 33(1): 43–55.

Pentland, D, Kantartzis, S, Giatsi Clausen, M and Witemyre, K (2018) *Occupational Therapy and Complexity: Defining and Describing Practice*. London: Royal College of Occupational Therapists.

Pirrie, A, Fang, N and O'Brien, E (eds) (2021) *Dancing in the Dark: A Survivor's Guide to the University*. London: Tilosophy Press.

Pooley, E A and Beagan, B L (2021) The Concept of Oppression and Occupational Therapy: A Critical Interpretive Synthesis. *Canadian Journal of Occupational Therapy*, 88(4): 407–17.

Royal College of Occupational Therapists (RCOT) (2022) Equity, Diversity and Belonging. [online] Available at: www.rcot.co.uk/equity-diversity-and-belonging (accessed 14 December 2022).

Sterman, J, Njelesani, J and Carr, S (2021) Becoming Anti-Racist Occupational Therapy Practitioners: A Scoping Study. *OTJR: Occupation, Participation and Health*, 41(4): 232–42.

Thambinathan, V and Kinsella, E A (2022) When I Say ... Anti-Racist Praxis. *Medical Education*. [online] Available at: https://doi.org/10.1111/medu.14997 (accessed 9 December 2022).

Williams, M T (2020) Microaggressions: Clarification, Evidence, and Impact. *Perspectives on Psychological Science*, 15(1): 3–26.

CONCLUSION: LEARNING TO LOVE

Geetha Marcus and Stefanie Van de Peer

Writing and editing a book on academic activism is a risky undertaking. As we curated this work and wrote our chapters, as a collective, we had conversations about the ethics of speaking out about our experiences, being honest about the implications of these experiences, and also – importantly – the way these experiences reflect the sector in which we work. As educators, we are people with considerable privilege and power: standing in front of a classroom at a university means we have had a specific type of education, and it also means we take up a space of authority. These positions of privilege imply intersectional luck, wealth and systems of support. How do we navigate those critically?

Likewise, as academics, we are practised in critical thinking, not only with regard to our research field but also in our practice as teachers and lecturers. We are all required to attain a fellowship of the higher education institute, and in the process of achieving that, every applicant is invited to critically reflect on their responsibilities towards their students, and how the student body is changing – both in societal ways and in the way it interacts with the institutional context of the university. In the process of writing the chapters for this book, as a collective, we reflected on our responsibilities towards our students and the ways we interact with them as an intercultural community, and on the ways we represent the institution that employs us to do so. How do we align our anti-racist educational practices with the ways in which this institution is a part of a larger institutionalised system? The system is, by design, discriminatory, as getting an education is costly and financial inequalities are consistently aligned with racial ones.

The work we reflect on is centred on Queen Margaret University, a small university in Edinburgh that carries social justice centrally in its identity. However, many of us are at an early stage in our careers and as such have had diverse experiences, as post-doctoral work is hard to come by and often temporary or otherwise precarious. A significant number of us have also had experiences in the professional world and in community work before coming to higher education as a career, and in most cases our work outside of academia continues. All of us have a practice rooted in community work that informs our teaching and our research, and that also informs the reflexive work done in this book. What Queen Margaret University has offered us is the opportunity to come together as a collective through the Lightning Talk efforts of our institution to take the decolonising turn in education seriously, beyond the discourse. This work continues. We want to believe that our institution is attempting to put into place positive measures to enable critical engagement with the role of an educational institution in anti-racism in Scotland. Anti-racist work ought to be encouraged from the top and led from the grassroots.

Nevertheless, there are those who still believe that decolonising our curricula consists of simply diversifying the syllabi we teach. This is a highly problematic attitude to anti-racist education, as it simplifies and disrespects the conversation, and indeed silences critical engagement with the deeper roots of and assumptions about canons, cultures and priorities. We all know of colleagues who are unable or unwilling to understand the full impact of their words in front of a classroom, and the consequences of the privileges we take for granted in our positions. Where equality, diversity and inclusion (EDI) committees or HR training opportunities continue to fail is in reaching those that need it the most. Those who remain unaware of their implicit bias or their racist privileges will not join such committees or do such training courses, refusing to reflect on their mindset and heart-set. Those opportunities are usually taken up primarily by those able to practise humility in their self-reflexive thinking and in 'doing' self-criticality – or, at times, as self-seeking opportunities to gain promotion. There is perhaps not enough transparency around processes of promotion, salary increase and pay grades negotiated at the hiring stages. Research shows that pay gaps persist, and those between ethnically diverse colleagues are the most pernicious.

While these inequalities may remain hidden and private, the continued legacies of racialisation in society informs academic institutions as well. Chapters here include testimonies of experiences of micro-aggressions as well as direct racism and verbal violence. One of the main questions to come out of all these chapters concerns where and by whom knowledge is produced. This refers back to the positions of privilege we all hold. How do we challenge persistent worldviews or expose the apparent universality of Western forms of thinking as Eurocentric? Beyond the obviously White or Western canonisation of knowledge, how do we expose existing and persistent core ideologies in our classroom language? And how do we move beyond the usual, assumed and expected personality traits of students in specific programmes of education? Some programmes hold student interviews prior to their being accepted onto the programmes. How can those doing the interviews – both students and staff – avoid explicit as well as inherent bias? And how do we avoid the assumed universality of European or Western standards? While it could be argued that this bias is based in the history of the location of learning and practice, Scotland and the United Kingdom more generally are increasingly intercultural societies, and this is reflected in the student body, with more than 100,000 Chinese students, followed by 84,000 Indian students and more than 21,000 Nigerian students currently at UK universities. Anti-racism education is therefore an increasingly acute and even urgent call to action.

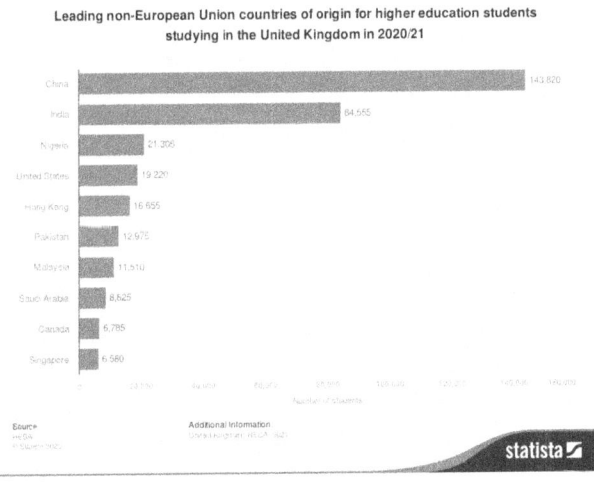

Figure 15.1: Leading non-EU countries of origin for higher education students studying in the United Kingdom in 2020/21 (Statista, 2022)

As a university dedicated to social justice, Queen Margaret University is committed to being outward looking and inclusive, and calls itself a University Without Borders. The institution is also in the process of applying for the title of University of Sanctuary, a network of universities that commit to supporting refugees and people in the asylum system. The requirements are a declaration of intention to commit to offering Sanctuary Scholarships and other opportunities for people seeking sanctuary. A large part of the Universities of Sanctuary application is about communication and ensuring the opportunities created are effectively and efficiently offered to those in need of sanctuary, reaching out into communities often not included for diverse reasons. It is precisely that aspect of communication that appears in the previous chapters as crucial in the authors' understandings of anti-racist work. Whether it is through dialogue, conversations, critical dialogue, sensitive language or inclusive, accessible policy documents, it is an institution's responsibility to ensure that its communication about inclusivity and equality reaches the intended beneficiaries.

Indeed, a central ideology behind anti-racism is a critical self-reflexivity on the part of those in the privileged position of being teachers or lecturers at university. Beyond explicit awareness of the epistemologies of a discipline, openness, honesty and conversational relationships between lecturers and students are some of the values inherent to anti-racist communication. It is an individual development for each of us, in front of a classroom, to achieve a level of confidence that will enable us to engage with the discomfort of the necessary conversations we need to have in anti-racist teaching practices. Being able to stop and address racism and bias – both implicit or explicit – and naming it and calling it out in plain language is crucial but requires practice and courage. It also requires the humility necessary to stop a class and move beyond the topic of the week in order to engage with racist language (ab)use and attitudes. This is highly uncomfortable, but as the case studies in this book have shown, it leads to the most effective learning processes. Sometimes shutting up and listening, as a teacher, is more important than ensuring your message comes across. We need to encourage young people to engage in the conversation and to ask them questions in a way that will enable them to be self-critical. Care, compassion and connection are key to effecting change, and evidence suggests those three c-words are needed to challenge the neoliberal agenda. The relationships we build with our students are the loci for anti-neoliberal attitudes. Instead of continuing to see ourselves as service or (worse) goods providers and, as such, encouraging students to see themselves as customers, we ought to take time to stop and think self-reflectively about our practice as educators.

A deep understanding of the meaning and position of research, scholarship and education in our workloads equally aids in our deconstruction of the neoliberalist attitudes to which we are all subject. The way we teach needs to become grounded in a collaborative relationship between our students and us, between our research and our teaching and between the students among themselves. Co-creative relationships in the classrooms result in better mutual understanding: explaining why we teach specific topics, and how we approach them, is at the root of clarity between teacher and learner. Posing emancipatory questions enables the exploration of individual perspectives, involves the questioning of assumptions and is intended to bring about change or improvement. Learning involves risk and controversy, and emanates from tutors or lecturers who are not afraid of confrontation, and who engage in brave and inclusive conversations where mutual respect, trust, compassion, humility and forgiveness are advocated. Such a humanist approach is rooted in dialogic action that espouses reflection and campaigns that challenge exclusionary practices. Anti-racism is a pact of alliances, a tool for exercising human wisdom. As seen in most of the chapters in this book, anti-racism comes from real-life experience, from seeing oneself and one's students as part of civil society, where formal education sits comfortably alongside informal and non-formal learning and social movement scholarship.

The most effective learning happens in the spaces where we are challenged, where things we took for granted or never stopped to think about surprise us and change us. The disorienting dilemma one of the chapters explains as a 'developmental challenge' or 'life crisis' that challenges one's 'embedded beliefs' is part of that anti-neoliberalist attitude to teaching, and is part of the anti-racism we embed in our teaching practice. We must not shy away from shocking our students or from admitting our own shock at some of the learning we do. The shock of the new, of the different, of the Other, is inherent to the internationalisation of the university institution, where the idea of neoliberal globalisation needs to be countered by a political transnationalism that recognises the specific experiences of individual students and staff as human beings, so that our approach can be humanistic and rooted in solidarity instead. Different perspectives and newness, as experienced through the lives, eyes and languages of our intercultural students and colleagues, are the shocks we need to start to learn again through our teaching encounters. There is a need to dismantle the hierarchy of knowledges and perspectives deeply engrained for centuries. Anti-racist, decolonised education calls for a re-balancing of frameworks. It is not about 'throwing anything out' or 'cancelling cultures'.

That is also how, in the chapters in this book, each author tells their own story of learning through the shock, the discomfort of realising their own privilege and their own bias as a lecturer-activist. What makes an activist? Is it precisely the shock or surprise about one's own ignorance, and one's complicity in the wider community's neglect of an element of social injustice? In each chapter, the authors have shown, though stories and testimonies shaped by case studies and experiences, how their own vulnerability in the face of a fundamental realisation about their own positionality became a strength. The journey towards learning anti-racism continues. We offer these narratives as examples and inspiration for other lecturers so that we can, as a community of educators in higher education in the United Kingdom and internationally, develop our commitment to anti-racism at increasing pace, moving away from the glacial process mired in discourse and not in action.

We urge everyone to action, to speaking up when provoked by any shape racism may take, and to shutting up when othered stories and othered voices need to not just be heard but listened to. That is the journey towards learning to love: understanding each other's humanity and practising solidarity with those who are challenging us to step away from the position of power and to sit down to stop and think self-reflexively about who we are and what we teach. And most importantly, to embody pedagogies that reflect and sustain our integrity and common humanity.

Index

accountable spaces, 195–6
Africa in Motion (AiM) film festival, 119
  curating an anti-colonial film syllabus, 128–30
agency, 20–2, 48, 65
Agents for Environmental Justice, 78
Ahmed, Sara, 3, 17, 22, 28, 38–9
Andreotti, V, 50–1, 52–3
Anti-Racist Early Years Collective (AREYC), 40–1
antisemitism, 83, 84–6
anti-social science, 181
AREYC *see* Anti-Racist Early Years Collective (AREYC)
art, socially engaged, 135–42
Asian Arts Agency, 156
Ataekong, Anthony, 152–3

Balani, S, 127–8
Ballantyne, Elaine, 164
Band Aid concert, 111
Battle of Algiers, 125
Bayoh, Sheku, 2
Bhopal gas disaster (1984), 80
Biswas, Abani, 155
'Black and Global Majority Scholars in UK Theatre, Dance, and Performance Studies', 153
Black and minority ethnic (BME) communities, 17, 28, 79, 167, 188
Black feminism, 18, 23, 39
Black Lives Matter movement, 79, 151, 205

Blaisdell, Caralyn, 34–5
body-as-machine view, 191
Bosma, P, 124
Boycott, Divestment and Sanctions (BDS) against Israel, 85–6
brave spaces, 22, 62, 110, 112–13, 129, 195–6
Brexit, 179
British Theatre, Dance and Performance Studies
  anti-racist collective, 153–4
  and decolonisation, 151
Bruce, L, 169

CAPS Independent Advocacy, 164
Caramel, 125
casual racism, 208–9, 210, 211
Chahine, Youssef, 122
Chartered Society of Physiotherapy (CSP), 189, 191
children's right to be heard, 35–8
children's right to non-discrimination, 36
Church, Kathryn, 164
co-creation, 93, 114, 126, 128, 223
collaborative anthropology, 135–42
colonisation, understanding, 170
Colston statue, dethroning of, 79
Comic Relief programme, 110–11
communal guilt, 4
communicative action, 194–5
complexities, within racist systems, 5
conscientisation, 64

consciousness, 22, 154, 208, 209
constructive activism, 68
contextualised learning, 51
cosmopolitan imagination, 49–50, 51
cosmopolitanism, 54
cost of living crisis, 91–2
Costa, Lucy, 165
counter spaces, 113
Covid 19 pandemic, impact of, 36, 91–2, 97–8
creative and critical compass, anti-racism as, 152–3
Critical Dialogue Groups for Youth Solidarity, 61, 62, 64, 114
   as an alternative to the seminar format, 71–2
   conscientisation, 64–5
   praxis, 65
   racial concept, 65–7
   students' responses to criticism of voluntourism, 65–7
   Ubuntu/Umunthu, 68–9
   White fragility, dehumanising condescension of, 68
critical race dialogues, 78–9
critical race theory, 113
critical self-reflexivity, 222
critical thinking, 7, 94, 127, 129, 219
CRP *see* culturally responsive pedagogy (CRP)
cultural relativism, 23–4
culturally responsive pedagogy (CRP), 17, 24–5
   cultural landscapes and functional dimensions, 26
   learning environment, 27–8
culturally sustaining pedagogy, 25

culture
   definitions of, 23
   misunderstanding of, 170
   in physiotherapy, 190
curative approach, to an anti-colonial film syllabus, 124, 128–30
curriculum, decolonisation/diversification of, 86–7, 151–2

Dabiri, Emma, 167
Daboo, Jerri, 151
De Lissovoy, N, 54
Dean, John, 156
decolonial pedagogy, study visits, 53–5
decolonial thinking, 4
decolonisation, 3, 4, 67, 77
   anti-colonial solidarity scholarship, 82–6
   of curriculum, 86–7, 151–2
   of education, 78–9
   of film studies, 119–30
   of physiotherapy curriculum, 187–97
   research, in postcolonial India, 79–82
   of universities, 6–7
'Decolonising the Curriculum/Diversifying the University' project, 151
defragmentations, anti-racist education, 182–4
dialogic exchanges, 135
DiAngelo R, 66, 68
Dignity at Work policy, 212
disciplinary paths, 38

disorienting dilemmas, 187–8, 193, 223
Djebar, Assia, 122
Drama for Life, 144

early years pioneers, 38–40
Eddo-Lodge, R, 66
Edge of Heaven, The, 123
Education Incubator project, 151
education systems, formal, 19
education, critical race dialogues, 78–9
emancipatory questions, 223
Ending Homelessness Together action plan, 73
environmental justice movements, 78, 80
Equality and Human Rights Commission (EHRC), 2
Equality, Diversity and Belonging Strategy, CSP, 189
equitable exchange, 135
Eromosele, F, 169–70

Faye, Safi, 122
feminism, 21–2, 23
see also Black feminism
film studies, 119–30
first order thinking, 50
First People of Color Environmental Leadership Summit, 78
Floyd, George, 1, 3, 79
foreign language films, 119
four-point conceptual framework, for radical pedagogy, 52–3
freedom, and love, 158–9
Freire, Paolo, 127, 128

Fresa y Chocolate, 122
Friends of the Earth Scotland, 78

glacial progress, 5
global health, 178–9, 181
global learning, 50, 51–2
Global South, media representations of, 110–12
Gross, Akiea, 39–40
Grotowski, Jerzy, 155

health inequalities, 96–7
see also global health
hidden curriculum, 194
higher education, anti-racist agenda in, 55–6
Hitchcock, Alfred, 125
homelessness, 94, 96
hooks, bell, 7, 17, 28, 126
humanisation, 64, 68, 72, 73
humanist approach, 223

Ignorant Schoolmaster, The, project, 142
Inch'Allah Dimanche, 123
India, postcolonial, 79–82
intellectuals, 19, 21
intercultural learning, 47, 52
intercultural performance pedagogies, 155–7
internal audit, and culturally responsive pedagogy, 26
International Holocaust Remembrance Alliance (IHRA) definition of antisemitism, 84–5
international students, 177, 179–80, 182

internationalisation, 223
Israel, Boycott, Divestment and Sanctions against, 85–6

Jerusalem Declaration on Antisemitism, 85
Jewish National Fund (JNF), 83
Johnson, Boris, 3
Joseph Rowntree Foundation, 91

Kachale, Blessings, 109–10
Kazepides, Tazos, 135
Kelly, U, 71
Khaldun, Ibn, 86–7
Kill Your Darlings project, 136, 143
knowledge creation, 33

La Haine, 122
Last Resort, 123
Lawrence, Stephen, 2
learning
    to learn, 53
    to listen, 52
    to love, 219–24
    to reach out, 53
    to unlearn, 52
learning spaces, 50–1, 158
LeFrançois, Brenda, 165
legislation, policy rhetoric and meaningful action, gap between, 5
Levinas, E, 136
liminal places, 50, 51
Live Aid, 111
living as an anti-racist, 159
Lorde, Audre, 17, 28
love, and freedom, 158–9

Macpherson Report, 2
Mad People of Colour, 166
mad studies, 163, 171
    definitions of, 163–4
    possibilities for anti-racist teaching, 167–71
    undoings of, 165–7
Malawi, 104
    see also Critical Dialogue Groups for Youth Solidarity; STEKA; STEKAskills
Mandela, Nelson, 7
Manley, Elizabeth Anne, 191
Martin, Jane Roland, 17
Maseko, Abigail, 103, 114–15
Maseko, Godknows, 61, 104
Maseko, Helen, 61
McWhorter J, 68
media representations, of the Global South, 110–12
microaggressions, 203, 208–9, 211
Milk Café, 93
Milòn Méla, 155, 156
mindset, 27
Mirza, Heidi, 17, 28
Mistry, Joyti, 121
model physiotherapists, 190
Mohammed, Khadija, 41
Moolaade, 125
Morrison, Toni, 111
Mouffe, Chantal, 141
mutual learning, 46, 94

Nair, Kottakkal Sasidharan, 156
Ndale, Sandra, 69, 70, 103, 106
    Walid on, 106–7

neoliberal agenda, challenging, 6–7
neoliberalism, deconstruction of, 223
New Scots (Refugee, Asylum Seeking and Migrant) Women, 93
No Recourse to Public Funds (NRPF) policy, 94–7, 98
non-performance, 2–3
Nwonka, Clive, 119

occupational therapy, discourses in, 12, 203
    anti-racism approaches, 212–13
    within critical gaze, 209–10
    journey forward, 213–14
    questions to think with, 210
Omolú, Augusto, 156, 157
Oor Mad History project, 164
Organic Theatre, 156
Othering, roots of, 154–5
'Our Rights, Our Communities' project, 93

Paget, (Mary) Rosalind, 191
Pailey, Neajai, 67
Palestine, Zionist colonisation of, 82–6
Palmer, Margaret, 191
Paris is Burning, 125
Perez, M S, 38–9
performance practice, anti-racist, 158–9
person-centred practice, 188–9
Perth Museum and Art Gallery (PMAG), 135
physiotherapist, being and becoming, 189–90

physiotherapy
    canons of knowledge in, 191–3
    curriculum, decolonisation of, 187–9, 196–7
    person-centredness in, 188–9
physiotherapy, anti-racist action in, 193
    accountable spaces, 195–6
    communicative action, 194–5
    informal and hidden curriculum, addressing, 194
    self and profession, reflecting on, 193–4
Piet Zwart Institute, 142, 143, 146
postcolonial theory, 48, 52
poverty, 91–2, 98
power, disparity in, 3
practice-based learning, 212
provisional meaning, 51

racial injustice and destitution, 94–6
racialisation, living legacies of, 3–5
racialised body, 150–1
radical pedagogy for activism, 52–3
Ranciere, Jacques, 142
relationships of equity, 142
Research Excellence Framework, 81
Rest of Us, The – Stories, 151
Reville, David, 164
Revolution or Nothing, 153, 154
Robinson, Lucy, 191

safe spaces, xvii, xviii, 47, 109–10, 112, 150, 195
Sanctuary Scholarships, QMU, 222
Sarma, Pavithra, 41

School of kNOw, 144–6
'sciences', and anti-racist education, 180–2
Scottish Centre for Social Justice at QMU, 9, 93, 97–8
Scottish Government Equality Unit, 93
Scottish Palestine Solidarity Campaign, 86
second order learning, 50
self and profession, reflecting on, 193–4
Self/Other relationship, 49, 50, 53, 54
self-censorship, 120
self-reflection, 127
Sembène, Ousmane, 122
Sewell Report (Johnson), 3
Sheku Bayoh Inquiry, 2
silence, silencing and agency, 20–2
social media, 5, 61, 62, 209
Social Renewal Board, 92
socially engaged art, 135–42
Society of Trained Masseuses (STM), 191
solidarity scholarship, anti-colonial, 82–6
STEKA, 61, 63, 64, 65, 103, 104
  support at, 110
  Vocational Skills Centre, 115
STEKAskills, 61, 103, 104
Stern, Kenneth, 84, 85
students' voicefulness, 129
study visits, 45, 46–8
  decolonial pedagogy, 53–5
  theoretical influences, 48–53

Tanger, Le Rêve des Brûleurs, 123
Tavernaro-Haidarian, L, 70
Tembo, Shaddai, 41
Theatre of Sources project, 155
Thompson, Gift, 62, 71, 72, 73, 103, 114
Thompson, John, 182–3
'three awakenings' model, 52
three Cs of generative love, 8, 17, 27, 28, 222
Tobacco Factory Theatre, 156, 157
transformative learning, 49, 50, 51
  dimensions, 51–2
  significance of, 27, 50
troublesome knowledge, 51

Ubuntu/Umunthu, 68–9, 70, 72, 73
uncomforted, learning to be, 142–3
United Nations
  Convention on the Rights of the Child (UNCRC), 35–6
  Sustainability Development Goals (SDGs), 64
universities, possibilities of anti-racist education in, 179–80
unlearning, 146, 212

voluntourism, 63
voluntourism, students' responses to criticism of, 65–6
  decolonisation, 67
  race, 66
voluntourism trips, 62

Wagstaff, Caroline, 41
Wayne, John, 125

Webster, Jonathan, 156–7
Welles, Orson, 125
West Beirut, 125
White feminists and Black feminists, compared, 21
White fragility, 66, 68
White gaze, 110–12, 150
White mad studies, 166
    See also mad studies
White privileges, 66, 152, 153
White saviours, 63, 111

White supremacy, 11, 19, 21, 149, 152, 153
Women's Aid, 78
World Zionist Congress, 83

Xala, 125

Year Zero, 122

Zionist colonisation of Palestine, 82–6

For Product Safety Concerns and Information please contact our EU
representative GPSR@taylorandfrancis.com
Taylor & Francis Verlag GmbH, Kaufingerstraße 24, 80331 München, Germany

www.ingramcontent.com/pod-product-compliance
Lightning Source LLC
Chambersburg PA
CBHW060600230426
43670CB00011B/1911